TRIUMPH TO TRAGEDY

WORLD WAR II BATTLE OF PELELIU, INVASION
OF IWO JIMA, AND ULTIMATE VICTORY ON
OKINAWA IN 1945

DANIEL WRINN

D1473862

CONTENTS

OPERATION ICEBERG

GET YOUR FREE COPY OF WW2: SPIES, SNIPERS AND THE WORLD AT WAR

Never miss a new release by signing up for my free readers group. Learn of special offers and interesting details I find in my research. You'll also get WW2: Spies, Snipers and Tales of the World at War delivered to your inbox. (You can unsubscribe at any time.) Go to danielwrinn.com to sign up

OPERATION STALEMATE

1944 BATTLE FOR PELELIU

SEIZING "THE POINT"

On September 15, 1944, five infantry battalions of the 1st Marine Division embarked in amphibian tractors. They clambered across 700 yards of coral reef to smash into the island of Peleliu.

Marines in the amphibian tractors (LVTs) were told the

operation would be tough but quick. A devastating amount of naval gunfire had been unleashed before their landing.

The 1st Division Marines still had grim images of their sister division, the 2nd's bloody attack across the reefs at Tarawa—two months earlier. But the 1st Division Marines peered over the gunwales of their landing craft and saw an incredible scene of blasted and churned earth along the shore.

Geysers of smoke and dust caused by exploding bombs and large-caliber naval shells gave the Marine's hope. Maybe the enemy would become quick casualties from the pre-landing bombardment. Or at least, they'd be too stunned to react and defend against the hundreds of Marines storming the beach.

Ahead of the Marines were waves of armored amphibian tractors mounted with 75mm howitzers. They were tasked to assault any surviving enemy strongpoints or weapons on the beach before the Marines landed. Ahead of these armored tractors, naval gunfire was lifted toward deeper, more dug-in targets. Navy fighter aircraft strafed north and south along the length of the beach defenses—parallel to the assault waves. Their mission was to keep the enemy defenders subdued and intimidated on the beach as the Marines closed in.

Naval gunfire was shifted to target the ridge northeast of the landing beaches and used to blind enemy observation and limit Japanese fire on the landing waves. This ridge would later be known as the Umurbrogol Pocket (or just the Pocket) and was one of two deadly unknowns to command planners.

The other unknown was the natural traits of the Pocket. Aerial images showed it as a gently rounded north-south hill that commanded the landing beaches 3,000 yards distant. From these early images, this elevated terrain was camouflaged in jungle scrub, almost entirely unaffected from the preparatory bombardment and artillery fire directed at it.

But instead of a gently rounded hill, the Pocket was a complex system of sharply uplifted coral knobs, ridges, valleys, and sinkholes. It rose 300 feet above the island and offered superb positions for tunnels and cave defenses. The enemy had made most of what this terrain provided during their extensive occupation and defensive preparations before the Allied assault.

Another problematic issue for the Marines was the plan developed by Colonel Nakagawa, the Japanese commander of the force on Peleliu and his superior, General Inoue on Koror Island. The Japanese defense tactics had changed considerably from their defeats on Guadalcanal and Cape Gloucester.

Instead of depending on spiritual superiority, Japanese defenders would use their *bushido* spirit and *banzai* tactics to throw Allied troops back into the sea. Japanese forces would delay and try to bleed attacking Marines as long as possible. The enemy planned to combine the devilish terrain with a resolute discipline. Japanese soldiers would only relinquish Peleliu at a horrible price in blood to the Marine invasion. This wicked surprise marked a new and vital change to Japanese defensive tactics compared to what they employed earlier in the war.

Nothing during the trip to the beach revealed any elements of the revised Japanese tactical plan. They bounced across a mile of coral fronting the landing beaches. Amphibian tractors passed several hundred mines intended to destroy any craft approaching or running over them. These mines were aerial bombs detonated by wire control from observation points on shore. But the preliminary bombardment had disrupted the wire controls and the mines did little to slow or destroy any assaulting tractors.

As the LVTs neared the beaches, they came under fire from mortars and artillery. This fire against moving targets generated more anxiety than damage, as only a few vehicles were lost. But this fire did show that the preliminary bombardment had not eliminated the enemy's fire capability. Even more disturbing was when the leading waves of LVTs nearing the beaches were hit by heavy artillery and anti-boat gunfire from concealed bunkers on the north and south flanking points.

Enemy defenses on White Beach 1 were especially deadly and effective. The 3/1 Marines under Colonel Steve Sabol were in a savage beach fight with no means of communication to understand the situation. Japanese guns knocked out several amphibian tractors carrying essential control personnel and equipment.

The mission of seizing "The Point" had been given to Captain George Hunt (a decorated veteran of the New Britain and Guadalcanal campaigns). Hunt developed his plans, which entailed specific assignments for each element of his company. These plans were rehearsed until every Marine knew his role and how it fit into the company's strategy.

H-hour on D-Day brought heavier than expected casualties. One platoon was pinned down all day in beach fighting. Survivors wheeled left as planned, onto the flanking point. While they advanced, they pressed their assault on several enemy defensive emplacements. Pillboxes and casements were carpeted with small arms fire, and smoke from demolitions and grenades.

The climax came when a rifle grenade hit the gun muzzle and ricocheted into a casement, setting off explosions and flames. Enemy defenders ran out of the rear of the block house with their clothes on fire and ammunition exploding in their belts. Marines waited in anticipation of the enemy's flight and cut them down with small arms fire as they burned alive.

Captain Hunt's Marines held the Point, but his company

was reduced to platoon strength with no other nearby units. Sketchy radio communications got through to bring in supporting fire and a desperately needed resupply. One LVT made it to the beach before dark with mortar shells, grenades, and water—evacuating casualties as it departed. This ammunition made all the difference in that night's brutal struggle against a determined enemy's attempt to recapture the Point.

* * *

The next afternoon, Colonel Raymond Davis of the 1/1 Marines moved his Company B to establish contact with Captain Hunt to help hold the desperately contested positions. Hunt's company regained the platoon survivors that were pinned down on the beach fight during the day.

The newly reinforced company recovered their artillery and naval gunfire communications, which proved critical during the second night. That evening the enemy counterattacked the Marines at the Point. The Japanese were narrowly defeated. By midmorning, survivors of the two Marine companies had secured the Point and looked out on 500 dead Japanese soldiers.

On the right of Colonel "Chesty" Puller's struggling 3rd Battalion, Colonel Russell Honsowetz, commanding the 2nd Battalion, took artillery, mortar, and machine-gun fire from still effective enemy beach defenders during their landing.

The 5th Marines' two assault battalions also took heavy enemy fire as they fought through the beach defenses toward the clearing's edge, looking out eastward over the airfield.

On the right flank, the 3/7 Marines crossed in front of an imposing defensive fortification flanking the beach. Luckily, it wasn't as close as the Point position and did not suffer heavy damage. But its enfilading fire, along with natural obstructions on the beach, caused Company K to veer off their planned landing and end up out of position and out of contact. After the confused and delayed battalion regrouped, they used a line of large anti-tank ditches to guide their eastward advance.

Any further delay would be a disaster to the division. Momentum was the key to success. The divisional plan on the right called for the 7th Marines to land two battalions in a column on Orange Beach 3. As the 3/7 advanced, it would be followed by the 1/7. These units would tie into the right flank and attack southeast on the beach.

After a bloody hour of fighting, all five battalions were ashore. The closer each battalion got to the Pocket, the more tenuous its hold was on the shallow beachhead. For another two hours, three more of the division's four remaining battalions joined the attack and pressed the momentum that General Rupertus had ordered.

Colonel Puller landed his forward command group close behind the 3/1 Marines. He was ready to fight, even if his location would deny him the best position for supporting fire. With reduced communications and inadequate numbers of LVTs to follow in waves, he struggled to improve his regiment's situation.

His left flank had two platoons desperately struggling to gain control of the Point. Puller landed the 1st Battalion behind the 3/1 to reinforce the fight for the left flank but was hindered by multiple losses in the LVTs. The 1st Battalion companies had to be landed singly and committed piecemeal into the action.

On the regiment's right flank, the 2/1 Marines recaptured the west edges of the scrub, looking out to the airfield.

In the beachhead's southern sector, the 1/7 Marines were delayed by the heavy LVT losses. This successful early opposition was felt throughout the rest of the day. Most of the 1/7 eventually landed on the correct beach, but many Marines were driven leftward from heavy enemy fire and landed in the 5th Marines' zone.

This caused the 1/7 to join in with the 3/7 and advance east to assault prepared enemy positions.

The battle raged with heavy opposition from both east and south. In the midafternoon, Marines ran into a blockhouse (supposedly destroyed by pre-landing naval gunfire) but had not been touched and put up a strong resistance.

The cost in Marine lives and lost momentum by having to assault these heavily defended blockhouses was harsh and unnecessary.

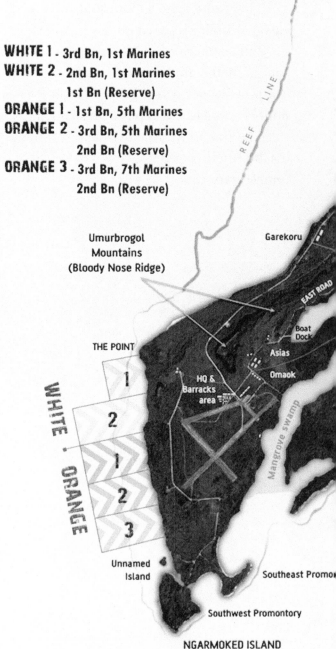

PACIFIC
OCEAN

WHITE 1 - 3rd Bn, 1st Marines
WHITE 2 - 2nd Bn, 1st Marines
    1st Bn (Reserve)
ORANGE 1 - 1st Bn, 5th Marines
ORANGE 2 - 3rd Bn, 5th Marines
    2nd Bn (Reserve)
ORANGE 3 - 3rd Bn, 7th Marines
    2nd Bn (Reserve)

REEF LINE

Umurbrogol
Mountains
(Bloody Nose Ridge)

Garekoru

EAST ROAD

Boat
Dock

THE POINT

Asias

HQ &
Barracks
area

Omaok

WHITE · ORANGE

Mangrove swamp

1

2

1

2

3

Unnamed
Island

Southeast Promo

Southwest Promontory

NGARMOKED ISLAND

NGESEBUS
ISLAND

KONGAURU ISLAND

ate Refinery

Akarakoro Pt

ation

Amiangal Mt

Radar Hill

Hill Row

Hill 80

Kamilianlul Mt

NGABAD ISLAND

Station

ISLAND A

wamp

REEF LINE

BEACH PURPLE

PELELIU
15 SEPTEMBER 1944

| 0 | 500 | 1000 | 2000 | 3000 |

YARDS

MAP by AKHIL KADIDAL

THE JAPANESE DEFENDERS

General Sadae Inoue, a fifth-generation warrior with a robust military reputation, commanded the *14th Infantry Division.* He'd just arrived from the *Kwangtung Army* in China. In March 1944, Inoue met Japanese Premier Tojo in Tokyo to discuss the war.

Tojo decided Japan could no longer hold the Palaus against the Allied naval dominance in the Western Pacific. Tojo gave General Inoue command of all Japanese forces in the Palaus. His orders: take the *14th Infantry* and kill Americans while denying its use to the Allies for as long as possible. He ordered Inoue to sell the Palaus at the highest possible cost in blood and time.

As the enemy sailed for the Palaus, Inoue flew ahead and surveyed his new locale for two days before deciding Peleliu was the key to his defense. The earlier Task Force 58 strikes confirmed his decision. Peleliu had been under the administrative command of a rear admiral. The admiral used his forces to build blockhouses and reinforced concrete structures above ground while improving the existing caves and tunnels under Peleliu's rich natural camouflage of jungle, scrub, and vines.

In these underground installations, the admiral and his troops survived the March attacks from Task Force 58. The above-ground structures and planes were demolished. when the Japanese emerged, they repaired what they could with a focus on the underground installations. Together with Korean labor troops, their numbers swelled to 7,000 (most lacking training and leadership for any infantry action).

Colonel Nakagawa arrived on Peleliu with his *2nd Infantry Regiment*—a 6,500-man reinforced regiment. They were veterans from the war in China and had two dozen 75mm artillery pieces, a dozen tanks, fifteen 81mm heavy mortars, over a hundred .50-caliber machine guns, and thirty dual-purpose anti-aircraft guns. There were many heavy 141mm mortars and naval anti-aircraft guns already on the island.

Colonel Nakagawa had been awarded nine medals for his leadership against the Chinese. His regiment was regarded as elite veterans within the Japanese Army.

Immediately upon arriving, Nakagawa reconnoitered his battle position from the ground and air. He identified the western beaches (the White and Orange Beaches) as the most likely landing sites. Nakagawa ordered his troops to dig in and construct beach defenses. But a conflict arose when the senior naval officer, Admiral Itou, resented taking orders from a junior army officer.

From Koror, General Inoue sent General Murai to Peleliu. Murai assumed command and maintained a liaison with

Nakagawa. Murai was a highly regarded, personal representative of General Inoue and considered senior to the admiral.

Murai left the mission firmly in Nakagawa's hands. Throughout the campaign, Nakagawa exercised operational control and was assisted and counseled but not commanded by General Murai.

Nakagawa fully understood his objective and the situation and firepower the Allies possessed. He turned his attention to making the fullest use of his primary advantage—the terrain. Nakagawa deployed and installed his forces to inflict all possible damage and casualties at the landing. Then his troops would defend in-depth to the last man. Peleliu offered a vertical and a horizontal dimension to its defense.

Nakagawa registered artillery and mortars over the width and depth of the reef on both eastern and western beaches. With a planned heavy concentration along the fringe of the western reef, he expected the Allies need to transfer follow-on waves from landing craft to the reef crossing amphibian vehicles. He registered weapons from the water's edge to subject landing troops to a hellish hail of fire. Offshore, he laid over 500 wire-controlled mines.

Nakagawa ordered the construction of beach obstacles using logs and rails and ordered multiple anti-tank ditches dug. He put troops in machine-gun and mortar pits along the inland from the beaches supported by all available barbed wire. He constructed concrete emplacements to shelter and conceal anti-tank and anti-boat artillery on the north and south beaches.

Inland, he used the already built blockhouses with adjacent reinforced buildings. He made them into mutually supporting defensive complexes and added communication lines in the trenches.

Nakagawa believed the western beaches were the most

probable route of attack. But he did not leave the southern and eastern beaches undefended. He committed one battalion on each beach to organize defenses. The eastern beaches were thoroughly prepared with contingents of defenders to move into central Peleliu if the battle expanded from the west as he expected.

Colonel Nakagawa assigned 600 infantry and artillery to defend Ngesebus and 1,100 Naval personnel to defend northern Peleliu. The only troops not under his command were the 1,500 defenders on Angaur.

The central part of his force and effort was committed to the 500 tunnels, caves, and firing embrasures in the coral ridges of central Peleliu. The naval units' prior extensive tunneling into limestone ridges rendered the occupants mainly immune to any Allied bombardments. Only an occasional lucky hit in the cave's mouth or a point-blank direct fire could damage the hidden defenses and the enemy troops.

Tunnels were designed for several purposes: command centers, hospitals, barracks, storage, ammunition dumps, and cooking areas with freshwater springs and basins—and of course, firing embrasures. He added elaborate concealment and protective devices including a few sliding steel doors.

Nakagawa expected an intense pre-landing bombardment. He believed his troops would endure it and carry out their mission of delaying and bleeding the Allies for as long as possible before Peleliu fell.

General Inoue was busy with his troops on Koror. He prepared for expected Allied attacks against Babelthuap. The Allied plan, Operation Stalemate, also called for the invasion of Babelthuap. As the expected invasion drew closer, Inoue made a statement to his troops, reflecting Tojo's instructions to bleed and delay the American forces. He pointed out the necessity to expect and endure the naval bombardment and how to use terrain to inflict casualties on the attacking force.

General Inoue said: "Dying and losing the territory to the enemy would contribute to opening a new phase of the war. We are ready to die honorably."

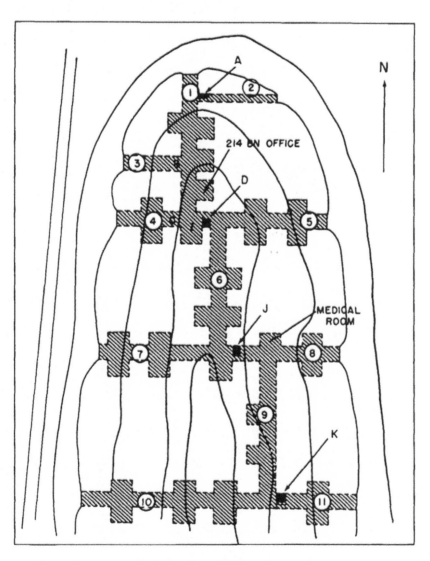

Map of most elaborate tunnel system on Peleliu

D-DAY CENTER ASSAULT

The 1st Marines fought to secure the left flank. The 7th Marines battled to isolate and reduce enemy defenses on the southern end of Peleliu. The 5th Marines were tasked with driving across the airfield to cut the island in half, reorient north, and secure the island's eastern half.

The 2/5 Marines under Major Gordon Gayle landed on Orange Beach 2 and advanced east through scrub jungle and dunes. They moved in and out of the anti-tank barrier to the west edge of the clearing surrounding the airfield.

Gayle's battalion passed through the lines of the 3/5 Marines and attacked scattered resistance through the scrub in dugouts and bomb shelters near the southern end of the airfield. The 3rd Battalion's mission was to clear that scrub and maintain contact with the 3/7 Marines on the right flank, while the 2/5 Marines advanced across the open area to reach the far side of the island.

The 2/5 Marines advanced in the center and right, fighting entirely across the island by midafternoon. They kept contact with the 1/5 Marines and moved to reorient their attack northward.

The Japanese anti-tank ditch along the center and right of the Orange Beaches was notable because of the several command posts along its length.

The 1st Tank Battalion's M-48A1 Shermans—a third of which were left behind at the last moment—finally crossed the reef. These tanks had developed special reef-crossing maneuvers in anticipation of terrain obstacles.

Moving the fire and logistical support onto the beach was challenging and under direct observation from Japanese observers. This was an inescapable risk because of Peleliu's terrain. As long as the enemy had observation posts atop the Umurbrogol Point over the airfield and beach—there was no alternative but to advance rapidly and coordinate fire support.

The rapid beach advance caused heavy casualties. General Rupertus' concern for early momentum seemed to be correct. Marines on the left flank assaulted the foot of the Pocket's ridges and swiftly got to the crest. In the center, the 5th Marines advanced and secured all likely routes to outflank the Pocket. In the south, the 7th Marines destroyed the now cut-off forces before they could regroup and join the fight in central Peleliu.

The 5th Marines moved across the airfield to the western edge of the lagoon. They separated the airfield area from the eastern peninsula. They created a line of attacking Marines across the eastern and northern part of the island, believed to be the center of the enemy's strength.

Colonel Hanneken's 7th Marines pushed south and divided the Japanese forces. Hanneken's troops were fully engaged and mostly concealed against enemy observation.

It was becoming clear that the D-Day line objectives would not be met in either the north or south. General Rupertus was alarmed by the loss of his momentum, and he ordered the 2/7 (his last uncommitted infantry battalion), under Colonel Spencer Berger, into the fight. No commander onshore felt a need for the 2/7 Marines. Colonel Hanneken cleared an assembly area for them where they wouldn't be in the way.

General Rupertus was now fully committed. He told his staff that he'd "shot his bolt." On the crowded beachhead, more troops were not needed—they needed more room to maneuver them and more artillery.

Rupertus decided to land himself and the key elements of his command group onshore. His chief of staff, Colonel John Selden, convinced the general to stay on the flagship because it was too dangerous. So Rupertus ordered Colonel Selden ashore.

The shortage of LVTs stalled the timely landing of the following waves. Neither Selden's small command post group nor Berger's 2/7 Marines could get past the transfer line. The landing craft had to return to the ships, despite their orders to land.

At 1700, Colonel Nakagawa launched his counterattack. Marine commanders had been alerted to the Japanese capability to make an armored attack on D-Day and were well prepared. The enemy assault came from north of the airfield and headed south across the 1st Marines' line on the eastern edge of the airfield clearing.

This attack went directly into the 5th Marines' sector, where the 1/5 was dug in across the southern area of the airfield. Marines opened up on the enemy attackers' infantry and tanks. A bazooka gunner in front hit two tanks. The CO of the 1/5 Marines had his tanks in defilade behind the front lines. They fired on the enemy armor, running through the front lines as they advanced. The Marines' lines held, and they fired on the enemy infantry and tanks with all available weapons.

Major John Gustafson of the 2/5 was in the forward command post halfway across the airfield and had his tank platoon close at hand. While the enemy had not yet come into his zone, he launched a platoon of tanks into the fight. In minutes it was over. The enemy tanks were destroyed, and the Japanese infantry was ripped apart.

While Colonel Nakagawa's attack was bold, it was a failure. Even where the Japanese tanks broke through Allied lines, the Marines did not retreat. Instead, all anti-tank fire of every caliber concentrated on the enemy armor. Japanese light tanks were blown apart into pieces on the battlefield. Over one hundred were destroyed, although that figure may be exaggerated because of the amount of fire directed their way. Each Marine anti-tank gunner and grenadier thought they destroyed each tank they fired at and reported it that way.

* * *

With the Japanese counterattack repulsed and the enemy in shambles, Marines resumed their attack. They moved north along the eastern half of the airfield and advanced halfway up the length of the clearing before stopping to re-organize for the night. This was the farthest advance of the day over favorable terrain on the division's front. This advance provided the needed space for logistics and artillery deployment to support the next day's attack.

But this quick advance left a hole in the right flank. The 3/5 Marines were supposed to keep contact with the north-facing 2/5. But 3/5 command and control had been destroyed. The battalion's XO, Major Robert Ash, was killed earlier in the day from a direct hit into his LVT.

When the Japanese attack started, a mortar barrage hit the 3/5 command post in the anti-tank ditch and killed several staff officers and caused the evacuation of the battalion commander. At 1700, the 3/5 Marine companies weren't in contact with each other—nor their battalions.

The 5th Marines CO ordered his XO, Colonel Lewis Walt, to take command of the 3/5 and redeploy them in between the gap of the 5th and 7th Marines. Walt moved the 2nd Battalion's reserve company to his right flank in a tie-in position to form a more continuous regimental line. By 2200, he came under several sharp counterattacks from central and southern defenders throughout the night.

Enemy attacks came from the north and south. None had any significant success but were persistent enough to require an ammunition resupply. At dawn, dozens of Japanese bodies laid ripped to pieces north of the Marine lines.

Elsewhere across the front, there were more menacing night counterattacks. None drove the Marines back or penetrated Allied lines in significant strength.

In the south, the 7th Marines expected substantial night attacks from the enemy battalion opposing them. Marines were dug in and in strength. They had communications to call in fire support, including naval gunfire and star shell illumination—they easily turned back the sporadic enemy attacks.

At the end of the first twelve hours ashore, the 1st Marine Division held its beachhead across their projected front.

Marine positions were strong everywhere except on the extreme left flank. General Smith, from his forward command post had communication with all three regimental commanders. The report he received from Colonel Puller was not a realistic assessment of the 1st Marines' weak hold on the Point. This was because of Colonel Puller's own limited information.

Besides all three infantry regiments, the 1st Division had three battalions of light artillery emplaced onshore. All thirty tanks were also now onshore. The shore party was operating on the beach under sporatic enemy fire and full daylight observation. The division was preparing to press their advance on D +1. Their objective was to capture the commanding crests on the left, advance farther into the center, and destroy isolated enemy defenders in the south.

By the end of the day, at least two colonels on Peleliu had misleading information about their situations and gave inaccurate reports to their superiors. When General Smith finally got a telephone wire into the 1st Marines' command post, he was told the regiment had secured the beachhead and was on the objective line. He was not told about the gaps in his lines nor of the gravity of the 1st Division's struggle on the Point— where thirty-eight Marines battled to keep the position.

Colonel Nakagawa reported that the Marines' landings attempt had been routed. He also reported that his brave counterattack had thrown the Marines into the sea.

THE UMURBROGOL POCKET

General Rupertus was irritated that after his failed efforts to land, his division reserve into the southern sector of the beachhead. Now he was informed that his northern sector—on the extreme left flank—needed reinforcements. Rupertus ordered the 2/7 into Colonel Puller's sector to assist.

Division headquarters afloat had reported the Marine D-Day casualties had exceeded 1,100, of which 210 Marines were killed in action. While not a substantial percentage of the total divisional strength, this number threatened the overall cutting-edge strength. Most of those 1,100 casualties were from each of the division's nine infantry battalions (with the exception of the center). General Rupertus was still not on the O-1 objective line—the first of his eight planned phase lines.

Rupertus had inaccurate information about the 1st Marines' situation. The general was determined to get ashore and see what he could do to reignite the lost momentum. He had a broken ankle from a pre-assault training exercise. His foot was in a cast, but his gimpy leg dragging in a sandy trench would not hold him back from seeing the situation on Peleliu for himself.

On Colonel Nakagawa's side, he saw a different situation from his high ground because of the incredible reports being sent out from his headquarters. The Marine landing force had *not* been routed. He watched while a division of Marines deployed across two miles of beach. While the Marines had been punished on D-Day, they were still in the fight.

Nakagawa predicted the next assault would be preceded by a hailstorm of naval artillery, gunfire, and aerial bombardments. Also, that they'd be supported by the US tanks that annihilated the Japanese armor on D-Day.

In Nakagawa's D-Day counterattack, he lost one of his five infantry battalions.

Across Peleliu, he lost hundreds of beach defenders in fighting across the front, and in futile night attacks. Still, he had several thousand courageous, well-armed and well-trained soldiers ready to fight and die for the empire. They were deployed through strong defensive complexes and fortifications, with abundant underground support facilities. Nakagawa's troops were determined to kill as many Marines as they could before they fell.

Colonel Nakagawa had the terrain advantage. He focused his defensive strategy around the occupation and organization of that terrain. Until he was driven from the commanding crests of the Point, he still had a dominant position. He could observe and direct hidden fire on the attackers while his forces were largely invisible to the Marines and their fire superiority. Continuing to hold this terrain was a key component of his overall defensive strategy.

The Marines were assaulting fortified positions, and precise fire preparations were needed. Marines on the left flank were under extreme pressure to advance rapidly, sacrificing speed for careful preparation. General Rupertus understood that enemy weapons and observation dominated the

Marine position and troops were getting picked off at the enemy's leisure. Rupertus' concern for momentum was a priority and would save Marine lives.

The rapid advance burden was on the 1st Marines—on the left flank—and on the 5th in the airfield area. In the south, the 7th Marines already held the edge of the airfield's terrain. The scrub jungle screened the regiment from enemy observation.

Colonel "Chesty" Puller's 1st Marines had suffered the most casualties on D-Day. They fought through the most formidable terrain and assaulted the toughest positions. They had to attack and relieve Company K of the 3/1 on the Point and then assault the Pocket ridges north to south.

Puller's Marines (aided by the 2/1) swung leftward and secured the built-up area between the airfield in the ridges. When Puller was at the foot of the cliffs, his Marines fought in a savage, scratch and scramble attack against the enemy troops in the ridges.

Puller closed the gaps on his left flank and swung his entire regiment north. With the help of the 3/1, he reinforced Company K on the Point. Then he moved north, keeping his left on the beach and his right close to the West Road, along the foot of the Pocket. While the terrain allowed for tank support, maneuverability was tight, and hard fighting was involved.

The rapid rate of movement along the boundary and the more open zone created a pressing need for reserves. Tactically, it was necessary to press east into and over the rough terrain and destroy enemy defenses. That job was given to the 1st and 2nd Battalions of the 1st Marines and the 2nd Battalion of the 7th Marines. But more troops were still needed to move north and encircle the rugged landscape of the Umurbrogol Pocket area. By September 17, reserves were needed along the 1st Division's western (left) advance, but neither division nor III Amphibious Corps had reserves.

The 3/1 Marines battled up easier terrain on the left flank. In the center, the 1/1 Marines advanced between the coral ridge and an open flat zone. One of their early surprises, as they approached the foot of the ridge area, was another enemy blockhouse. Admiral Oldendorf had reported that blockhouse destroyed from pre-landing naval gunfire, but the Marines who first encountered it reported the enemy placement as "not even having a mark on it."

This blockhouse was part of an impressive defensive complex. It was connected and supported by a web of adjacent emplacements and pillboxes. It had four-foot-thick walls of reinforced concrete. The naval gunfire support team from the USS *Mississippi* was called on to help. They annihilated the entire complex. The 1/1 Marines advanced again until running into the far more challenging Japanese ridge defense systems. Major Davis, in command of the 1/1 Marines (later to earn a Medal of Honor in Korea) said the attack into and along the ridges: "was the most difficult assignment I'd ever been tasked with."

All three of the 1st Marines' Battalions battled beside each other onto the Pocket and its wicked, cave-filled coral ridges. The initial reserve, the 2/7 Marines, was assigned to the 1st Marines and immediately thrown into the fight. Colonel Puller fed companies into the battle piecemeal. Shortly afterward, the 2/7 took the central zone of action between the 1st and 2nd Marine Battalions.

The 1st Marines continued to assault the stubborn enemy defenders in their underground caves and fortifications. Every new advance opened the Marines to new fire from the incredible number of cliffs and ridges and concealed positions in the caves above and below the newly won ground.

Nothing exemplified this tactical dilemma better than the September 19 seizure and withdrawal from Hill 100. This ridge bordered the Horseshoe Valley on the eastern limit of the Pocket. The 2/1 Marines landed with 240 Marines. Now they had only 90 Marines left when they were ordered to take Hill 100. The Japanese called it East Mountain (Higashiyama).

Marines were at first supported by tanks but lost that support when the leading two tanks slipped off the approach causeway. The Marines continued with only mortar support into the face of heavy machine gun and mortar fire. When the Marines reached the summit at twilight, they discovered the ridge's northeast extension continued to even higher ground, where Japanese troops poured fire on the hill.

Just as threatening was fire from enemy caves on the

parallel ridge to the west—known as Five Brothers. Into the setting darkness, Marines supported by heavy mortars hung on. Throughout the night, a series of enemy counterattacks on the ridge top were turned back. Marines repulsed them with mortars and hand-to-hand brawls, knives, and rifles. Marines even threw rocks when their grenade supplies ran low.

Marines were still clinging to the ridge-top when dawn broke. Only eight Marines were left. The remaining Marines, under the command of Captain Everett Pope, withdrew and successfully evacuated their wounded. The dead were left behind on the ridge until October 3, when the ridge was finally captured for good. Another example of the enemy's expert use of mutually supporting positions on the Umurbrogol Pocket.

By D +4, the 1st Marines was a regiment in name only. They'd taken over 1,500 casualties. General Rupertus had continued to urge Puller's under-strength Marines forward. General Geiger (commander of III Amphibious Corps and Rupertus' superior) was an experienced ground operations commander from Guam to Bougainville. He understood the lower combat efficiency that these types of losses imposed on a committed combat unit.

On October 2, General Geiger, after visiting Puller in his forward command post and observing the exhausted condition of his Marines, met with General Rupertus and his staff. Rupertus wasn't willing to admit that his division needed to be reinforced, but Geiger overruled him. He ordered the Army's 321st Regiment Combat Team and 81st Infantry Division (on Angaur) to be attached to the 1st Marine Division.

Geiger ordered Rupertus to stand down and send the 1st Marines to the division's rear area base on Pavuvu, in the Russell Islands.

On September 21, the 1st Marines had 1,749 casualties.

They reported killing over 4,000 Japanese soldiers and capturing ten heavily defended coral ridges. They reported the destruction of three blockhouses, twenty-five pillboxes, fourteen anti-tank guns, and over 140 defended caves.

The 1st Marines' assault battalions had captured much of the crest required to deny the enemy observation and effective fire on the airfield and logistical areas. Light aircraft flew on September 25 from the scarred and still under repair airfield.

With the Pocket now in Allied control, the division's logistical lifeline was assured. While the Japanese still had some observation capability on the airfield, they could only harass rather than threaten.

The Marine front lines were now close to the final Japanese defensive positions. While intelligence couldn't verify it—the terrain and situation suggested that all assault requirements had been met, and it was time for siege tactics.

Enemy defenders learned that when aerial observers were overhead, they could no longer run their weapons out of caves and fire on the beach or the airfield. After one or two rounds, they were answered with a quick counter-battery fire or a dreaded aerial attack from carrier-based planes.

On September 24, Marines used attack planes operating from the airfield on Peleliu.

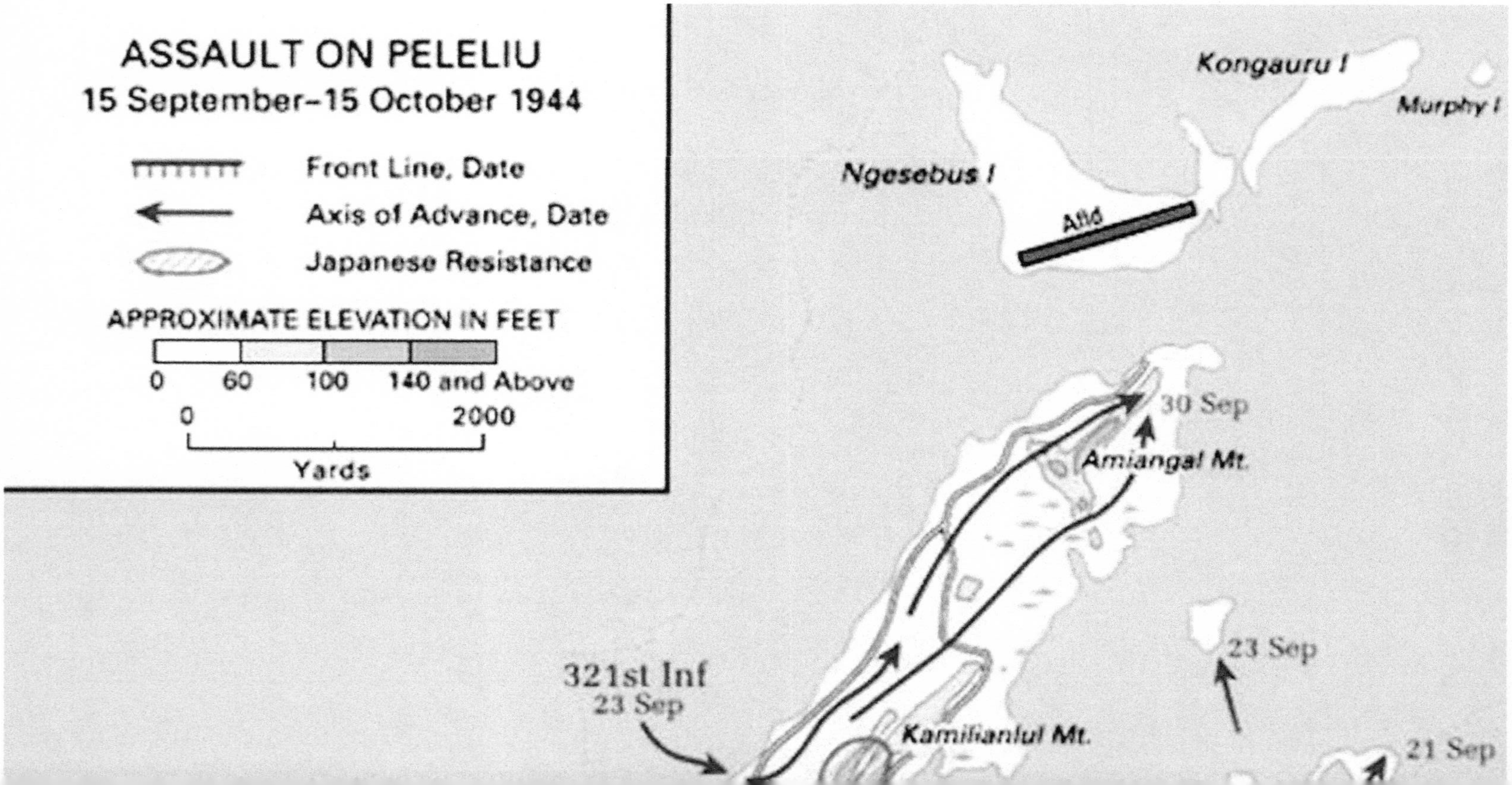

ASSAULT ON PELELIU
15 September–15 October 1944

Front Line, Date
Axis of Advance, Date
Japanese Resistance

APPROXIMATE ELEVATION IN FEET

0   60   100   140 and Above

0   2000
Yards

Kongauru I
Murphy I
Ngesebus I
Akd
Ngabad
21 Sep
23 Sep
30 Sep
Amiangal Mt.
Kamilianlul Mt.
321st Inf
23 Sep

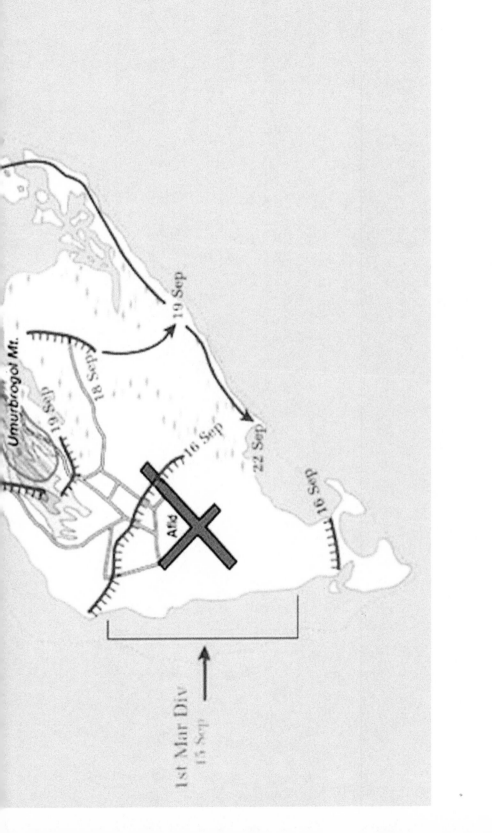

PELELIU'S EASTERN PENINSULA

On D +1, when the 1st Marines launched their bloody assault on the Pocket, the 5th Marines (on the right flank) found less opposition and easier terrain to navigate.

The 1/5 fought southwest to northeast across the airfield through a built-up area similar to what the 2/1 Marines faced. The battalion took fire from the Pocket and assorted small arms from hidden defenders in the rubble-filled built-up area.

The 1/5's tank-infantry attack carried the day. Marines had control of the east to west cross-island road—the next step in securing Peleliu's eastern peninsula.

The 2/5 Marines had a more difficult time. Their progress was opposed by infantry from the woods, and artillery directly from the Pocket, which targeted their tanks supporting the attack along the wood's edge.

Whether the Japanese troops in those woods were posted to defend that position or just trying to survive was never established. The battle took all day, and Marine battalions suffered heavy casualties. By nightfall, the 2/5 Marines had fought past the north end of the airfield and halted to spend the night in the woods, concealing the approaches to the eastern peninsula.

The two-battalion Marine assault was deeply engaged on its front and right. Regimental headquarters near the beach was hit by an artillery barrage that, coupled with the 3/5 Marines' CO and XO losses, prompted a considerable rearrangement of command assignments. The barrage at the regimental command post took out most of the staff and buried the regimental commander in the crumbling Japanese anti-tank trench.

Luckily, it was a temporary burial, and the regimental commander, Colonel Harris, crawled out with a twisted and battered leg but could still hobble. Two of his staff officers were casualties, and the sergeant major was killed. Harris didn't evacuate but needed help in his CP. Harris ordered Colonel Walt back from the 3rd Battalion and had the XO of the 2/5, Major John Gustafson, take command of the 3/5.

Fortunately, the 3/5 Marines were having a quiet day,

unlike their hair-raising regrouping on the night of D-Day. After daylight, the 2/5 attacked to the north, and the 3/5 stretched along the east edge of a mangrove lagoon, separating Peleliu from the eastern peninsula. From that position, the 3rd Battalion 5th Marines tied into the 3/7 Marines as they attacked south.

This maneuver protected each regiment's flank against enemy movement across the lagoon and into the rear of the attacking Marines. While no such threat developed, a more pressing concern emerged for the 3/5 Marines. Major Gustafson was tasked with getting the 3/5 into position to bolster and relieve the 1/5 Marines as they closed in on their objective.

The next day, the 5th Marines tied in with the 1st on their left and secured the foot of the East Road. To the right, the 2/5 Marines hacked their way through the jungle north of the airfield and alongside a road leading to the eastern peninsula. A thick and almost impenetrable scrub reduced progress to a crawl. The scrub concealed most of the advancing Marines from enemy observation on the high ground to the northwest.

The 5th Marines' position overlapped with the northeast sector. Securing that visual boundary meant frontline Marines were spared hostile, directed fire from Pocket. Like the 7th Marines, hidden mainly in the jungle to the South, this would lessen the need for a frontal assault.

Now Marines had the freedom to maneuver purposefully and coordinate supporting fire more carefully into enemy positions.

7TH MARINES IN THE SOUTH

In the south, starting on D +1, the 7th Marines' spirited assault against enemy fortifications smashed into the elite *2nd Battalion, 15th Regiment.*

Even though the enemy was isolated and surrounded by Marines, this Japanese battalion showed skill and an understanding of Colonel Nakagawa's orders and mission: to sell Peleliu at the highest price possible.

The 7th Marines attacked. The 3/7 were on the left and the 1/7 on the right. Marines had the advantage of assaulting the extensive and well-prepared defenses from the rear—with heavy fire support. Both sides fought bitterly, but by 1530 on September 8, the battle was over. Marines destroyed the fortified elite Japanese infantry battalion in their stronghold.

General Rupertus was informed that the 7th Marines' objectives had been met, through the courage, bravery, skill, and many casualties of the 7th Marines infantry companies. Now the 7th advanced out of their successful battle area and into another bloody assault—better known as a siege.

The 5th Marines were still battling bitterly for the eastern "lobster claw" peninsula. By the end of D +2, the 5th Marines stood at the approach to the eastern peninsula off the East Road—near the 1st Marines' vicious fight at the Pocket.

They'd planned an assault on the eastern peninsula across a narrow causeway the Japanese were sure to defend. But a recent reconnaissance revealed that the causeway was not defended. The 2nd Battalion advanced swiftly to seize the opportunity. They moved across in strength but were turned back by friendly fire. The battalion was strafed by Navy planes and then hit by an artillery airburst that killed eighteen Marines.

Still, a bridgehead across the causeway was established and on D +3 the 5th Marines moved in. By the afternoon, Marines advanced to capture and clear the eastern peninsula. Marines expected an attack against a strong defending force that never materialized, this provided an opportunity to secure Purple Beach quickly—a massive logistical prize.

Just before dark, two companies of the 3/5 Marines moved across the causeway to plan the next day's advance. They hoped for little resistance but armed their point units with war dogs to guard against a nighttime ambush. Their lead companies moved out just after dawn, while nearly ambushed, the war dogs warned the Marines and thwarted the enemy's attempted surprise attack.

By the end of D +4, the two battalions had secured the main body of the eastern peninsula and reached Purple Beach from the rear. While the Japanese defenses were extraordinary, many were unmanned. The enemy troops encountered were more interested in hiding than fighting. This added to the speculation that Colonel Nakagawa's trained infantry had been moved west. By D +5, Purple Beach was secured along with the southwest and northeast of the long peninsula of Purple Beach.

From that position and others near the island of Ngar-dololok, Marines could direct fire against the cave-infested ridges of central and northern Peleliu.

* * *

Now that eastern and southern Peleliu was captured, the Allies planned to encircle the Japanese defenders in central Peleliu and assault nearby Ngesebus and Kongauru in the north. While this was the obvious next tactical phase for the fighting, securing it was unnecessary for strategic and tactical goals.

General Oliver Smith, the 1st Marine Division's assistant

commander, believed that the island's mop-up operations should take priority. He wrote: "by the end of the first week, the division controlled everything on the island that was needed, or later even used."

The airfield was secured and under improvement and repair—and in use. There was now no threat to MacArthur's long-heralded return to the Philippines. Purple Beach, Peleliu's best strategic axis, was secured and provided a protected logistic access to the major battle areas. While enemy defenders in their caves on northern Peleliu could still some-what harass Allied rear installations, Marine counterattacks would quickly silence them.

Only two significant Japanese capabilities remained: they could reinforce Peleliu from Babelthuap and bitterly resist from their cave positions.

The Allied encirclement of the Pocket suffered from a lack of reinforcements.

The III Amphibious Corps reserves were fully committed to the seizure of Angaur. The Angaur operation's planning and timing were heavily affected by the Peleliu operation. Division planners proposed landing on Angaur before Peleliu, but General Julian Smith said that would cause the Japanese in northern Palau to reinforce Peleliu.

Division agreed that Angaur should only be assaulted after the landing on Peleliu was sure to succeed. But in the end, the assault on Angaur began before the Peleliu landing was resolved. The 81st Division's commanding general wanted to land as soon as possible and was supported by Admiral Bill Valenti. General Julian Smith argued that committing the III Corps' Reserve before the operations on Peleliu were more fully developed was premature and costly. Admiral Wilkinson ignored his advice.

On September 17, the III Corps' final reserve was assigned to the Western Attack Force and ordered to use "all available forces." Against General Smith's advice, Wilkinson committed the entire 323rd RCT and the 81st Division's other maneuver element. The 321st successfully occupied an undefended Ulithi, while reserves were desperately needed on Peleliu.

By September 20, the 81st Division had destroyed or cornered Angaur's 1,400 enemy troops, and Anguar was declared secure. The 322nd RCT would complete mop-up operations, and the 321st RCT was now available for further operations.

General Rupertus believed his Marines could do it without help from the Army. The III Corps' plan had the 81st Division reinforcing Marines on Peleliu and then relieving the 1st Marine Division for the mop-up. But General Rupertus refused to accept the help and continued to tell his commanders to "hurry up."

Rupertus also shrugged off suggestions from 5th Marines

"Bucky" Harris that he should take a look at the Pocket from the newly available light planes of the Marine Observation Squadron 3. Harris' newest aerial reconnaissance on September 19 changed his view of the Pocket from sober to serious. He believed attacking the Pocket from the north would be less costly than the original plan, and Rupertus told Harris that he had his own map.

The Marines' plan was built on the tactical concept that the 1st Marine Division would push in a northern line across the island's width after capturing the airfield. Once close to the southern edge of the Pocket, Marines would advance in four west-to-east phase lines. It was expected that the advance along with flatter zones east and west of the Pocket would be roughly the same pace as along the high central ground of Peleliu. Maybe this thinking was consistent with Rupertus' prediction of a three-day assault, but developments in Marine sectors to the west and east didn't change division-level thinking. Until additional forces were available, this linear advance may have seemed the only possible advance.

There was no re-examining the planned south-to-north advance, and for days, the Pocket was sealed off at its northernmost extremity. Still, the division commander kept ordering attacks from south to north following the initial landing plan. As "Bucky" Harris reported from his aerial reconnaissance of the overall Pocket, these attacks would only bring severe casualties. Heavily supported Marines could advance into "the Horseshoe" and "Death Valley," but their positions would soon prove untenable, and they'd need to withdraw by day's end.

The failure in this thinking may have come from the mapping use. The 5th Marines in early October created a newer sketch map to locate and identify the details within the Umurbrogol Pocket.

Even after General Geiger had ordered General Rupertus to stand down Puller's shattered 1st Marines on September 21, Rupertus made it known that *his Marines alone* would clear the entire island. After taking a closer look at the situation on the ground, General Geiger ordered the 321st RCT from Angaur and attached them to the 1st Marine Division—the encirclement of the Umurbrogol Pocket was possible.

Capturing Ngesebus and northern Peleliu became a priority. Allied forces discovered on September 23 that considerable enemy troop strength in the northern Palaus was being ferried by barge from Koror and Babelthuap. Even though the Navy patrol set up to protect against those reinforcements had discovered and destroyed some of the Japanese barges, many enemy troops had waded ashore on the early morning of September 23.

Colonel Nakagawa now had reinforcements on northern Peleliu.

NORTHERN PELELIU SEIZURE

General Rupertus held a meeting with III Corps staff and General Geiger. They formed a plan to encircle the Pocket and deny reinforcements to the enemy on northern Peleliu. The Army's 321st Infantry would advance up the West Road with the 5th Marines. After they reached the Pocket, Marines would pass through Army lines and continue north to assault Ngesebus and northern Peleliu.

The 321st Army Regimental Combat Team was now a battle-tested and hardened outfit. They would advance up the West Road along the edge of the elevated coral plateau. The plateau was 300 yards west to east and formed the western shoulder of the Pocket. It rose seventy feet, and its western cliff was a jumble of small ridges that dominated the road. This cliff would have to be cleared and secured to allow for an un-harassed use of the road.

After the 321st passed this cliff, they could probe east in search of any routes to the eastern edge of Peleliu. Any openings in that direction would be a chance to encircle the Pocket on the north. Following the 321st, the 5th Marines would press their attack into northern Peleliu. The 7th Marines (relieving the 1st) were stood down on the eastern peninsula and relieved the 5th Marines of their passive security role. This allowed the 5th to focus on the capture of northern Peleliu and Ngesebus.

The West Road would be used as a tactical route north and then as a communication line for continuing operations. The road was paralleled by the jagged cliff, which made up the western shoulder of the plateau. This was *not* a level plateau and had a moonscape of sinkholes, coral knobs, and karst.

With no defined ridges or patterns, the sinkholes varied from room size to house size, and some were over twenty feet deep and covered by jungle and vines. This plateau was ninety feet above the road. And another 300 yards to the east, it dropped off into a sheer cliff (known as the China wall). Marines who looked up at it from the eastern approaches to the Pocket claimed the western edge of the plateau was "virtually impassable."

The plateau was also impenetrable to vehicles. Coral sinkholes forced all infantry to crawl, climb, and clamber into small compartments of jagged and rough terrain. Having to evacuate any casualties would involve rough handling of stretchers and the wounded men.

The enemy defended this area with scattered small units who bitterly resisted movement into their moonscape. Japanese troops ignored individuals and only fired on groups or what they considered rich targets.

The tactical decision along the West Road was to seize and hold the cliffs and coral spires. From here, they could command the road and defend these positions against any attacks. Once these heights were secured, troops and trucks could move along the West Road. But until secured, this cliff gave cover and concealment to the enemy. Until these cliff positions were taken and held, the Japanese could only be temporarily silenced from heavy firepower.

On September 23, this was the situation the 321st launched their assault into. Following an hour-long naval bombardment against the high ground of the West Road. Army patrols moved in and were screened from the Japanese still on the cliff. These small-unit tactics worked well until larger units of the 321st moved out alongside the West Road. From here, the enemy unleashed hell from above.

Two battalions of the 321st advanced along an east-west line across the road and up to the heights. Soldiers secured the west edge of the cliff and advanced northward, but some elements of the cliff were outpaced to the west. Instead of fighting to seize the ridge, some units responsible for securing the cliff abandoned it and side-stepped down to the road.

Colonel Hanneken ordered the 3/7 to capture the high ground that the 321st had abandoned. After that, the 3/7 Marines were committed along the ridge within the 321st zone of action. This stretched the Marines, who still needed to maintain contact to their right. Farther north, the 321st pressed on and regained some of the heights above their advance and held onto them.

On the northern end of the Pocket, the sinkhole terrain blended into regular ridgelines. The 321st assaulted Hill 100, along with a nearby hill east of East Road, and designated it Hill B. This position was the northern cap of the Pocket. The 321st would fight for Hill B and the northern cap of the Pocket for the next three days.

The 321st probed the eastern path across the north end of the Pocket. They sent patrols north up to the West Road. In an area of buildings designated "radio station," they found the junction of East and West Roads. Colonel Bob Dark, commanding the 321st, sent a mobile task force (Task Force

Neal), heavy with flamethrowers and armor, to circle southeast and join with the 321st at Hill 100. Below that battle, the 7th Marines continued to put pressure on the south and east fronts of the Pocket.

As this was underway, the 5th Marines were ordered to help in the battle for northern Peleliu. The 5th motored, marched, and waded to the West Road and sidestepped the 321st to join in the fight. The Marines found flat ground, some open, and some covered with palm trees. The familiar limestone ridges broke the ground. But the critical difference here was that most of the ridges stood alone.

Marines were not exposed to flanking fire from parallel ridges like they were in the Pocket. The Japanese fortified the northern ridges with extensive tunnels and concealed gun positions. But these positions could be attacked individually with flamethrowers, demolitions, and tank tactics. Many of the enemy defenders were from Naval construction units and not trained infantrymen.

On the US side of the fighting, Colonel "Bucky" Harris was determined to direct all available firepower before sending his infantry into the fight. His newer aerial reconnaissance gave him a better understanding of the terrain.

On September 25, the 1/5 Marines secured the radio station complex. When the 3/5 arrived, they were ordered to seize the next high ground to the east of the 1/5's position. From there, they would extend the regimental line back to the beach. This broke contact with the 321st's operations in the south but fulfilled Colonel Harris's plan to advance north as rapidly as possible without overextending their lines.

By suddenly establishing this regimental beachhead, the 5th Marines had surprised the enemy with powerful forces in position to engage them fully in their cave defenses the next day.

5TH MARINES NORTHERN ATTACK

On September 26, the 321st launched a three-pronged attack against Hill B. The 5th Marines attacked the four hills running east to west across Peleliu (Hills 1,2,3, and Radar Hill). This row of hills was perpendicular to the south of the last northern ridge—Amiangal.

These hills were defended by 1,500 enemy infantry, artillery, naval engineers, and the shot-up reinforcing infantry battalion, which landed on the night of September 23. The enemy were well protected in the caves and interconnected tunnels within the hills and ridges.

As the fighting started, Colonel Harris side-stepped his 2nd Battalion west of the hills and attacked Amiangal Ridge to the north. By dark, the 2nd Battalion had secured the southern end of the ridge but took heavy fire from positions in the central and northwestern slopes.

The Marines now confronted the most wide-ranging set of tunnels and caves on Peleliu. They were trying to invade the homes and defensive positions of a long-established naval construction unit. Most of whose members were better miners than infantrymen. As night settled, the 2nd Battalion cut itself loose from its southern units and formed a small battalion beachhead for the night.

The next morning, the 2/5 Marines tried to advance along the route leading to the northern nose of Amiangal Ridge. They ran into a wide and deep anti-tank ditch that denied them the close tank support they'd successfully used earlier. Again, the 5th Marines asked for point-blank artillery.

This time division responded. Major George Hanna's 155mm Gun Battalion moved one of its pieces into position. This gun was 175 yards from the face of the ridge. The sight of that gun prompted enemy machine-gun and small arms fire, inflicting casualties upon the artilleryman.

Enemy fire was quickly suppressed by Marine rifle fire and then by the 155mm gun. Throughout the morning, the heavy 155mm fire pounded across the face of the ridge and

destroyed or closed all identified caves on the west face—
except one. That cave was a tunnel mouth that led down to the
ground level in the northwest base of the hill. It was too close
to Marine lines to permit the 155mm to fire on it.

After a bulldozer filled in a portion of the anti-tank ditch,
tank-infantry teams moved into blast and bulldoze the tunnel
mouth closed. Marines swept over the slopes above the tunnel
and secured the crest of the northern nose of Amiangal.
While Marines held the outside of the hill, stubborn Japanese
defenders still occupied the interior.

A maze of interconnected tunnels extended throughout
the length of the small Amiangal mountain. Enemy
defenders would blast open the previously closed cave or
tunnel mouth and surge out in a banzai attack. Apart from
the surprise, these counterattacks were a rare and welcome
opportunity for Marines to see and kill their enemy in
daylight. These tactics were inconsistent with the overall
enemy strategy on Peleliu and shortened the fight for the
island's northern end.

As the fighting raged on, the 5th Marines assembled its 3rd
Battalion with supporting tanks, amphibian tractors, naval

gunfire, and air support to assault and secure Ngesebus 700 yards to the north of Peleliu on September 28.

This operation involved a single, reinforced battalion against 500 prepared and entrenched enemy infantry. In just over forty hours, the 3/5 Marines fought the most cost-effective single battalion battle in the Peleliu campaign.

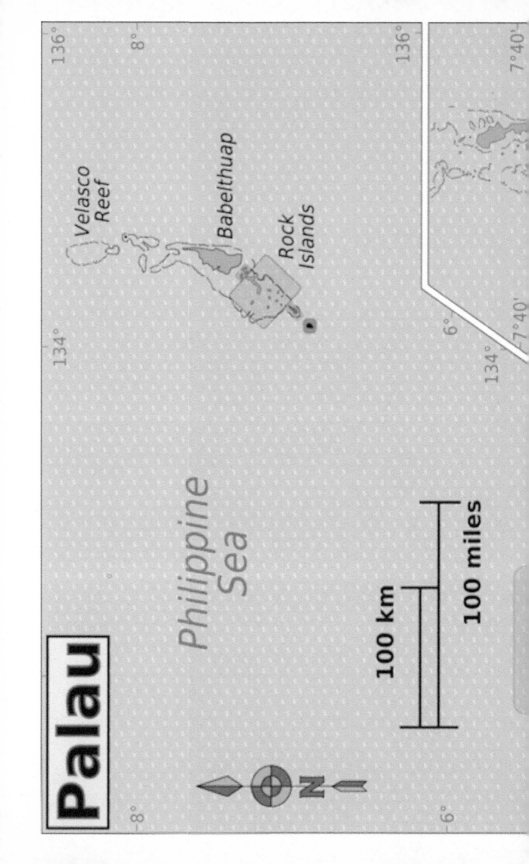

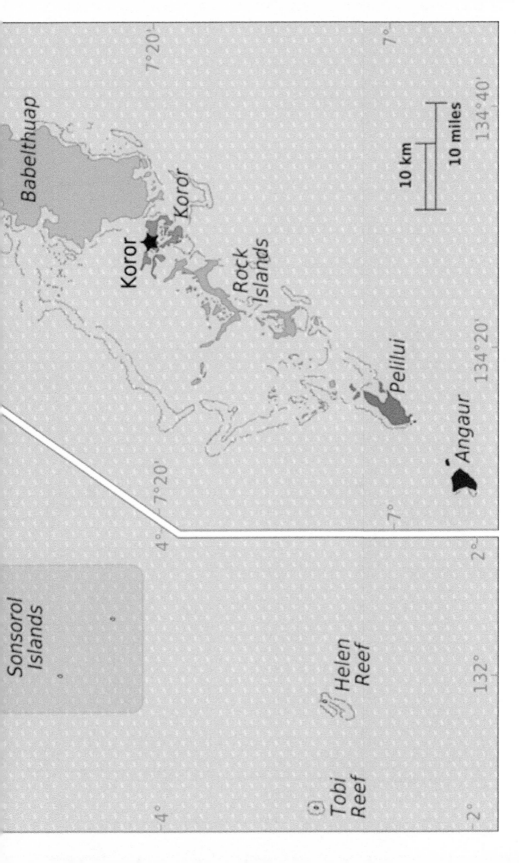

SEIZURE OF NGESEBUS

The 3rd Battalion got ashore with no casualties. They immediately knocked out all the enemy's beach defenses. Then they turned their attention to the cave positions in the ridges and blockhouses. The ridges here were like those in northern Peleliu in that they stood individually and not part of a complex ridge system.

This denied enemy troops the opportunity to have a mutual defense between cave positions. The attacking Marines could use supporting tanks and concentrate all their fire on each defensive system—without taking fire from their flanks.

By dusk on September 28, the 3/5 Marines had overrun most of the enemy opposition. The next day at 1500, Ngesebus was declared secure. The island was turned over to the 321st, and the 3/5 Marines were put into the division reserve.

The seizure of Ngesebus by one depleted infantry battalion illustrates an enduring principle of war: effective concentration of means. General Rupertus concentrated all his available firepower: divisional and corps artillery, two cruisers, a battleship, nearly all the division's remaining armor, armored and troop-carrying amphibian tractors, and all Marine aviation on Peleliu.

This concentrated support allowed the heavily depleted 3/5 Marines to secure Ngesebus and destroy 477 of Colonel Nakagawa's battle-hardened, entrenched soldiers in forty-one hours at the cost of forty-eight Marine casualties.

As the 3/5 Marines were securing Ngesebus, the rest of the 5th Marines fought the Japanese still hunkered down in northeast Peleliu. After seizing Akarakoro Point past Amiangal Mountain, the 2/5 Marines turned south and swept through enemy defenses east of the mountain with flamethrowers and demolitions. Then they moved southward to Radar Hill, the stronghold of Hill Row.

Radar Hill was under attack from the south and west by the 1/5 Marines. After two days, two battalions were on the top side of the hills. But inside, there were still stubborn enemy defenders continuing to resist.

Marines solved this problem by blasting the cave and tunnel mouths closed—silencing the enemy forever.

FIGHT FOR THE POCKET

The Umurbrogol Pocket was the scene of the bloodiest and most costly fighting along with the campaign's best and worst tactical decisions.

Its terrain was the most challenging on the island. Pre-landing planners didn't realize the Pocket for what it was: a complex cave fortress perfect for a suicidal defense. The southern slopes (known as Bloody Nose) dominated the landing beaches and airfield through where the Pocket had to be assaulted.

After Colonel Puller's 1st Marines conquered those heights through a costly and brave assault, command sent in artillery controlled by aerial observers. This radically changed the situation. The Pocket's defenders could only delay and harass Allied forces with sporadic fire attacks and nighttime raids. After D +4, enemy defenders in the Pocket could no longer seriously threaten the division's mission.

After more enemy observation sites were secured, General Rupertus continued to urge his Marines forward. He pressed his commanders to keep up momentum. As though the seizure of the Pocket was as crucial as securing the commanding heights guarding it from the south. But the challenging terrain and fanatical defenders became entangled with Rupertus' determined character.

This was only sorted out by time and the intervention of General Geiger. Most of the offensive into the Pocket between September 21-29 was directed into the cave mouths, ridges, and twin box canyons. Infantry, tanks, air support, and flame-throwing LVTs penetrated the low ground but were then surrounded on three sides. Enemy positions inside canyons and ridges were hidden from observation. Japanese troops were protected in their caves and were skilled at making the captured low ground untenable.

Other attacks to seize the heights of the eastern ridges were initially successful. Small infantry units scrambled up onto the bare ridge tops but came under fire from facing parallel ridges and caves. They were also harassed by strong enemy counterattacks who left their caves under cover of darkness in suicide attacks.

On September 20, the 7th Marines relieved the 1st Marines along the southwest front of the Pocket and resumed the attack the next day. These assaults achieved limited success behind heavy fire support and smoke. But these positions became impossible to maintain after the fire support and smoke lifted. Assault troops were withdrawn under renewed fire support to their original jump-off positions. There was little to show for the day's bloody fighting.

On September 22, against the west shoulder of the Pocket (Wildcat Bowl), Allied troops gained ground on their early advances—most of which were surrendered at day's end. Marines came under heavy fire from concealed defenders in their mutually supporting cave positions. The 7th Marines had advanced to within a hundred yards of Colonel Nakagawa's cave position. But several supporting hilltops and ridges would have to be reduced before a direct attack on the cave would have any hope of success.

The fight for the Pocket was turning into a siege, but the 1st Marine Division believed they could break through enemy opposition. Rupertus ordered continued battalion and regimental assaults believing they would soon bring victory.

When the 321st's eastward probes brought them within grasp of sealing off the Pocket from the north, they deployed two battalions to complete the encirclement. This assault would absorb the 321st Infantry's full attention until September 26, while the 5th Marines were fighting in northern Peleliu. The 7th Marines continued to pressure the Pocket from the south. When the 321st broke through on the 26th, their mission was expanded to assault the Pocket from the north.

The 321st broke through in the north and cleared the sporadically defended Kamilianlul Ridge. Their attack along adjacent ridges allowed for the Allied forces' consolidation on the north side of the Pocket—now 400 yards wide. On September 29, the 7th Marines were ordered to relieve the Army units in the northern sector.

Now that the 2/7 and 3/7 Marines were on static guard duty, hundreds of non-infantry were stripped from combat positions and put into support units. These "infantillery" units were assigned to hold the earlier held sectors. They faced the karst plateau between the Pocket and West Road.

On the 30th, with the 7th Marines' flexibility restored, they moved south and secured Boyd and Walt's Ridge. They controlled the East Road, but enemy defenders still harassed them from caves on the west side.

On October 3, the 7th Marines organized a four-battalion attack. This plan called for the 1/7 and 3/7 to attack Boyd's

Ridge from the north, while the 2/7 would attack Walt's Ridge from the south. The 3/5 would make a diversionary southern attack into Horseshoe Canyon and Five Sisters to its west.

This regimental attack committed four battalions (closer to company strength) against the heights in the southern edge of the Pocket. The assault succeeded, but with heavy casualties. Four of the Five Sisters were scaled but were untenable and had to be abandoned. The next day, the 7th Marines made another attack to seize—then give up positions on Five Sisters.

During this fight, the 3/7 Marines' push led to a rapid advance that gained them Hill 120. They hoped this would provide a jump-off point for the next day's operation against the ridge to the west. But Hill 120, as with so many others in the Pocket, came under enemy crossfire, making it completely untenable.

The 3/7 withdrew and suffered heavy casualties. Among

these was Captain "Jamo" Shanley, who commanded Company L. When several of his men fell wounded, Captain Shanley dashed forward under heavy fire to rescue two men, bringing them behind a tank. When he returned to help another wounded Marine, a mortar round exploded behind him—killing him instantly. His XO was shot by a Japanese sniper when he ran up to help, but collapsed on top of Shanley with a bullet in his brain.

Captain Shanley was awarded a gold star for the Navy Cross he earned in Operation Backhander at Cape Gloucester on New Britain, where he led his company in the seizure of Hill 660 in the Borgen Bay area.

The 7th Marines had been in the savage Umurbrogol Pocket struggle for two weeks. Under the *advice* of General Geiger, Rupertus relieved them but was still determined to have his Marines secure the Pocket and turned to his only remaining regiment. Colonel Harris moved in with his 5th Marines. He planned to attack from the north and chip off one ridge at a time.

SUBDUING THE POCKET

On September 30, Peleliu aerial reconnaissance convinced Allied planners that siege tactics were required to clear positions in the Pocket. Colonel Harris believed in being lavish with ammunition and stingy with Marine lives. Harris would use all available fire support before ordering advances.

The 2/5 Marines were in position on October 5, but only reconnoitered positions where heavier firepower could come into play. Bulldozers prepared paths on the north end of the box canyons for tanks and LVT flamethrowers to operate. Light artillery batteries were placed along the West Road to fire point-blank into cliffs at the north end of the Pocket.

Cliffs considered "troublesome" were obliterated by direct fire. The rubble created a ramp for tanks to climb into better firing positions. Light mortars were used to strip vegetation from areas with suspected enemy caves. Planes loaded with napalm-filled belly tanks were also used to bomb enemy targets selected by the 5th Marines as their key objective.

While the 2/5 Marines picked off enemy firing positions in the north, on October 7, the 3/5 assaulted Horseshoe Ridge with tanks. This time the mission wasn't to seize and hold but to destroy all targets on the faces of Five Sisters and the lower western face of Hill 100.

When all the ammunition was used, tanks withdrew to rearm and then returned accompanied by flame-throwing LVTs and small infantry fire teams. This tactic killed many cave-dwelling Japanese, along with finally silencing their heavy weapons. Before this, single enemy artillery pieces firing from Horseshoe Ridge had harassed the airfield. After the October 7 assaults, no further enemy attacks occurred.

For six more days, the 5th Marines provided all available support to small incremental advances from the north. Light mortars were used to clear vegetation and routes of advance. Both tanks and artillery were used at point-blank range, firing into suspected caves or rough coral areas.

Napalm aerial bombardments cleared vegetation and drove the Japanese defenders farther back into their caves. All advances were limited and aimed at seizing new firing positions. Small platoons and squads made these advances. After Hill 140 was taken, they had a firing site for a 75mm howitzer. The howitzer was wrestled in, disassembled, reassembled, sandbagged, and then fired from position. The 75mm fired into the mouth of a huge cave at the base of the next ridge from where enemy fire had come from for days.

Sandbagging the 75mm howitzer posed several problems. The only available loose sand or dirt had to be carried in from the beach or came from occasional debris slides. The use of sandbags in forward infantry positions increased, and this technique was later widely used when the 81st Infantry Division took over Pocket operations.

SECURING THE EASTERN RIDGES

The 2/5 carefully advanced through several small ridges and knobs and finally seized two murderous box canyons. Direct fire could now be poured into the west face of Boyd and Walt Ridges. But these cave-filled western slopes were protected by other caves on the parallel ridge known as Five Brothers.

After a week of siege-like activity pushed the northern boundary of the Pocket another 600 yards south, the 3/5 Marines were called in to relieve the 2/5. The forward positions being relieved were so close to the enemy that snipers picked off several incoming Marines (even the company commander).

During this exchange, a small enemy group reoccupied a position earlier secured by frequent interdiction fires. Even through these losses and interruptions, the relief was completed on schedule, and on October 13, the 3/5 Marines continued their slow and deliberate advance.

Terrain prohibited any advance south of Hill 140, so the 3/5 shifted southwest, paralleling the West road and into the coral badlands. This terrain was earlier judged unsuitable, but with the aid of fire-scouring napalm bombs, it was traversed. Major "Cowboy" Stout's VMF-114 bombs fell incredibly close to the advancing 3/5 Marines front and the stationary units east of the West Road.

The 1/7 Marines launched a similar effort. Together, these two battalions advanced and secured one-half of the depth of the coral badlands. Between the West Road and the China Wall this clearing allowed the "infantillery" unit to advance their lines eastward and then hold as far as the infantry had cleared.

In early October, the 5th and 7th Marines' actions had reduced the Pocket to an oval shape 700 yards north to south and 350 yards east to west. According to Colonel Nakagawa's radio report, he still had over 700 troops within the Pocket, and eighty percent were still effective.

Division command suggested enclosing the Pocket with

barbed wire and designating it as a prisoner of war closure. The Pocket no longer counted in the strategic balance nor in completing the effective seizure of Peleliu. General Rupertus wanted to subdue the Pocket before turning it over to General Mueller's 81st Army Division for mop-up operations. Rupertus' successful seizure of northern Peleliu and Ngesebus had ended the enemy's capability to reinforce the isolated Japanese troops on Peleliu.

Without pressing for a declaration that Peleliu had been secured (which would formalize the completion of the 1st Marine Division's mission), General Geiger ordered Rupertus to relieve the 5th and 7th Marines with his freshest and largest infantry regiment, the 321st RCT (still attached to the 1st Marine Division). General Rupertus replied that "very shortly," his Marines would subdue and secure the Pocket.

Admiral Nimitz sent a message to General Geiger. He directed him to turn command over to General Mueller's 81st Division, relieve the 1st Marine Division, and begin mop-up operations and garrison duty on Peleliu.

MOPPING UP PELELIU

On October 20, General Mueller took responsibility for mop up operations on Peleliu. He described the tactical situation as a siege—and ordered his troops to proceed accordingly.

For six weeks, his two infantry regiments, the 322nd and 323rd, plus the 2nd Battalion of the 321st Regiment, did just that. They used sandbags as an assault device, carrying sand up from the beaches and inching them forward. They pressed closer to enemy caves and dug-in strong points. They used tanks and flamethrowers and even improved on the vehicle-mounted flamethrower. They made a gasoline pipeline from a road-bound gas truck, enabling them (with booster pumps) to launch napalm hundreds of feet into the enemy's defensive area. They took advantage of the 75mm howitzer on Hill 140 and found other sites to put howitzers and fire point-blank into enemy caves.

To support the growing need for sandbags on ridge-top foxholes, army engineers strung high lines to transport them (along with ammo and rations) up to the peaks and ridge tops. Army troops still took casualties, even with these siege tactics, as they ground down the stubborn Japanese defenses. The Umurbrogol Pocket siege consumed the 81st Division's full attention and both regimental combat teams until November 27, 1944.

This prolonged siege operation was carried out within twenty miles of a much larger enemy force of 25,000 soldiers in the northern Palaus. The US Navy had the enemy isolated with patrols and bombing from Marine Aircraft Group 11 operating from Peleliu.

As costly and challenging as the Allied advances were, Japanese defenders had similar demanding, and even more discouraging, situations in their underground positions. Sanitation was crude. They had little to no water, rations were nearly nonexistent, and ammunition was even more scarce. As time wore on, some Japanese were given the opportunity to leave the defenses and make suicidal banzai night attacks. Very few were ever captured.

In late November, General Murai suggested in a radio message to General Inoue on Koror to make one final banzai attack for the honor of the empire. Inoue turned him down. By this time, Nakagawa's only external communications were by radio to Koror. As he'd expected, all local wire communications were destroyed.

Tanks and infantry carefully pressed on in their relentless advance. The 81st Divisions' engineers improved the roads and ramps leading into the heart of the final Japanese position. Flamethrower and tank attacks steadily reduced each cave position as the infantry pushed its foxhole sandbags forward.

On November 24, Colonel Nakagawa sent his final message to Koror. He'd burned the colors of the *2nd Infantry Regiment* and split the remaining fifty-six men into seventeen infiltration parties. They would slip through Allied lines and "attack the enemy everywhere."

On the night of November 24, twenty-five Japanese soldiers (including two officers) were killed. One soldier was captured the following day. His interrogation, along with post-war records, revealed that General Murai and Colonel Naka-gawa committed *Seppuku* (Japanese ritual suicide by disembow-elment) in their command post.

The final two-day advance of the 81st Division was indeed now a mop-up operation. Carefully conducted to eliminate any holdout opposition. By noon on November 27, north-moving units, guarded by other infantry units, met face-to-face with the battalion moving south near the Japanese command post. Colonel Arthur Watson, commanding the 323rd, reported to General Mueller that the operation was over.

The tenacious determination of the enemy was symbolized by the last thirty-three prisoners captured on Peleliu. In March 1947, a small Marine guard attached to a navy garrison on the island found unmistakable signs of a Japanese military pres-ence in a cave.

Patrols captured a straggler, a Japanese sailor who said there were thirty-three Japanese soldiers under the command of Lieutenant Yamaguchi. While the straggler reported some dissension in the ranks, a final banzai attack was still under consideration.

The Navy garrison commander moved his personnel and their dependents to a secure area and radioed Guam for rein-forcements and a Japanese war crimes witness. Admiral Michio Sumikawa flew in and traveled by Jeep along the roads near the suspected enemy positions. Through a loudspeaker, he recited the existing situation.

No response. The Japanese sailor who'd been captured earlier went back to the cave armed with letters from Japanese families and former officers on the Palaus, informing the hold-outs that the war was indeed over.

On April 21, 1947, the holdouts surrendered. Lieutenant Yamaguchi led a haggard twenty-six soldiers to a position of eighty battle-dressed Marines. Yamaguchi bowed and handed over his sword to the on-scene US Navy commander.

CONDITIONS ON PELELIU

Robert "Pepper" Martin from *Time* magazine was one of the
few civilian correspondents who chose to share the fate of the

Marines on Peleliu. He wrote the following account: "Peleliu was a horrible place. Suffocating heat and sporadic rain—a muggy rain that brings no relief—only more misery. Coral rocks soak up heat during the day, and it's only slightly cooler at night.

"The Marines were in the finest possible physical condition, but they wilted on Peleliu. By the fourth day, there were as many casualties from heat as from wounds. Peleliu was worse than Guam in its bloodiness, climate, terror, and tenacity of the Japs. The sheer brutality and fatigue has surpassed anything yet seen in the Pacific, indeed from the standpoint of troops involved in the time taken to make the island secure.

"On the second day, the temperature had reached 105 degrees in the shade. There was little to no shade in most places where the fighting was going on, and arguably there was no breeze anywhere. It lingered at that level of heat as days dragged by (temperatures were recorded as high as 115 degrees).

"The water supply was a serious problem from the start. While this had been anticipated, the solution proved less complicated than expected. Engineers discovered productive wells could be drilled almost anywhere on low ground. Personnel semi-permanently stationed at the beach found that even shallow holes dug in the sand would yield a mildly repulsive liquid that could be purified for drinking with halazone tablets.

"It continued to be necessary to supply the assault troops from scoured out oil drums and 5-gallon fuel cans. But steaming out the oil drums didn't remove the oil, which resulted in many troops drinking water and getting sick. When the captains of the ships in the transport area learned of this and the shortage of water, they rushed cases of fruit and fruit drinks to the beaches to ease the problem.

"The water situation was a problem for troops operating on the relatively open and level ground. Once the fighting entered the ridges, just traversing the difficult terrain without having to fight caused the debility rate to shoot up quickly. An emergency call was sent to all the ships offshore—requisitioning every available salt tablet for the 1st Marines."

The statement that heat casualties equaled wound casualties was misleading. Most evacuated troops were returned to duty after a day or two of rest. Their absence from the front lines did not permanently impair the combat efficiency of their units. But these several cases strained the already overburdened medical core.

III AMPHIBIOUS CORPS

The III Amphibious Corps commander, General Roy Geiger, was responsible for planning the seizure of the southern Palaus (Peleliu, Ngesebus, and Angaur). But Geiger and his staff were distracted during these critical planning weeks with the liberation of Guam on August 10.

The Guam operation took a month longer than planned. Someone else needed to plan the assault for the operation in the Palaus. A temporary headquarters, X-Ray Corps, under General Julian Smith was formed. The two main assaults of the southern Palaus campaign were assigned to the Army's 81st Infantry (Angaur) and the 1st Marine Division (Peleliu-Ngesebus). The 81st Division was also tasked with placing one regimental combat team as a core reserve.

While this separation of division level planning was convenient, it caused a gross imbalance of force allocation, neither recognized nor corrected as plans progressed. The 1st Marine Division had nine infantry battalions (8,000 Marines) to attack over 10,000 enemy defenders on Peleliu. General Mueller's 81st Infantry Division had six infantry battalions (5,400 soldiers) allocated to attack 1,500 Japanese defenders on Angaur.

The circumstances and the terrain between the two islands were also imbalanced. Peleliu was much larger and had a more complex landscape. The defensive fortifications were far more developed, and it offered fewer predictable landing beaches than on Angaur.

Only the later rapid shifting of plans accounted for such force allocation imbalances not being corrected at the Corps or Expeditionary Troops level. The effect of these imbalances was magnified on September 17. Higher-level changes in these plans (naval decisions) took away all the III Amphibious Corps reserves.

* * *

Operation Stalemate would be conducted by two divisions, one from the Marines, and one from the Army. In the Pacific since mid-1942, the 1st Marine Division was a combat-tested veteran organization that launched the first offensive landing in the Pacific on Guadalcanal.

After a brief rest and recovery in Australia, and training newly joined Marines, the division made its second amphibious assault at Cape Gloucester (Operation Backhander) on New Britain on December 26, 1943. When the 1st Division landed on Peleliu on September 15, 1944, its regiments had officers and enlisted Marine veterans from both landings and fresh troops ready to fight. Before World War II ended, the 1st Marine Division took part in one last battle: Operation Iceberg: victory on Okinawa.

GENERAL WILLIAM RUPERTUS

General Rupertus commanded the 1st Marine Division during their time on Peleliu. He'd been with the division since the beginning of 1942. As a brigadier general, he was General Vandegrift's assistant division commander during the Guadalcanal campaign.

He took command of the division at the start of Operation Backhander (battle for Cape Gloucester on New Britain) on December 26, 1943. Rupertus was commissioned in 1913 and commanded a Marine ship's detachment in World War I. Following the Great War, he was assigned to duty in China and Haiti. After the Peleliu campaign, he was made Commandant of the Marine Corps schools in Quantico. On March 25, 1945, the general died of a heart attack while still on active duty, aged fifty-five.

GENERAL PAUL MUELLER

General Mueller commanded the 81st Division and was a graduate of the West Point class of 1915. He commanded an infantry battalion in France in World War I and during the interwar period had several infantry commands and staff billets. In August 1941, he took command of the 81st at Fort Rucker, Alabama, and trained extensively until his division was called to battle in Angaur and Peleliu.

General Mueller served on active duty until retiring in 1954. He died ten years later on September 25 at seventy-one years of age.

ARMY'S 81ST INFANTRY DIVISION

The Wildcats formed in August 17 at Camp Jackson, South Carolina. They saw action in France at the Argonne in World War I. They were deactivated at the end of the war. In June 1942, the 81st was reactivated and sent to several Pacific training bases before their first combat assignment on Angaur.

After successful operations on Angaur, they relieved units of the 1st Marine Division on Peleliu. Once Peleliu was secure, the Wildcats trained for Operation Olympic—the invasion of Japan. But the Japanese surrendered after two atomic bomb attacks. Instead of invading Japan, the 81st became an occupying force. On January 30, 1946, the 81st Infantry Division was once again deactivated.

JAPANESE FIGHTING TACTICS

After the December 1941 surprise attacks, Japanese military planners believed they could quickly secure an Asian empire in the Pacific. Japan would defend her territories until the bitter end. The Empire of Japan would tire and bleed out the Allies before negotiating Japanese dominance in the Pacific.

This strategic concept was in line with the medieval Japanese code of *bushido*. The Japanese believed in their army's moral superiority over lesser races. This led the Japanese to expect their 19th-century *banzai* tactics would bring them success. Experience and expectations clashed until their 1942 encounters with the Allies, particularly in the Solomon's. It took several confrontations with the Allies to learn that modern infantry weapons and tactics would defeat them.

To Allied troops, these Japanese misconceptions were disturbing but cost-effective. It was less costly and easier to mow down banzai attacks than dig stubborn defenders out of fortified positions.

By the spring of 1944, these hard lessons had been understood in the highest levels of Japan's Army Command. When General Tojo directed General Inoue to defend the Palaus deliberately and conservatively, he ordered Japanese troops to dig in and hunker down, making the final defense a costly and bloody affair.

NAVAL GUNFIRE SUPPORT

In many of the 1st Division Marines' earlier operations (especially on Guadalcanal) they were on the receiving end of naval gunfire. At Cape Gloucester, the character and disposition of the Japanese defenses didn't call for extensive pre-landing fire support, nor did following operations ashore.

The naval gunfire Guadalcanal veterans were exposed to often damaged planes and installations onshore. Its effect on the dug-in Marines was sobering and scary, but rarely destructive.

During the planning for Peleliu, division staff had no trained naval gunfire planner. When one arrived, he was hindered by a cumbersome communications link back to higher headquarters.

General Holland M. Smith's FMF (Fleet Marine Force) in Honolulu would provide essential targeting information for the division's plan. The FMF would also plan and allocate available gunfire resources to the targets deemed necessary by the division staff planners.

This preoccupation with the ongoing Marianna's

campaigns and illness of Admiral Jesse Oldendorf, the naval gunfire support group commander, further limited and constrained preparations. Heavy enemy ammunition expenditures in the Marianas also reduced the available ammunition for the Peleliu operation.

During the delivery of Allied preparatory fires, there was no Japanese response. This persuaded Oldendorf to report all known targets destroyed and to cancel any further preparatory fires scheduled on D +3. An unintended benefit of this change in naval gunfire resulted in more shells being available for post-landing support.

But the costly effect of this inadequate naval gunfire support was that the flanking positions north and south of the landing beaches were destroyed. The selection of naval gunfire targets could have been done more thoroughly. Colonel "Chesty" Puller, the 1st Marines commander, specifically asked for the destruction of positions dominating his landing on his division's left flanks.

This failure was paid for in blood, bravery, and time during the battle for the Point.

After D-Day, there were several instances of well called and delivered naval gunfire support. Night illuminations during September 16 and the destruction of two significant blockhouses were effective support for the Ngesebus landing.

REEF-CROSSING TACTICS

Peleliu's coral reef would not permit landing craft within 700 yards of the beach, so the landing craft deposited tanks at the reef's edge. The depth of the reef's edge allowed the tanks to operate in *most* areas without being submerged.

A plan was devised to form tanks into small columns, each led by an LVT. As long as the amphibious tractor was grounded on the reef, the tanks could follow. When an LVT encountered a depth that floated it, tanks were halted while the amphibious tractor felt for a more suitable, shallow path. This brought the tanks onshore in small columns as quickly as possible. This tactic was crucial for timely employment of armor onshore before D-Day was over.

Two other reef crossing innovations were used on D-Day. Several amphibious trailers were towed behind landing craft, and later, at the reef's edge, they were towed in by the LVTs. Once onshore, trucks pulled them the rest of the way in. This allowed for vital supplies to be brought into points in the rear of the fighting.

Newly available cranes were placed on barges near the

reef's edge. They lifted nets full of ammunition and other essential supplies from boats to tractors at the transfer lines. Crawler cranes were landed early and positioned by the shore party to lift net loads from LVTs to trucks for a swift forward delivery.

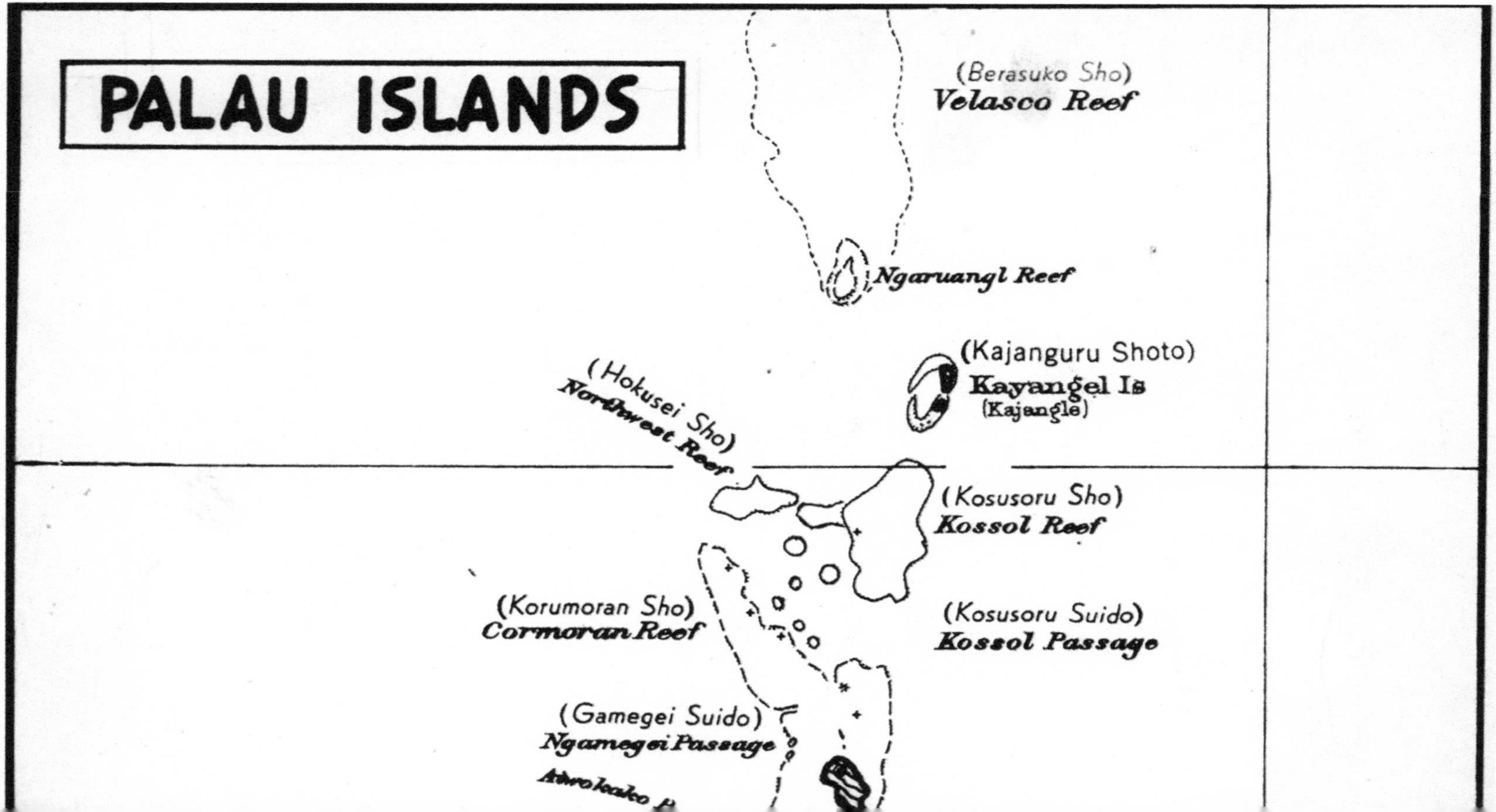

PALAU ISLANDS

(Berasuko Sho)
Velasco Reef

Ngaruangl Reef

(Kajanguru Shoto)
Kayangel Is
(Kajangle)

(Hokusei Sho)
Northwest Reef

(Kosusoru Sho)
Kossol Reef

(Kosusoru Suido)
Kossol Passage

(Korumoran Sho)
Cormoran Reef

(Gamegei Suido)
Ngamegei Passage

Atorokoko P

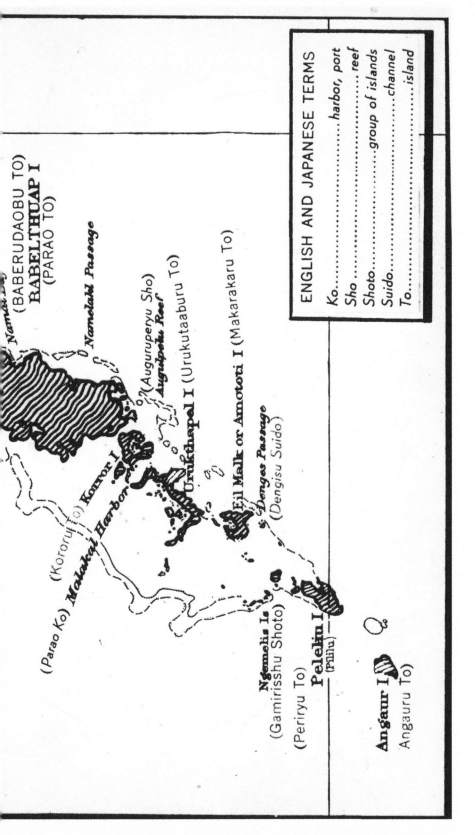

(BABERUDAOBU TO)
RABELTHUAP I
(PARAO TO)

Namelabi Passage

(Auguruperyu Sho)
Augulpelu Reef

Grukthapel I (Urukutaaburu To)

Eil Malk or Amototi I (Makarakaru To)

Denges Passage
(Dengisu Suido)

Korror I

(Kororu ○) **Korror I**

(Parao Ko) *Malakal Harbor*

Ngemelis Is
(Gamirisshu Shoto)

(Periryu To)
Peleliu I
(Piliu)

Angaur I
Angauru To)

ENGLISH AND JAPANESE TERMS
Ko..................harbor, port
Sho.............................reef
Shoto.............group of islands
Suido.........................channel
To..............................island

CONQUEST OF PELELIU

Was the seizure of Peleliu necessary?

What were the advantages to the US war effort from securing Peleliu?

It assured the absolute domination of all the Palau Islands. It also added to the security of General MacArthur's right flank as he continued westward with his Philippines campaign. Within the Palaus group, the conquest destroyed enemy facilities that survived Admiral Mitscher's destructive strike in March 1944.

Securing Peleliu also ensured a total denial of support to Japanese forces from the submarine base at Koror. Reducing the already waning enemy submarine capability east of the Philippines.

The Allied position on Peleliu contributed to neutralizing 25,000 enemy troops in northern Palau. The Peleliu landing *did not* contribute to the RLT 323's (regimental landing team) unopposed seizure of Ulithi. Admiral Halsey had earlier believed his forces could seize Ulithi without first taking Peleliu.

The most significant visible benefit of a subdued Peleliu was its use as a link in the flight path and communication lines from Hawaii to the Philippines. It was convenient but not a necessity.

Survivors of the *Indianapolis* during the July 29, 1945 sinking were saved indirectly by the seizure of Peleliu. After delivering atomic bomb parts to Tinian, the ship was heading for the Philippines when it was torpedoed. The *Indianapolis* sunk in twelve minutes. There was no received report of the contact or the sinking. Four days after it sunk, the 316 survivors (from a crew of 1,197) were spotted by a Navy patrol bomber flying out of Peleliu. This sighting directly led to the rescue and most likely would not have happened but for the Allied occupation of Peleliu.

PRICE OF PELELIU

Marine Casualties were 6,526. This included Navy doctors and corpsmen with 1,252 killed. The Army's 81st Division had 3,088 casualties, 404 were killed in action. Total US troop casualties were 9,616 (1,657 killed) on Peleliu, Angaur, and Ngesebus

The Japanese were successful in implementing their bleed and delay strategy. Their actions cost them an estimated 11,000 casualties (all but a small portion killed). Only 202 prisoners of war were captured, and of them, only nineteen were Japanese military (twelve Navy and seven Army). The rest were Korean laborers. Statistically, less than two out of every thousand Japanese military defenders were captured.

The bloody battle at Peleliu was a warning for the remaining Allied operations being conducted across the Pacific. Even with total naval and air superiority and a four to one troop advantage—the conquest of Peleliu cost one Allied casualty and 1,590 rounds of ammunition per Japanese soldier killed or driven from his position. A couple of months later, the attacks on Iwo Jima and Okinawa would confirm this grim calculation.

On September 13, 1944, two days before D-Day, Admiral Halsey recommended to Admiral Nimitz that the Peleliu landing should be canceled. But by that time, it was too late: Peleliu would be added to the long list of brutal battles in which Allied forces fought, suffered, and ultimately prevailed.

Seventy-seven years later, the question of whether Operation Stalemate was necessary remains debatable. The heroism and commendable conduct of the 1st Marine Division, its Navy corpsmen, and soldiers of the 81st Infantry on that miserable island will forever be written in blood.

OPERATION DETACHMENT

1945 BATTLE OF IWO JIMA

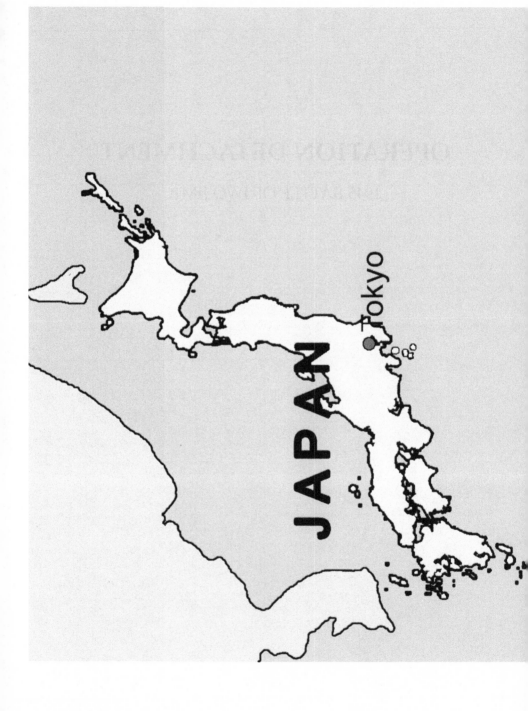

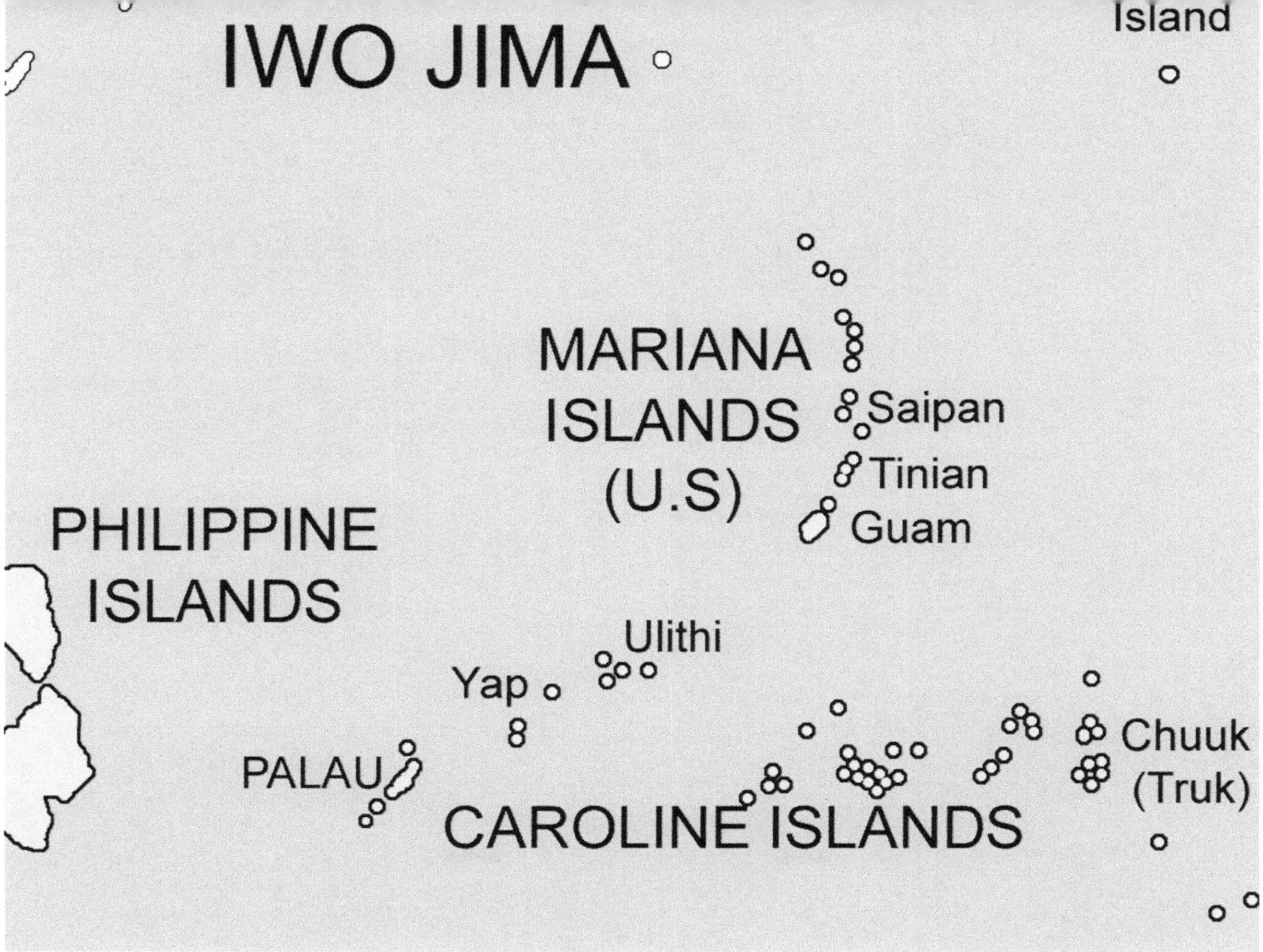
IWO JIMA
Island
MARIANA
ISLANDS
(U.S)
Saipan
Tinian
Guam
PHILIPPINE
ISLANDS
Ulithi
Yap
PALAU
CAROLINE ISLANDS
Chuuk
(Truk)

THE PACIFIC OFFENSIVE

March 4, 1945 was the second week of the Allied invasion of Iwo Jima. By now, the assault elements of the 3rd, 4th, and 5th Marine Divisions were drained, and their combat efficiency was seriously reduced.

The thrilling sight of the American flag being raised by the 28th Marines on Mount Suribachi had happened ten days earlier—a lifetime ago on Sulfur Island. The Amphibious Corps landing forces had already suffered 13,000 casualties, including 3,000 dead. The front was a jagged serration across Iwo Jima's fat northern half. Smack in the middle of the primary Japanese defenses. The Allied landing force had to advance uphill against a well-disciplined, entrenched, and rarely visible enemy.

In the center of the island, the 3rd Marine Division spent the night turning back a small, but determined, enemy counterattack, which found a gap between the 21st and 9th Marines. Savage hand-to-hand combat had cost both sides heavy casualties. The counterattack ruined the division's preparation for a morning advance, but both regiments made gains against stubborn enemy opposition.

In the east, the 4th Marine Division secured Hill 382 at the cost of their combat efficiency plummeting below fifty percent. By nightfall, it would fall another five percent. The 24th Marines, supported by flame-throwing tanks, only advanced one hundred yards before stopping to detonate two tons of explosives against enemy cave positions. The 23rd and 25th Marines entered the most challenging terrain yet—a broken ground with visibility less than a few feet.

On the western flank, the 5th Marine Division took Hill 362-B (Nishi Ridge) at the cost of over 500 casualties. They'd engaged a sizeable enemy force throughout the night. While the enemy attacks lacked coordination, exhausted Marines were barely able to hold them off. Most rifle companies were now at less than half strength. The division reported the net gain for the day as "practically nothing."

* * *

The battle took its toll on the enemy garrison as well. Japanese General Tadamichi Kuribayashi knew his *109th Division* had inflicted heavy casualties on the assaulting Marines, but his losses were comparable. The Allied capture of the critical hills the day before denied him his prized artillery observation sites.

Kuribayashi's brilliant chief of artillery, Colonel Chosaku Kaido, had been killed. Kuribayashi moved his command post from the central highlands to a large cave on the northwestern coast. Imperial Headquarters in Tokyo had reached him by radio that afternoon, but the general was in no mood for heroic rhetoric. He replied: "Send air and naval support, and I will hold the island. Without them, I cannot hold."

That afternoon, the combatants witnessed a glimpse of Iwo Jima's fate. Through the overcast skies, a giant silver bomber (the largest aircraft yet seen), the B-29 "Dinah Might," came in for an emergency landing on the scruffy island airstrip. Allied troops held their breath as the bomber swooped in and landed with a thud. Clipping a field telephone pole with its wing and rumbling to a stop three feet from the end of the strip.

Pilot Fred Malo and his ten-man crew didn't stay long. Every enemy gunner within range wanted to bag this prize. Mechanics made hurried field repairs, and the sixty-five-ton Super Fortress scrambled through a hail of enemy fire, returning to its base on Tinian.

The battle of Iwo Jima raged for another twenty-two days and claimed 11,000 more Allied casualties and the lives of nearly the entire Japanese garrison. A historic and colossal fight between two well-armed veteran forces. This was the bloodiest and biggest battle in the history of the Marine Corps. But after March 4, leaders on both sides had no doubts as to the ultimate outcome.

OPERATION DETACHMENT

Iwo Jima was an amphibious landing where assault troops saw the value of the objective. They were finally within a thousand miles of the Japanese homeland—and contributing clearly in support of the Allied bombing campaign.

This bombing campaign was a new wrinkle on an old theme. For forty years, Marines had been developing the skills to seize advanced naval bases in support of the fleet. In the Pacific war—especially at Tinian, Saipan, and now Iwo Jima —they secured advanced airbases to further the bombing of the Japanese home islands.

Allied forces had waited for the arrival of the B-29s for years. These long-range bombers became operational too late for the European Theater—but they'd been hitting Japan since November 1944 with disappointing results. The problem wasn't the planes or the pilots, but a little spit of volcanic rock halfway across the path from Saipan to Tokyo—Iwo Jima.

Radar on Iwo gave the enemy two hours' advance notice of every B-29 strike. Japanese fighters on Iwo's airfields would swarm and harass the unescorted Super Fortresses going in and especially returning to base. Enemy fighters picked off the B-29s crippled from antiaircraft fire. This caused the B-29s to fly higher and with a reduced payload.

The Joint Chiefs decided Iwo Jima must be secured with an Allied airfield built there. This would stop Japanese bombing raids and early warning interceptions. The airfield would offer fighter escorts through the treacherous portions of the B-29's missions and greater payloads at longer ranges. Iwo Jima in Allied hands would also provide emergency airfield support and landing for crippled B-29s returning from Tokyo and protect the Allied flank for the Okinawa invasion. Admiral Chester Nimitz was given three months to seize and develop Iwo Jima: codename Operation Detachment

Iwo Jima translates to "Sulfur Island" in Japanese. An ugly, foul-smelling, barren chunk of volcanic rock and sand—not even ten square miles in size. According to a Japanese Army officer: "an island of sulfur, no sparrow, no swallow, no water."

Less poetic Marines described Iwo's resemblance to a pork chop with a 556-foot volcano. Mount Suribachi dominated the southern end of the island and overlooked all potential landing beaches. Iwo rose unevenly over onto the Motoyama Plateau in the north before falling sharply off into the coast and steep cliffs and canyons. The northern terrain was a defender's dream: an intricate, broken, cave-dotted jungle of stone. Ringed by volcanic steam and a twisted landscape that seemed like a barren moon wilderness. More than one surviving Marine compared the eerie silence to something out of Dante's *Inferno*.

Iwo Jima in 1945 had two redeeming characteristics: the military value of its airfields and the psychological status of the island as a historical Japanese possession. The Allies were now within Japan's Inner Defense Zone. According to a Japanese officer: "Iwo Jima is the doorkeeper to the Imperial capital."

Even with the slowest aircraft, Tokyo could be reached in three flight hours from the island. In the Iwo Jima battle, 20,000 Allied and Japanese troops would be killed during brutal fighting in the last winter months of 1945.

No one suggested taking Iwo Jima would be easy. Admiral Nimitz assigned this mission to the same team who'd done so well in the earliest amphibious assaults in the Gilberts, Marshalls, and Marianas. Admiral Raymond Spruance would commend the 5th Fleet, Admiral Richmond Kelly Turner would commend the expeditionary forces, and Admiral Harry Hill would command the attack force.

Operation Detachment required unrelenting military pressure on the enemy and an accelerated planning schedule. The Amphibious task force preparing to assault Iwo Jima was getting squeezed on both ends. Admiral Hill desperately needed amphibious ships, shore bombardment vessels, and landing craft that were currently in use by General Douglas MacArthur and his reconquest of the Philippines. Poor weather and stiff enemy resistance combined to delay the completion of that operation.

The Joint Chiefs reluctantly postponed D-Day on Iwo from January 20 to February 19. The new schedule provided no relief for Allied planners. D-Day on Okinawa could be no later than April 1 because of the monsoon season. This tight timeframe held grim implications for Marine landing forces.

General Harry Schmidt would command the V Amphibious Corps in the assault. Schmidt's landing force consisted of three Marine divisions (3rd, 4th, and 5th). Schmidt would have the honor of commanding the largest US Marine force ever committed into a single battle—a force totaling over 80,000 troops.

Over half of these troops were Marine veterans from earlier fighting in the Pacific. Realistic training had prepared new Marines for the hard fight to come. The Iwo Jima assault force was arguably the most proficient amphibious force the world had yet to see.

Two senior Marines shared the limelight on Iwo Jima, and history has done them both an injustice. General Holland M. Smith, who then commanded the FMF (Fleet Marine Force), was tasked to participate in Operation Detachment as the Expeditionary Troops' Commanding General. This was an unnecessary billet. Schmidt had the rank, experience, staff, and resources to execute core level responsibility without being second-guessed.

General Smith was an amphibious pioneer and veteran of landings in the Gilberts, Marshalls, and the Marianas. According to him: "My sun had nearly set by then. I think they asked me along in case something happened to Harry Schmidt." Smith would try to keep out of Schmidt's way, but his decision to withhold the 3rd Marines (Expeditionary Troops Reserve) remains as controversial as it was in 1945.

General Smith proved himself an asset to the Iwo Jima campaign. He was always a voice in the wilderness in the top-level planning stage. Smith predicted severe casualties unless more effective preliminary naval bombardment was provided. He diverted visiting dignitaries and the press away from Schmidt and always offered a realistic counterpoint to some of the rosier staff estimates. According to Smith: "It's a tough proposition, that's why we're here."

General Schmidt's few public statements left him saddled with predicting Iwo Jima would be conquered in ten days. According to post-war accounts, Schmidt resented Smith's perceived role: "I was the commander of all troops on Iwo

Jima at all times. Holland Smith never had an onshore command post, never issued a single order, and never spent a single night ashore. Isn't it important from a historical standpoint that I commanded the greatest number of Marines ever to be engaged in a single action in the entire history of the Marine Corps?"

General Smith did not disagree with those points. While Smith proved to be useful, Schmidt and his staff should be credited for planning and executing the difficult and bloody Iwo Jima campaign.

The V Amphibious Corps' conquest of Iwo Jima was even more remarkable due to tough enemy opposition on the island. General Kuribayashi was one of the most fearsome opponents of the war. Kuribayashi was a fifth-generation samurai hand-picked by the emperor. The Japanese general combined combat experience with an innovative mind and an iron will.

Although this would be his only struggle against US forces, he learned much about his opponents from earlier service in the US. Kuribayashi appraised with an unblinking eye the results of previous Japanese attempts to repel Allied invasions of Japanese-held garrisons.

Aside from the heroic rhetoric, Kuribayashi saw little value in the defend-at-the-water's-edge tactics and suicidal *banzai* attacks that branded Japan's failures from Tarawa to Tinian. Kuribayashi was a realist. He did not expect much help from Japan's depleted fleet and air forces. His best chance was to fortify Iwo's forbidding terrain with an in-depth defense, similar to the defense on Peleliu. Kuribayashi would shun coastal defenses, anti-landing, and banzai tactics. Instead, he'd wage a battle of attrition: a war of patience, nerves, and time. A delay and bleed strategy. Would the Allied forces lose heart and abandon the campaign?

A passive policy this late in the war was radical to senior Japanese Navy and Army leaders. It was counter to the deeply ingrained *Bushido* samurai code: a warrior code that viewed the defensive as only an unpleasant delay before the glorious offensive could resume—where the enemy would be destroyed by fire and sword. Imperial Headquarters was nervous. There was evidence of a top-level request for guidance in defending against Allied storm landings from Nazi Germany, whose experience trying to defend Normandy at the water's edge had proven disastrous.

Japanese command was unconvinced. Kuribayashi used his connection to the Emperor to avoid being relieved. But it was not a complete victory—the Navy insisted on building blockhouses and gun casements along the obvious landing beaches. Kuribayashi demanded assistance from the finest mining engineers and fortification specialists in the Empire.

The island favored the defender. Iwo's volcanic sand mixed with cement produced an exceptional concrete for installations. The soft rock was easy to dig. Over half of the Japanese garrison put their weapons aside and picked up picks and spades. When Allied bombers from the Seventh Air Force began a daily pummeling of the island in early December 1944, Kuribayashi just moved everything underground: weapons, command post, barracks, and aid stations. The engineering achievements he accomplished were extraordinary. Kuribayashi masked gun positions, created interlocking fields of fire, and miles of tunnels linking key defensive positions. Every cave had multiple outlets and ventilation tubes. One installation inside Mount Suribachi ran seven stories deep. Allied troops rarely encountered a live Japanese on the island until the bitter end.

Allied intelligence, aided by documents captured in Saipan and by an almost daily flow of aerial surveillance, was puzzled

by the Japanese garrison's disappearing act. The photo inter-
preters, using stereoscopic lenses, listed 775 potential targets,
but all were covered, hardened, and masked. Allied planners
knew there was no fresh water available on the island. They
saw the rainwater cisterns and knew what the average monthly
rainfall would deliver. They determined the enemy garrison
couldn't survive under those conditions in numbers greater
than 12,000 for long. But Kuribayashi's force was twice that
size. His troops had existed on half rations of water for
months before the battle even began.

Unlike the earlier amphibious assaults on Guadalcanal and
Tarawa, Allies would not have a strategic surprise on Iwo.
Japanese headquarters believed Iwo would be invaded after
the loss of the Marianas. Six months before the battle, Kuribayashi wrote to his wife: "the Americans will most definitely
invade Iwo Jima—do not look for my return."

Kuribayashi ruthlessly worked his men to complete the
defensive and training preparations by February 11, 1945. The
general met his objective. Kuribayashi had a mixed force of
recruits and veterans, soldiers and sailors. His artillerymen and
mortar crews were the best in the Empire. Still, he trained and
disciplined them all. Each fighting position had the commander's "Courageous Battle Vows" prominently posted above the
firing apertures. Troops were cautioned to maintain their position and to take ten Marine lives for each Japanese death.

General Schmidt issued the operational plan on December
23, 1944. This plan wasn't fancy. Mount Suribachi towered
over the potential landing beaches, but the 3,000 yards of
black sand along the southeastern coast were more sheltered
from the prevailing winds. It was here the V Amphibious
Corps would land on D-Day. The 4th Marine Division on the
right, the 5th on the left and the 3rd in reserve. The primary
objectives were the lower airfield and Suribachi. Then, the

assault force would swing into line and attack north shoulder to shoulder.

Anticipating a significant enemy counterattack on the first night, General Holland Smith said: "We welcome their counterattack. That's generally when we break their back."

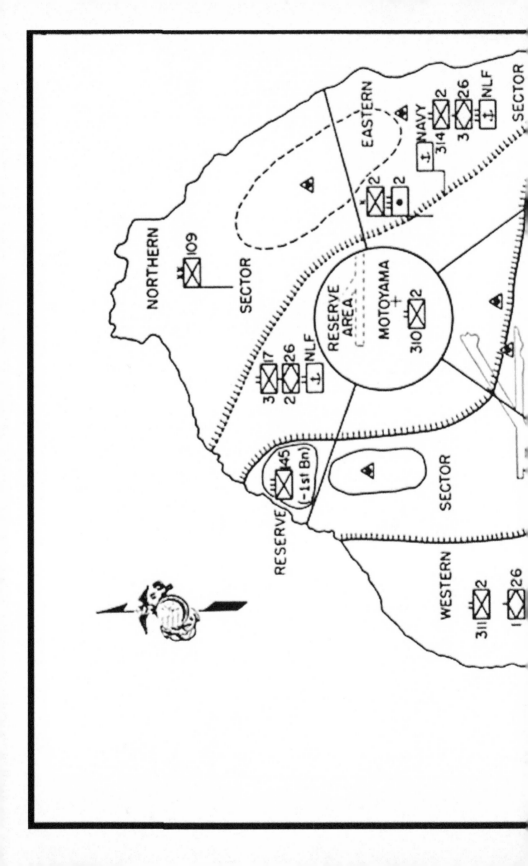

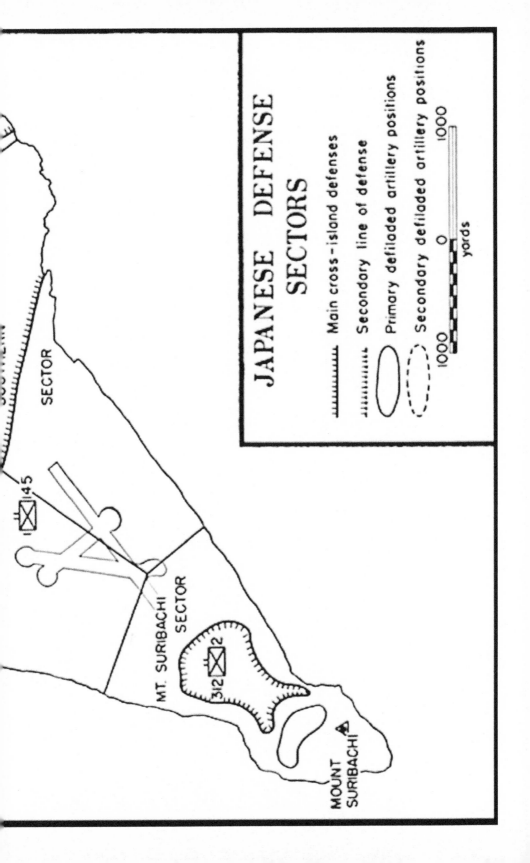

JAPANESE DEFENSE SECTORS

Main cross-island defenses
Secondary line of defense
Primary defiladed artillery positions
Secondary defiladed artillery positions

1000   0   1000
yards

SECTOR

145

MT. SURIBACHI SECTOR

3½2

MOUNT SURIBACHI

KURIBAYASHI'S BIG MISTAKE

The physical separation of the three Marine divisions from Hawaii to Guam had no apparent adverse effect on their training. The proficiency of small units in combined arms assaults on fortified positions and amphibious landing were where it counted most. Each division was well prepared for the invasion.

The 3rd Marine Division had just completed their part in the liberation of Guam. Their field training often included active combat patrols to root out and destroy stubborn enemy survivors.

On Maui, the 4th Marine Division prepared for their fourth assault landing in thirteen months with quiet confidence. According to Major Fred Karch: "We had a continuity of veterans that was unbeatable."

The 5th Marine Division prepared for their first combat experience on the big island of Hawaii. The unit's newness would prove misleading. Over half of the officers and men were veterans, including several former Marine Raiders and Parachutists who'd fought in the Solomons. Colonel Don

Robertson took command of the 3rd Battalion, 27th Marine Regiment with less than two weeks before embarkation and immediately ordered them into the field for sustained live-fire exercises. Their confidence and competence impressed and convinced Robertson that these Marines were professionals.

Among the veterans preparing to deploy on Iwo Jima were two Medal of Honor recipients from Guadalcanal. Gunnery Sargent John Basilone and Colonel Robert Galer. The Marine Corps preferred to keep these distinguished veterans in the US for morale (bond raising) purposes, but both men wrangled their way back into the fight. Basilone led a machine gun platoon and Galer led a new radar unit for the Landing Force Air Support. The Guadalcanal veterans were amazed at the abundance of amphibious shipping available for Operation Detachment. Admiral Turner commanded 497 ships (140 of these were configured for amphib operations). This armada was ten times the size of the Guadalcanal task force.

But there were still problems. Many of the ships and crews were so new that each rehearsal featured an embarrassing collision or other accident. New bulldozers (TD-18s) were an inch too wide for the LCMs. Newly modified M4A3 Sherman tanks were so heavy that the LCMs rode with a dangerously low freeboard. The 105mm howitzers overloaded the DUKWs (amphibious trucks) to the point of unseaworthiness. These factors would soon prove treacherous in Iwo Jima's unpredictable surf.

Still, the massive Allied armada embarked and began the familiar move westward in good shape, well-trained, well-equipped, and thoroughly supported.

* * *

General Kuribayashi had benefited from the Allied delays of Operation Detachment due to the Philippines campaign. He felt as ready and prepared as possible. When the Allied armada sailed from the Marianas on February 13, he was warned. He deployed one infantry battalion into the lower airfield and ordered the bulk of his garrison into their assigned fighting holes—to await the inevitable storm.

Two issues divided the Navy/Marine team as D-Day on Iwo approached. The first was Admiral Spruance's decision to detach Task Force 58 (the fast attack carriers under Admiral Marc Mitscher) to attack strategic targets on Honshu (Main island of Japan) with the simultaneous bombardment of Iwo. Marine officers suspected a Navy/Air Force rivalry at work: Mitscher's targets were aircraft factories that the B-29s had missed a few days earlier. Mitscher took all eight Marine Corps fighter squadrons assigned to the fast carriers, plus the new fast battleships with their 16-inch guns. While Task Force 58 returned in time to offer fire support on D-Day, they were off again for good, two days later.

There was a continuing argument between senior Navy and Marine officers over the extent of the preliminary naval gunfire. Marines looked at their intelligence reports on Iwo Jima and requested ten days of preparatory fire. The Navy said it did not have the time nor the ammunition to spare; three days would have to suffice. Generals Smith and Schmidt pleaded their case to Admiral Spruance. Their request was denied. Admiral Spruance ruled that three days of preparatory fire along with the daily hammering administered by the Seventh Air Force would be good enough to get the job done.

Lieutenant Colonel Don Weller was the Task Force 51 naval gunfire officer, and no man knew the business more thoroughly than him. Weller had absorbed the Pacific War's lessons well. Especially the terrible failures at Tarawa. He argued the issue was not the weight of shells and other caliber but rather the time. The destruction of heavily fortified enemy targets took deliberate and pinpoint firing from close range. They had to be assessed and adjusted by aerial observers. His seven hundred plus hard targets would need time to knock out —a lot of time.

Admiral Spruance did not have time to give for strategic, tactical, and logistical reasons. Three days of firing would deliver four times the shells than Tarawa and would be one and a half time as much delivered against the larger Saipan. It would have to do.

Iwo's notoriously foul weather and strong enemy fortifications dissipated the three-day bombardment. According to General William Rogers: "We got about 13 hours with the fire support during the 34 hours of available daylight."

General Kuribayashi committed his only known tactical error during this battle. On D minus 2, a force of one-hundred Navy and Marine frogmen approached the eastern beaches. They were escorted by a dozen rocket-firing LCI (Landing Craft Infantry). Kuribayashi believed this was the main assault and authorized the coastal batteries to open fire. This exchange was hot and heavy with the LCIs getting the worst of it, but the US battleships and cruisers hurried to blast the casement guns that were suddenly revealed on Suribachi's right flank.

That night, seriously concerned about the hundreds of Japanese targets untouched by two days of firing, Admiral Turner authorized a "war council" on his flagship and junked the original plan. He ordered the gunships to concentrate exclusively on beach areas. This was done with considerable effect on D minus 1 and D-Day morning.

Kuribayashi noted most of the positions the Imperial Navy insisted on building along the beach were destroyed—just as he predicted. But his central defensive force that crisscrossed the Motoyama Plateau remained intact. "I pray for a heroic fight," Kuribayashi told his staff.

The press briefing held the night before D-Day on Admiral Turner's flagship was uncommonly somber. General Holland Smith predicted heavy casualties: upwards of 15,000, which shocked everyone. A man clad in khakis without a rank insignia then stood and addressed the room. It was the Secretary of the Navy, James Forrestal: "Iwo Jima, like Tarawa, leaves very little choice. Except to take it by force of arms, by character, and by courage."

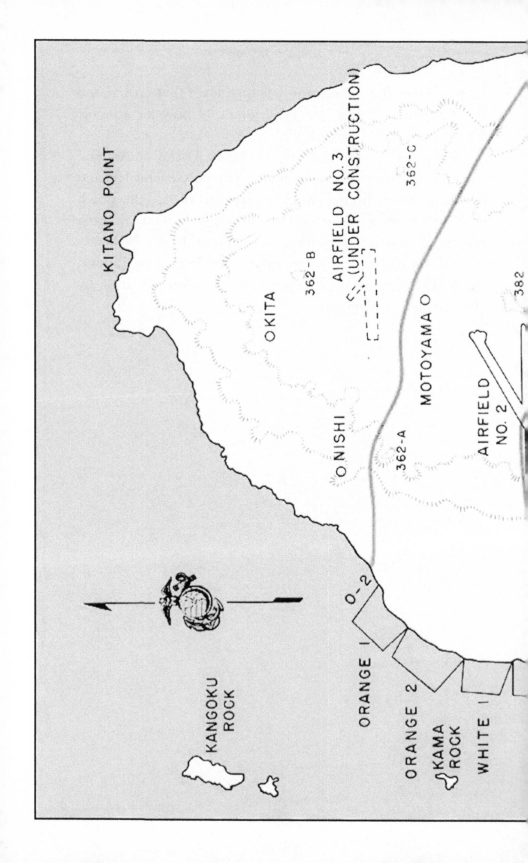

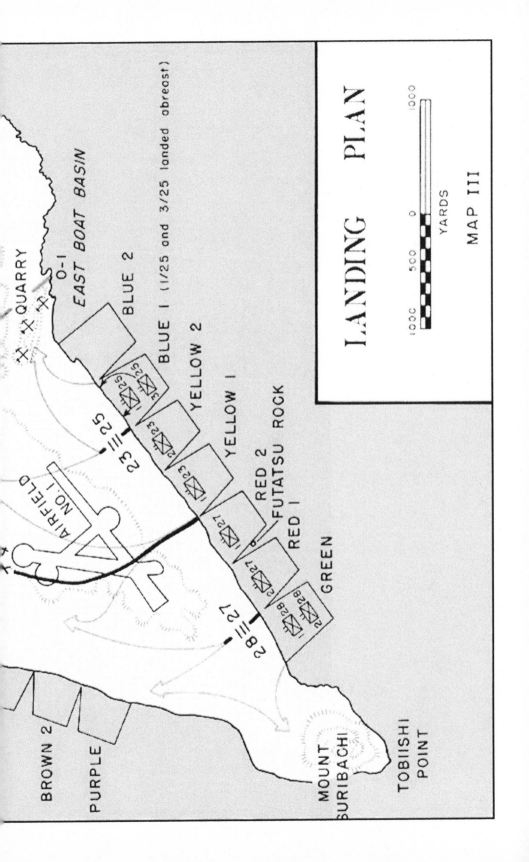

LANDING PLAN

YARDS

MAP III

EAST BOAT BASIN

QUARRY

O-1

BLUE 2

BLUE 1 (1/25 and 3/25 landed abreast)

YELLOW 2

YELLOW 1

RED 2

FUTATSU ROCK

RED 1

GREEN

AIRFIELD NO. 1

23 ≡ 25

28 ≡ 27

BROWN 2

PURPLE

MOUNT SURIBACHI

TOBIISHI POINT

D-DAY ON IWO JIMA

On D-Day morning, February 19, Iwo's weather conditions were ideal. At 0645, Admiral Turner signaled: "Land the landing force."

Shore bombardments had engaged the enemy island at near point-blank range. Battleships and cruisers steamed in as close as 1,500 yards to level their guns against their island targets. Many of these older battleships had performed this dangerous mission in other theaters of the war. The *Nevada*, raised from the muck and ruin of Pearl Harbor, led the bombardment force. The battleship *Arkansas*, built in 1912, had joined the armada from the Atlantic where she'd battered German positions at Normandy during the Allied landing on June 6, 1944.

Colonel "Bucky" Buchanan devised a modified form of the "rolling barrage" used by the bombarding gunships against beachfront targets. This concentration of naval gunfire advanced gradually as troops landed. Always 400 yards to the front. Air spotters would regulate the pace. This innovation was appealing to the division commanders who'd served in

World War I France. In those days, a rolling barrage was often the only way to break a stalemate.

The amount of shelling was shocking. Admiral Hill later wrote: "there were no proper targets for shore bombardment remaining on D-Day morning." This was an overstatement. No one denied the fury of firepower delivered against the landing beaches and surrounding areas. General Kuribayashi admitted in an assessment report to Imperial headquarters: "we need to reconsider the power of bombardment from ships. The violence of enemy bombardments is far beyond description."

When the task force appeared over the horizon, troop ships crowded with combat-equipped Marines gazed at the stunning fireworks. The Guadalcanal veterans among them watched with grim satisfaction as battleships hammered the island. The world had come full circle from the dark days of October 1942: when the 1st Marines and the Cactus Air Force suffered a similar shelling from Japanese battleships.

Sailors and Marines were eager to get their first glimpse of the objective. War correspondent John Marquand wrote of his first impressions on Iwo: "a silhouette like a sea monster, with a little dead volcano for a head and the beach area for the neck and a scrubby brown cliff for the body."

Navy Lieutenant David Susskind wrote his thoughts from the bridge of the troopship *Mellette*: "Iwo Jima was an ugly and rude sight. Only a geologist could look at it and not be disgusted."

A surgeon in the 25th Marines, Lieutenant Mike Keleher wrote: "the naval bombardment had already begun. I saw the orange-yellow flashes as the cruisers, battleships, and destroyers blasted away at the island with broadsides. We were close to Iwo, just like the pictures and models we'd been studying for weeks. A volcano was on our left and long flat beaches in a rough, rocky plateau was on our right."

General Clifton Cates studied the island through binoculars from his ship. Each division would land two reinforced regiments abreast. From left to right, the beaches were designated Green, Red, Yellow, and Blue. The 5th Division would land the 27th and 28th Marines on the left flank on Green and Red Beaches, While the 4th would land the 23rd and 25th Marines on the right flank at Blue Beach.

General Schmidt reviewed the latest intelligence reports with growing anxiety and requested that General Holland Smith reassign the reserve forces. Schmidt wanted the 3/21 Marines to replace the 26th Marines as the core reserve and release them to the 5th Division. Schmidt envisioned the 28th Marines cutting the island in half before turning to capture Suribachi. The 25th would scale the rock quarry, serving as the hinge for the entire corps to swing north. The 23rd and 27th Marines would then capture the first airfield, before pivoting north into their assigned zones.

General Cates was concerned about Blue Beach on the right flank. Blue Beach was directly under the observation and fire of suspected enemy positions in the rock quarry. Steep cliffs overshadowed their right flank, while Suribachi dominated the left. The 4th Division figured that the 25th Marines would have the most challenging objective to take on D-Day. General Cates said: "if I knew the name of the man on the extreme right of that squad, I'd recommend him for a medal before we even get there."

Iwo Jima was the pinnacle of a forced amphibious landing against a heavily fortified shore. A complex art mastered by the Fifth Fleet through many painstaking campaigns. B-24 bombers from the Seventh Air Force flew in to strike the smoking island. Rocket ships moved in to saturate shore targets. Fighter and attack squadrons from Mitscher's Task Force 58 joined in. While Navy pilots showed their skills at bombing and strafing, the troops started cheering at the sight of F4U Corsairs flown in from Marine fighter squadron 213.

Colonel Vernon McGee was the air officer for the Expeditionary Troops. He urged this special show for the men in the assault waves. "Drag your bellies on the beach," McGee said to the Marine fighters. The F4U Corsairs made an aggressive approach parallel to the island. They streaked low over the beaches and savagely strafed enemy targets. The Pacific War geography since Bougainville kept ground Marines separated from their air support. According to McGee: "it was the first-time many troops had ever seen a Marine fighter plane, and they were not disappointed."

Not long after the planes left, naval gunfire resumed. Gunfire carpeted the beach with a crescendo of high explosive shells. Ship-to-shore movement was underway, an easy thirty-minute run for the LVTs.

For Operation Detachment, there were enough LVTs to get the job done. Sixty-eight LVT (A)4 armored amtracs, with snub-nosed 75mm cannons, blasted the way forward with 385 troop laden LVTs following close behind. The assault waves crossed the line of departure on time and confidently chugged toward the smoking beaches.

On Iwo, there was no coral reef or killer neap tides to worry about. Navy frogmen cleared the approaches of tetrahedrons and mines. There was no premature secession of fire. The modified rolling barrage was in effect, and no vehicles were lost from enemy fire. Assault waves hit the beaches within two minutes of H-hour. Enemy observers watching the drama unfold from a cave on the slopes of Suribachi reported: "At 9 am, several hundred landing craft with amphibious tanks rushed toward shore like an enormous tidal wave."

Colonel Robert Williams, XO of the 28th Marines, later wrote: "The landing was a magnificent sight to see—two divisions landing abreast—you could see the whole show from the deck of a ship. At this point, so far so good."

The first obstacle didn't come from the Japanese, but from the beach and its parallel terraces. Iwo was a volcano with steep beaches that sharply dropped off into a narrow and violent surf zone. Soft black sand immobilized all wheeled vehicles and caused many tracked amphibious vehicles to belly down and get stuck.

The following boat waves had even more trouble. When ramps dropped and a Jeep or truck would drive out, they got stuck too. Then, plunging waves would smash into the stalled craft before they could unload, filling their sterns with water and sand and broaching them broadside. The beach quickly became a salvage yard.

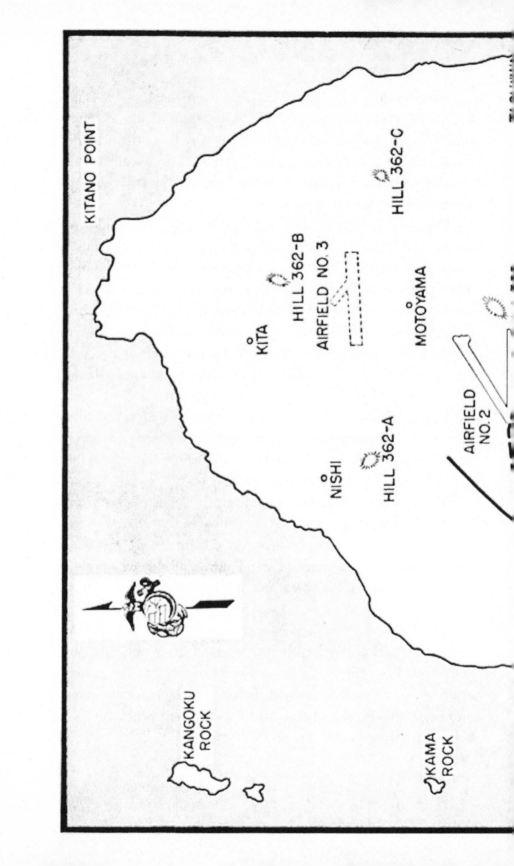

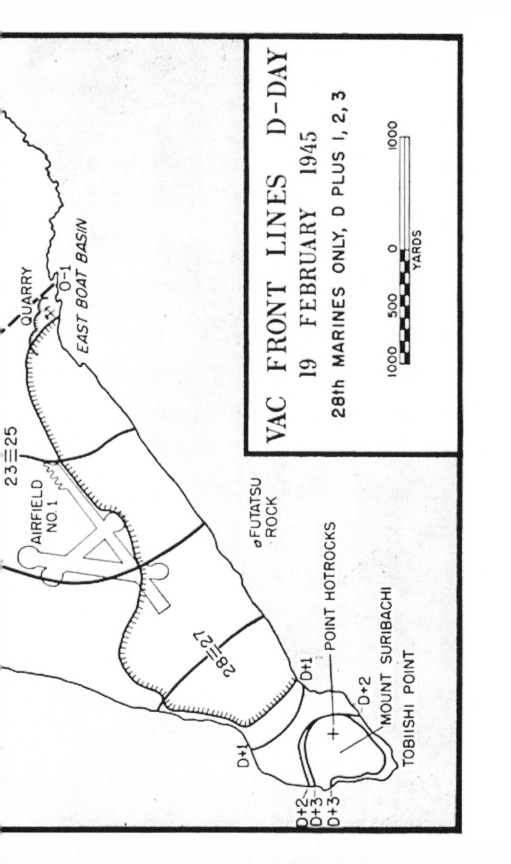

QUARRY

EAST BOAT BASIN

O-1

23 ≡ 25

AIRFIELD NO. 1

FUTATSU ROCK

28 ≡ 27

POINT HOTROCKS

D+1

D+2

MOUNT SURIBACHI

TOBIISHI POINT

D+1

D+2
D+3
D+3

VAC FRONT LINES D–DAY
19 FEBRUARY 1945
28th MARINES ONLY, D PLUS 1, 2, 3

1000   500   0   1000
YARDS
1000   0   1000

GETTING THE GUNS ASHORE

The heavily laden infantry was bogged down. According to Corporal Ed Hartman, a rifleman in the 4th Marine Division: "the sand was so soft, it was like trying to run in loose coffee grounds." The 28th Marines' first report after getting ashore: "resistance moderate, terrain awful."

The rolling barrage and carefully executed landing produced the desired effect: suppressing enemy fire while providing enough shock and awe to allow the first assault waves to clear the beach and advance inward. In less than fifteen minutes, 6,000 Marines were ashore. Many were hampered by increasing fire over the terraces and down from the highlands, but hundreds leaped forward and maintained their assault momentum.

The 28th Marines on the left flank had rehearsed this landing on the volcanic terrain of Hawaii's Big Island. Now, despite increasing casualties among company commanders and the usual landing disorganization, elements of the regiment used their initiative to advance across the narrow neck of the peninsula. This became much bloodier as enemy strong points along Suribachi's base sprung to life.

Ninety minutes after landing, elements of the 1/28 Marines reached the western shore—700 yards from Green Beach—Iwo had been severed. According to one Marine: "it was like we cut off the snake's head." This was the deepest penetration of what would become a costly and bloody day.

The regiments had difficulty getting across the black-sand terraces toward the airfield. The terrain was like an open bowl in a shooting gallery. In full view of Suribachi on the left and a rising table to the right. Any thoughts of this operation being a cakewalk quickly vanished as registered machine gun fire whistled across the open ground and mortar rounds dropped along the terraces. Through this hardship, the 27th Marines made good initial gains and reached the southern and western edges of the first airfield by noon.

The 23rd Marines on Yellow Beach took the brunt of the first round of enemy combined arms fire. Troops crossing the terrace were confronted by two massive concrete pillboxes—still lethal after the bombardment. Overcoming these positions proved costly in men and time and. More fortified positions rose from the broken ground beyond. Requests for tank support could not be fulfilled because of the congestion problems on the beach. Still, the regiment clawed its way several hundred yards toward the eastern edge of the airstrip.

The 25th Marines immediately ran into a "Buzz-Saw" trying to move across Blue Beach. General Cates was correct in his appraisal: "The right flank was a bitch, if there ever was one." The 1/25 Marines scratched, scrambled, and clawed their way 300 yards forward under heavy enemy fire in the first half-hour. The 3/25 Marines took the heaviest beating of the day on the extreme right flank while trying to scale the cliffs leading to the rock quarry.

According to Lieutenant Colonel Justice Chambers leading the 3/25 Marines: "Crossing that second terrace, there was fire from automatic weapons coming from all over. I could've held up a cigarette and lit it on the stuff going by. I knew immediately we were in for one hell of a fight."

But this was only the beginning. When the landing forces tried to overcome the enemy's infantry weapons, they were blind to an imperceptible stirring taking place among the rocks and crevices in the interior highlands. General Kuribayashi's gunners unmasked their big guns—giant mortars, heavy artillery, rockets, and antitank weapons held under the tightest discipline for just this precise moment. Kuribayashi had waited patiently until the beaches were clogged with troops and material. Gun crews knew the range and deflection at each landing beach by heart: all weapons had been pre-registered on these targets long ago. At Kuribayashi's signal, hundreds of weapons opened fire. It was shortly after 1030.

This bombardment was as horrifying and deadly as any Marines had ever experienced. There was no cover. Enemy mortar and artillery rounds blanketed every corner of the 3,000-yard-wide beach. Large caliber coastal defense guns and dual-purpose antiaircraft guns fired horizontally. This created a deadly scissor of direct fire from high ground on both flanks. Marines stumbled over the terraces to escape the rain of lethal projectiles only to encounter machine-gun fire and minefields. Landing force casualties mounted at a shocking rate.

Major Karch of the 14th Marines expressed a begrudging admiration for the Japanese gunners: "it was one of the worst blood-lettings of the war. They rolled artillery barrages up and down the beach—I don't see how anybody could've lived through such a heavy fire barrage. The Japanese were superb artillerymen—someone was going to get hit every time they fired."

At sea, naval gunfire support desperately tried to deliver fire against enemy gun positions shooting down from the rock quarry. It took longer to coordinate this fire: the first enemy barrages wiped out the entire 3/25 Marines Shore Fire Control Party.

When the Japanese fire reached a crescendo, assault regiments issued grim reports to the flagship. Within fifteen minutes, these messages buzzed over the command net:

From 25th Marines 1036: Catching hell from the quarry. Heavy mortar and machine-gun fire.

From the 23rd Marines 1039: Taking heavy casualties and cannot move forward. Mortars are killing us.

From the 27th Marines 1042: All units pinned down by mortars and artillery. Heavy casualties. Need tank support fast to move.

From the 28th Marines 1046: Taking heavy fire and forward movement stopped. Artillery and machine-gun fire heaviest yet seen.

The landing force was getting bled but did not panic. The abundance of combat veterans throughout the rank-and-file beach regiments helped the rookies focus on the objective. Communications were still effective. Aerial observers spotted some of the now exposed gun positions and directed effective naval gunfire. Carrier planes screeched in low and dropped napalm from their belly tanks. But heavy enemy fire continued to take an awful toll throughout the first day and night—but would never again be as murderous as that first hour.

Sherman tanks played hell getting into the action on D-Day. Later in the battle, these combat vehicles were the most valuable weapons on the battlefield. This day was a nightmare. The assault divisions had embarked many tanks on board LSMs (Landing Ship Medium), sturdy craft that could deliver five Shermans at a time. But it was a challenge to disembark them on Iwo's steep beaches. The LSMs' stern anchors couldn't hold in the loose sand and the bow cables parted under the strain.

One lead tank stalled on top of the ramp and blocked the others, leaving the LSM at the mercy of the violent surf. Other tanks threw tracks or got bogged down in loose sand. Several tanks that made it over the terraces were destroyed by huge horn mines or were disabled by accurate 47mm antitank fire from Suribachi. Still, the tanks kept coming. Their mobility, armor protection, and 75mm guns were a welcome addition to the scattered infantry along Iwo's lunar-looking, shell-pocked landscape.

The division commanders committed their reserves. The 26th Marines were ordered in just after noon, General Cates ordered two battalions of the 24th Marines to land at 1400. The 3/24 Marines followed several hours later. The reserve suffered heavier casualties than the initial assault units crossing the beach, because of the punishing enemy bombardment from all island points.

Aware of a probable Japanese counterattack in the night to come, and despite the fire and confusion along the beaches, both divisions ordered their artillery regiments ashore. This frustrating and costly process took most of the afternoon. The surf and wind picked up as the day wore on and caused more than one low-riding amphibious truck to swamp with its precious 105mm howitzer cargo. Getting the guns ashore was one thing; getting them up off the sand was another.

The 75mm howitzers did better than the heavier 105s. Marines could quickly move them up over the terraces—at significant risk. But the 105s had a mind of their own in the black sand. The effort to get each weapon off the beach was a saga. Despite unforgiving terrain and enemy fire, Marines managed to get the batteries in place and registered them to render close-fire support before dark.

Plunging surf and enemy fire turned the battlefield into utter chaos. Later that afternoon, Lieutenant Mike Keleher, the battalion surgeon, went ashore to take over the aid station. (A sniper had killed the previous surgeon.) Lieutenant Keleher was a veteran of three assault landings. He was shocked by the carnage on Blue Beach: "such a sight on the beach. Wrecked boats, bogged down jeeps and tractors and tanks. Burning vehicles and casualties. Limbs of dead Marines were scattered all over the beach."

PROWLING WOLVES

An enemy mortar shell took the life of the legendary John Basilone. He'd led his machine gun platoon in a brave attack against the southern portion of the airfield. All Marines on the island felt this loss. Farther east, Colonel Rob Galer (one of the Pacific War's first fighter aces) survived the afternoon's battle along the beaches and reassembled his scattered radar unit in a deep shell-hole near the base of Suribachi.

Later that afternoon, Colonel Donn Robertson led his Marines onshore to Blue Beach. He was shocked at the intensity of fire still directed at the troops so late on D-Day: "they were ready for us. I watched with pride and wonderment as young Marines landed under fire, took casualties, and stumbled forward to clear the beach. I asked myself, what impels a young man landing on the beach in the face of fire?"

Then it was Robertson's turn. His boat slammed into the beach too hard. The ramp wouldn't drop. His Marines had to roll over the gunwales into the churning surf and crawl ashore.

The savage battle to capture the rock quarry cliffs on the right flank raged. The beachhead was exposed to direct enemy fire all day. Marines had to storm them before any more supplies or troops could be landed. In the end, it was the fighting spirit of Captain James Headley and Colonel "Jumping Joe" Chambers who led the survivors of the Marines to the top of the cliffs.

The battalion paid a high price for this feat. They'd lost twenty-two officers and five hundred troops by nightfall. Assistant division commanders Generals Hart and Hermle of the 4th and 5th Marine Division spent most of D-Day on board the control vessels marking both ends of the line a departure—4,000 yards offshore. This was another lesson in amphibious techniques learned from Tarawa. Having senior officers close to the ship-to-shore movement provided landing force decision-making from the forward most vantage point.

By dust, General Hermle chose to come ashore. On Tarawa, he'd spent the night of D-Day out of contact on a fire-swept pierhead. This time he would be in the fight.

Hermle had the bigger operational picture in mind. He understood that the corps' commanders insistence on forcing the reserves and artillery units onshore despite the carnage to build combat power. Hermle knew that whatever the night brought, the Allies had more troops on the island than the Japanese could muster. His presence would help his division forget about the earlier days' disaster and focus on preparing for the inevitable enemy counterattacks.

Enemy mortar and artillery fire raked the beachhead. An enormous spigot of mortar shells (Marines called them "flying ashcans") and rocket-boosted aerial bombs were loud, whistling projectiles that tumbled end over end. Many of them sailed over the island, but those that landed along the beaches of the southern runways caused dozens of casualties. Few Marines could dig a proper foxhole in the sand. It was like trying to dig a hole in a barrel of wheat. With urgent calls to the control ship for plasma and stretchers and mortar shells came repeated sandbag requests.

War combat correspondent Lieutenant Cyril Zurlinden (soon to become a casualty himself) described his first night ashore: "On Tarawa, Saipan, and Tinian, I saw Marines killed and wounded in a shocking manner. But I never saw anything like the ghastliness that hung over the Iwo Jima beachhead. It was utter frustration, anguish, and a constant inner battle to maintain at least some semblance of sanity.

Accounting for personnel was a nightmare under those conditions. But assault divisions eventually reported a combined loss of 2,375 men to General Schmidt—503 killed and 1,755 wounded, 18 missing, and 99 combat fatigues. While these statistics were sobering, Schmidt had gotten

30,000 Marines ashore. A casualty rate of eight percent left the landing force in better condition than Saipan or Tarawa's first day. It was a miracle the casualties hadn't been twice as high. Did Kuribayashi wait too long to use his big guns?

The first night in Iwo Jima was an eerie affair. Mists of sulfur spiraled from the earth. Marines who were used to the tropics now shivered in the cold, waiting for Kuribayashi's samurai warriors to come screaming down the hills. Marines learned this Japanese commander was different. There would be no wasteful banzai attack tonight. Instead, small teams of infiltrators, "Prowling Wolves," would probe the Marine lines and gather intelligence. A barge full of the elite Japanese *Special Landing Forces* tried a counter landing on the western beaches—they died to a man under the alert guns of the 28th Marines and supporting LVT crews.

That night was one of continuous indirect fire from the Highlands. A high velocity round landed directly in a fighting hole occupied by the 1/23 Marines commander Colonel Ralph Hass and instantly killed him. Marines took other light casualties throughout the night, but at dawn, the veteran landing force stirred.

Five infantry regiments moved to the north, while the sixth turned to the business at hand in the south: Mount Suribachi

SURIBACHI-YAMA

Marines knew this dormant volcano as "Hotrocks."

The Japanese called it Suribachi-yama. Allied planners knew their drive north would never succeed without first securing that hulking rock dominating the southern plain. According to one Marine: "Suribachi took on a life of its own. It watched over us. It loomed over us. That mountain represented more evil to us than the Japanese."

Colonel Atsuchi commanded 2,000 enemy soldiers and sailors in the Suribachi garrison. The Japanese had honeycombed the mountain with machine-gun nests, tunnels, and observation sites. But Atsuchi had lost many of his large-caliber guns from the three-day naval bombardment. Atsuchi's command at Suribachi was semiautonomous. General Kuribayashi realized the invaders would soon cut communication lines across the island's narrow tip. Kuribayashi hoped Atsuchi could hold out for at least ten days and maybe even two weeks.

Some of the strongest defenses on Suribachi were down along the rubble-strewn base. Here, over seventy camouflaged concrete blockhouses protected the mountain's approaches. Another fifty blockhouses bulged from the slopes within the first hundred feet of elevation. Then came the caves, and the first of hundreds the Marines would face on Iwo Jima.

The 20th Marines took 407 casualties cutting across the neck of the island on D-Day. The following day in a cold rain, they prepared their assault. Colonel Chandler Johnson, commanding the 2/28 Marines, set the morning's tone as he deployed his tired troops forward: "it's going to be a hell of a day in one hell of a place to fight this damn war."

Several 105mm batteries opened up overhead. Gun crews fired from positions dug in the black sand next to the 28th Marine's command post. Troops learned that even their 155mm howitzers would hardly shiver the enemy's concrete pillboxes. As the preparatory fire lifted, infantry advanced into heavy mortar and machine-gun fire. Colonel "Harry the Horse" Liversedge requested tanks. But the 5th Tank Battalion was having a frustrating morning. Tanks desperately searched for a defilade spot to rearm and refuel for the assault. But in those first few days on Iwo, there was no such spot. Every time the tanks gathered to service their vehicles, they were walloped by enemy artillery and mortar fire from the entire island. Getting the tanks serviced to join in on the assault took most of the morning. After getting battered all day, the tankers would now only refit, rearm, and re-equip at night.

The day's slow start led to more setbacks for the 5th Tank Battalion. Enemy antitank gunners hid in the hodgepodge of boulders and knocked out the first approaching Shermans, crippling the assault's momentum. While the 20th Marines overran forty enemy strongpoints and gained 200 yards a day, they lost a Marine for every yard gained. The tankers redeemed themselves when a 75mm round caught Colonel Atsuchi poking his head out of a cave entrance—blowing him apart.

Elsewhere on the morning of D +1 were discouraging sites of chaos along the beaches from Kuribayashi's unrelenting artillery barrages and the violent surf. According to one Marine: "The wreckage was indescribable. I saw two miles of debris that was so thick there were only a few places our landing craft could still get in. The wrecked hulls of dozens of landing boats testified to the price we had to pay to put our troops ashore. Tanks and half-tracks laid there crippled from getting bogged down in the coarse sand. LVTs and amphibian tractors were victims of mines and well-aimed shells and were now flopped on their backs. Cranes were brought in to unload cargo and were tilted at insane angles. Our bulldozers were smashed in their own roadways."

Then bad weather set in and complicated the unloading.

Strong winds whipped sea swells into a nasty chop. The surf got uglier. These were the conditions Colonel Carl Youngdale faced while trying to land the 105mm howitzer batteries of his 4/14 Marines. All twelve of these guns were preloaded in amphibious trucks (DUKWs) one to a vehicle. Adding to that was the problem of marginal seaworthiness and contaminated fuel. Youngdale watched in shock as eight amphibious trucks suffered engine failures, swamped, and sank with a terrible loss of life. Two more amphibious trucks broached in the surf zone and spilled their guns into deep water. Youngdale managed to get the two remaining guns ashore and into firing position.

General Schmidt committed one battery of the 105mm howitzers to the narrow beachhead on D +1. These guns reached the beach intact, but it took hours to get the amphibious tractors to drag the heavy guns up over the terraces. The 105's were in place and firing before dark. The deep bark of the guns was a welcome sound to the Marines. Concerned about heavy casualties in the first twenty-four hours, General Schmidt committed the 21st Marines from the core reserve. But the seas were too rough. Troops had a harrowing experience trying to climb down the cargo nets and into the small boats—violently bobbing alongside the transports. Many Marines tumbled into the sea. The boating process took hours to complete. Once afloat, troops circled endlessly in the small Higgins boats waiting for the call to land. But after six hours of bobbing in the water and awful seasickness, the 21st Marines returned to the ships for the night.

Even the larger landing craft, the LSMs and LCTs, had a hard time breaching. Sea anchors were needed to keep the craft perpendicular to the breakers, and they rarely held fast in that soft bottom. Admiral Hill later wrote: "dropping that stern anchor was like dropping a spoon in a bowl of mush."

Hill contributed to the development of amphibious operations in the Pacific War. He and his staff developed armored bulldozers to land in the assault waves. They experimented with hinged *Marston* matting, used as a temporary road on airfields to get vehicles over soft sand. On the beach at Iwo, bulldozers were worth their weight in gold. The Marston matting was only partially successful: the LVTs chewed it up, but all hands could see the true potential.

Admiral Hill worked with the Naval Construction Battalion (Seabees) to bring the supply-laden pontoon barges ashore. But again, the surf prevailed and broached the craft, spilling the cargo. Now desperate, Hill's beachmasters turned to a round-the-clock use of amphibious trucks and LVTs to keep the combat cargo flowing. Once amphibious trucks got free of their crippling loads, they were fine.

Amphibian tractors could cross the soft beach without help. They resupplied and conducted medevac missions directly along the front lines. These vehicles suffered from inexperienced crews in the LSTs who wouldn't lower their bow ramps enough to accommodate the amphibious trucks and tractors approaching after dark. Many times, vehicles loaded with wounded Marines got lost in the dark or ran out of gas and sank. The amphibian tractor battalions lost over 147 LVTs at Iwo Jima. Unlike Tarawa, where enemy gunfire and mines accounted for less than twenty percent of this total. Thirty-four LVTs perished from Iwo's crushing surf, and eighty-eight sank in the deep water.

Once ashore and clear of the loose sand along the beaches, half-tracks, tanks, and armored bulldozers collided with the strongest minefield defenses yet encountered in the Pacific. Under Kuribayashi's direction, enemy engineers had planted irregular rows of antitank and horned anti-boat mines along the exits from both beaches.

The enemy accompanied these weapons by rigging

massive makeshift explosives from 500-pound aerial bombs, torpedo heads, and depth charges triggered by a pressure mine. The loose soil on Iwo had enough metallic characteristics to render standard mine detectors inaccurate. Marines and engineers were on their hands and knees in front of tanks, probing for mines with bayonets and wooden sticks.

While the 28th Marines battled to encircle Suribachi, the shore party and beachmasters struggled to clear the wreckage from the beaches. In the 5th Marine Division zone, the relatively fresh troops of the 1/26 and 3/27 Marines got bloodied. They forced their way across the western runways and took heavy casualties from time-fused airbursts and enemy dual-purpose antiaircraft guns. In the 4th Division zone, the 23rd Marines captured and secured the airstrip—advancing 800 yards with massive casualties.

Some of the most savage fighting was along the high ground above the Rock Quarry on the right flank. Here, the 25th Marines were engaged in the fight of their lives. Rifleman Richard Wheeler found the landscape, and the embedded enemy surreal: "there was no cover from enemy fire. Japs were in reinforced concrete pillboxes and laid down interlocking bands of fire that cut entire companies to pieces. Camouflage hid all their positions. The high ground on either side was honeycombed with layer after layer of Jap emplacements. They had a perfect observation of us. Whenever a Marine made a move, those damn Japs smothered the area with a murderous blanket of fire."

The second day of battle proved unacceptable on every front for the Marines. When the 1/24 Marines finally broke through along the cliffs late in the day, they were rewarded with back-to-back cases of friendly fire. A naval airstrike caused eleven casualties. Misguided salvos from an unidentified gunfire support ship took down another ninety troops. Nothing was going right.

The morning of D +2 promised more frustration. Marines shuddered in the chilly rain and wind. Admiral Hill twice closed the beach because of dangerous undertows and wicked surf. But during one of the grace periods, the 3/21 Marines came ashore, glad to be free of the heaving small boats.

The 20th Marines continued their attack on Suribachi's base. It was a slow, grinding, and bloody fight—boulder by boulder. On the western coast, the 1/28 Marines made the most of naval and field artillery gunfire support and reached the mountain's shoulder. Everywhere else, murderous enemy fire restricted any progress to a matter of yards. Enemy mortar fire from all over the volcano rained down on the 2/28 Marines, clawing their way along the eastern shore. Rifleman Richard Wheeler recalled: "it was terrible. Worst I can remember us ever taking. Jap mortar men played checkers with us as the squares."

The Marines used *Weasels*, handy tracked vehicles that made their first field appearance in this battle to hustle forward flamethrower canisters and evacuate the wounded. That night the amphibious task force experienced the only significant air attack of the battle. Forty-nine *kamikaze* pilots from the *22d Mitate Special Attack Unit* smashed into ships on the outer ring of Iwo Jima. In a desperate action, serving as a prelude to Okinawa's fiery hell, kamikaze pilots sank the escort carrier *Bismarck Sea* with heavy loss of life. They damaged several ships and knocked the veteran *Saratoga* out of the war. All forty-nine Japanese planes were destroyed.

On D +3, it rained even harder. Marines darted forward under fire, hitting the deck to return fire. They discovered that the loose volcanic sand, combined with rain, jammed their weapons. The 21st Marines at the vanguard ran headfirst into a series of enemy emplacements at the southeastern end of the Japanese defenses. Marines battled all day to scratch and claw and advance 200 yards. Casualties were disproportionate and horrific.

On the right flank, Colonel Chambers rallied the 3/25 Marines through the rough and rugged terrain above the Rock Quarry. While Chambers directed the advance of his decimated companies, an enemy sniper shot him in the chest. Chambers went down hard, thinking it was all over: "I faded in and out. I don't remember too much about it except a frothy blood gushing from my mouth. Then someone started kicking the hell out of my feet. It was Captain Headley yelling, 'get up, you were hurt worse on Tulagi.'"

Captain Headley knew Chamber's sucking chest wound was life-threatening. He tried to reduce his commander's shock until he could get him out of the line of fire. Lieutenant Mike Keller, the battalion surgeon, crawled forward with one of his corpsmen. They lifted Chambers onto a stretcher and through enemy fire, carried him down the cliffs to the aid station, and eventually onboard an amphibious truck to make the evening's last run out to the hospital ship. All three battalion commanders on the 25th Marines were now casualties. Chambers survived and received the Medal of Honor. Captain Headley took command of the shot-up 3/25 Marines for the rest of the fight.

The 20th Marines on D +3 made progress against Suribachi. They reached the shoulder on all points late in the day. Combat patrols from the 28th Marines linked up at Tobiishi Point: the southern tip of the island. Reconnaissance patrols reported they found few signs of life along the mountain's upper slopes and on the north side.

Admiral Spruance authorized Task Force 58 to strike Okinawa and Honshu at sundown. After that, they would go to Ulithi and prepare for the Ryukyuan campaign. All eight Marine Corps fighter squadrons left Iwo Jima for good. Navy pilots flying from the ten remaining escort carriers picked up the slack. While there was no question of the courage and skill of these pilots, the quality of close air support for the troops fighting ashore plummeted after the Marine fighter squadrons departed.

The escort carriers had too many other missions: combat air patrols, anti-submarine sweeps, downed pilot searches, and harassing strikes against neighboring Chichi Jima. Marines reported a slow response time for air support requests, light payloads, and high delivery altitudes. The navy pilots delivered several napalm bombs, but many failed to detonate. This wasn't the pilots' fault. The early napalm bombs were old wing-tanks filled with the mixture and activated by unreliable detonators. Marines on the ground were concerned about these notoriously inaccurate weapons being dropped from high altitudes.

On February 23, D +4, the 28th Marines were poised to capture Suribachi. This honor was given to Lieutenant Harry Schrier and Company E, 3rd Platoon. They were ordered to summit, secure the crater, and raise a 54" x 28" American flag for everyone to see. At 0800, Schrier led his forty-man patrol forward. The regiment had already blasted dozens of pillboxes with demolitions and flame. They'd rooted out snipers and knocked out the mass batteries. The combined arms hammering by planes, naval guns, and field pieces had finally taken their toll on the enemy. Any Japanese soldier who popped out of a cave to resist was cut to shreds. Marines carefully walked up the steep northern slope, sometimes resorting to crawling on hands and knees.

The Suribachi flag-raising drama has endured for so long because so many people observed it. All over the island,

Marines tracked the progress of the tiny column of troops during their ascent. Hundreds of binoculars from offshore ships watched Schrier's Marines climb. When they finally reached the top, they disappeared. Those closest to the volcano heard gunfire. Then at 1020, there was movement on the summit—the Stars & Stripes fluttered bravely in the breeze.

Cheers roared from the southern end of the island. Ships sounded sirens and whistles. Wounded men propped up on their litters to get a glimpse. Marines wept. Navy Secretary Forrestal was thrilled. He turned to General Holland Smith: "raising that flag means a Marine Corps for another five hundred years."

Three hours later, an even larger flag went up. Few knew that Associated Press photographer Joe Rosenthal had just captured the American war-fighting spirit on film. *Leatherneck* magazine Staff Sergeant Lou Lowery had taken a picture of the first flag raising and immediately got into a firefight with a handful of enraged enemy defenders. His photograph would become a valuable collector's item—but it was Rosenthal's that would enchant the free world.

Captain Tom Fields of Company D's 1/26 Marines heard his men yell: "Look up there!" and he turned in time to watch the first flag go up. His first thoughts were on the battle still at hand, and he remembered in the moment saying: "Thank God the Japs won't be shooting us down from behind anymore."

The 28th Marines captured and secured Mount Suribachi in three days at the cost of 900 casualties. Colonel Liversedge reoriented his regiment for operations to the north. Unknown to all, the battle of Iwo Jima still had another bloody thirty days before it would be over.

THE MEATGRINDER

It wasn't until the ninth day of battle that intelligence officers realized General Kuribayashi led the Japanese forces on Iwo Jima.

The unexpected early loss of the Suribachi garrison was a setback for Kuribayashi, but he still held a strong position. He had eight infantry battalions, two artillery and three heavy mortar battalions, and a tank regiment. Admiral Ichimaru had 5,000 naval infantry and gunners under his command, but unlike other besieged garrisons in the Central Pacific—these two Japanese leaders worked well together.

Kuribayashi was pleased with the quality of his artillery and engineering troops. His chief of artillery, Colonel Kaido, commanded from an impregnable concrete blockhouse in the east-central sector of the Motoyama Plateau. A lethal landmark the Marines called "Turkey Knob."

General Senda was an artillery officer with combat experience in Manchuria. He commanded the *2d Independent Mixed Brigade*, whose central units would be locked into a 25-day death struggle against the 4th Marine Division. The *204th Naval Construction Battalion* had built some of the most formidable defense systems on the island in his sector. One cave had an 800-foot-long tunnel with fourteen separate exits. It was only one of the hundreds defended to the bitter end.

Well-armed and confident enemy troops waited for the advance of the V Amphibious Corps. Kuribayashi ordered occasional company-sized attacks to recapture lost terrain or disrupt enemy assault preparations—but these were not sacrificial or suicidal. These mainly were preceded by stinging mortar and artillery fires and aimed at gaining limited objectives. General Kuribayashi's iron will kept his troops from large-scale, futile banzai attacks until the last few days.

An exception was on the evening of March 8. General

Senda, frustrated at the noose the 4th Division were applying, ordered 800 of his surviving troops into a ferocious counterattack. Finally, the Marines had targets out in the open. The suicidal Japanese attackers were cut to pieces with machine-gun and small arms fire.

For the first week of the drive north, the Japanese on Iwo had the assaulting Marines outgunned. The enemy's 120mm mortars and 150mm howitzers were superior to most of the weapons of the landing force. Marines found the enemy's direct fire weapons deadly. Especially the dual-purpose antiaircraft guns and the 47mm tank guns, buried up to their turrets. Retired General Donn Robertson said: "the Japs could snipe with those big guns. They also had the advantage of knowing the ground."

Most of the casualties in the first three weeks of battle were from high explosives: rocket bombs, grenades, mines, artillery, and hellacious mortars. Robert Sherrod (*Time* correspondent) wrote that the dead on Iwo Jima, both Japanese and Marine, had one thing in common: "they all died with the greatest possible violence. Nowhere in the Pacific War had I seen such badly mangled bodies. Many men were cut squarely in half."

The close combat was savage. Another constant stress for Marines was no secure rear area to put wounded troops. Kuribayashi's gunners hammered the beaches and airfields. Massive spigot mortar shells and rocket bombs tumbled from the sky. Japanese defenders were drawn to softer targets in the rear. Anti-personnel mines and booby-traps were everywhere and on a large scale for the first time in the Pacific.

Exhausted Marines stumbled out of the front line, seeking nothing more than a helmet full of water to bathe in and a deep hole to sleep in. Instead, Marines spent their rare rest repairing weapons, dodging incoming rounds, humping ammo, or having to repel another nighttime enemy probe.

General Schmidt planned to assault the northern Japanese positions with three divisions abreast. The 5th on the left, the 3rd in the center, and the 4th on the right. This northern drive would jump off on D +5: the day after securing Mount Suribachi. Preparatory fires along the high ground north of the second airfield would last for an hour. Then three regimental combat teams would advance abreast: 26th Marines on the left, 24th on the right, and the 21st in the center. For this assault, Schmidt merged all three divisions' Sherman tanks into one armor task force—commanded by Colonel "Rip" Collins. This would be the largest concentration of Marine tanks in the Pacific War: an armored regiment.

Marines recognized they were trying to force a passage

through Kuribayashi's primary defensive belt. The assault deteriorated into multiple desperate small unit actions along the front. While the 26th Marines (with the help of tanks) gained the most yards, it was still relative. Airfield runways were lethal killing zones. Mines and high-velocity direct fire destroyed Sherman tanks all along the front. On the right flank, Colonel Alexander Vandegrift (son of Marine Commandant Alexander Vandegrift) was wounded.

During the fighting on D +5, General Schmidt moved his command post onshore from the amphibious force flagship *Auburn*. Schmidt now had eight entire infantry regiments committed to the battle. General Holland Smith still had the 3rd Marines and expeditionary troops in reserve. Schmidt made his first of multiple requests to Smith to release that seasoned outfit. The V Amphibious Corps had already taken 6,845 casualties.

On February 25, D +6, enemy resistance intensified. Small Marine units escorted by tanks made progress along the runway. Each Marine was under the impression he was alone in the middle of a giant bowling alley. Often, holding newly gained positions across the runway proved more deadly than capturing them. Resupplying the troops became virtually impossible. Precious Sherman tanks were getting destroyed at an alarming rate.

General Schmidt got two battalions of 105mm howitzers ashore under the command of Colonel John Letcher. Well-directed fire from these heavy field pieces eased some of the pressure on the assaulting Marines. While fire from destroyers and cruisers was marginally effective, air support was a total disappointment. The 3rd Marine Division later complained that the Navy's assignment of eight fighters and eight bombers on station was utterly inadequate.

At noon, General Cates sent a message to Schmidt requesting the strategic Air Force in the Marianas immediately replace Navy air support. Colonel McGee, air commander on Iwo, took heat from the frustrated division commanders. He later wrote: "those little spit kit Navy fighters up there were trying to help but were never enough and were never where they needed to be."

In fairness, it's debatable if any service could have provided adequate air support within the opening days of the northern drive. The air liaison parties within each regiment played hell trying to identify and mark targets. The enemy kept a masterful camouflage. Japanese frontline units were often eyeball to eyeball with Marines, and the air support request net was often overloaded.

Navy squadrons flying from the decks of escort carriers eventually improved by adding heavier bombs and improving their response times. A week later, General Cates rated his air support as satisfactory. But the battle of Iwo Jima would continue to frustrate Allied forces; the Japanese never assembled legitimate targets in the open. Captain Fields of the 26th Marines wrote after the war: "the Japs weren't *on* Iwo Jima. They were *in* Iwo Jima."

Richard Wheeler, who survived Iwo Jima with the 28th Marines, wrote two books about the battle. "This was one of the strangest battlefields in history. One side fought wholly above ground, and the other operated within it. During the battle, American aerial observers marveled that one side of the field had thousands of figures milling around or in foxholes while the other side was deserted. But the strangest of all was that the two contestants sometimes made troop movements simultaneously in the same territory with one maneuvering on the surface and the other using tunnels below."

As the Marines fought like hell to capture the second

airfield from the Japanese, the terrain features rising to the north caught their attention. While there were three hills named 362 on the island, Marines had different nicknames for them: "Amphitheater" and "Turkey Knob." But the bristling complex of hills and terrain would be forever known as "The Meatgrinder."

The 5th Marine Division earned their spurs and lost many of their precious veteran leaders fighting on "The Gorge" and attacking Nishi Ridge (Hills 362-A and B).

The 3rd Marine Division focused their assault north of the second airfield and then onto the heavily fortified Hill 362-C beyond the airstrip. Finally, they attacked the moonscape jungle of stone, soon to be known as "Cushman's pocket."

Colonel Robert Cushman commanded the 2/9 Marines on Iwo. Cushman and his Marines were veterans of heavy fighting on Guam but were stunned by their first sight of the battlefield. Burned out and smoldering Sherman tanks dotted airstrips. Casualties streamed to the rear. The terrific and horrific echo of machine-gun fire was everywhere. Cushman mounted his troops on the surviving tanks and rumbled across the field. They met the same reverse-slope defenses that dogged the 21st Marines. But after three days of savage fighting, Cushman's Marines secured the two Hills north of the second airfield, Peter and 199-Oboe.

General Schmidt made the 3rd Division attack in the center of his main effort. He gave the 3rd priority fire support from the corps artillery. He directed the other two divisions to allocate half of their regimental fire support to the center. The other commanders were not pleased. Neither the 4th Marine Division, who took heavy casualties in the Amphitheater, nor the 5th Division, who struggled to seize Nishi Ridge, wanted to dilute their organic fire support.

General Graves Erskine argued the main effort should

receive the primary fire. Schmidt never solved this problem. His corps artillery was too late, and he needed twice as many battalions and bigger guns: the 8-inch howitzers, which the Marines had not yet fielded. Schmidt had plenty of naval gunfire support available and used it abundantly. But unless targets were in ravines facing the sea—he lost the advantage of observed direct fire.

General Schmidt's fire support problems were eased on February 26. Two Marine observation planes flew in from the carrier *Wake Island* and were the first planes to land on Iwo's recently recaptured, fire swept main airstrip. These were single-engine observation planes (Grasshoppers). They were followed the next day by similar planes from VMO-5. The pilots of these fragile planes had already had an exciting time in the waters off Iwo. Many were launched from the experimental catapult on *LST-776*: "like a peanut from a slingshot."

All fourteen of these observation planes took heavy enemy fire airborne and while serviced on the airstrips. But these two squadrons flew 612 missions supporting all three divisions. Few units contributed as much to the eventual suppression of Kuribayashi's murderous artillery fire. The mere presence of the small planes overhead caused Japanese gunners to cease fire and button-up against the inevitable counter-battery fire soon to follow. Grasshopper pilots would fly predawn or dusk missions to extend a protective umbrella over the troops. This was risky flying because of Iwo's unlit fields and snipers hidden in the hills.

When the 4th Marine Division finally secured Hill 382 at the highest point north of Suribachi, they still suffered heavy casualties moving through the Amphitheater against Turkey knob. The 5th Marine Division seized Nishi Ridge and bloodied themselves on Hill 362-A's elaborate defenses.

Colonel Tom Wornham, CO, 27th Marines: "they had inter-locking fields of fire the likes of which I'd never seen before."

General Cates redeployed the 28th Marines into the fight. On March 2, an enemy gunner fired a high-velocity shell that killed Colonel Chandler Johnson one week after his glorious seizure of the Suribachi Summit. The 28th Marines captured Hill 362-A—at the cost of 200 casualties.

The same day, Colonel Lowell English, CO 2/21 Marines, took a bullet in his knee. Colonel English was upset that his battalion was not rotating to the rear: "We took heavy casualties and were disorganized. I had less than 300 Marines left of the 1,200 I came ashore with." Colonel English received orders to turn his Marines around and plug a gap in the front lines. "It was an impossible order. I couldn't move that disorganized battalion a mile back to the north in thirty minutes."

But General Erskine did not want excuses: "tell that *God-damned* English he'd better be there."

Colonel English replied: "you tell that son of a bitch I will be there, and I was, but my men were still half a mile behind me, and I got a hole in my knee!"

The 26th Marines fought their bloodiest and most successful attack of the battle on the left flank—finally securing Hill 362-B. This all-day battle cost 500 Marine casualties and produced five Medals of Honor. For Captain Frank Caldwell of Company F, 1/26 Marines, it was the worst day of his life. His company took forty-nine casualties on that hill—as well as the first sergeant and all the original platoon commanders.

The first nine days of the V Amphibious Corps' northern drive produced a net gain of only 4,000 yards at a horrific cost of 7,000 Marine casualties. Several of these pitched battles in The Meatgrinder would've been worthy of a separate book. The fighting was one of the most brutal and bloody in the Marine Corps' history.

On D +13, March 4, came the turning point. After alarming and frightful losses, Marines had torn through a substantial chunk of General Kuribayashi's primary defenses. Forcing the enemy commander to shift his command post to a northern cave. On this afternoon, the first crippled B-29 landed. In terms of Allied morale, it couldn't have come at a better time. General Schmidt ordered a standdown on March 5 to enable the exhausted assault forces a brief rest and the opportunity to absorb replacements.

The issue of replacement troops throughout this battle is controversial—even seventy-seven years later. General Schmidt had suffered losses approaching the equivalent of an entire division (6,561 Marines). Schmidt urged Holland Smith to release the 3rd Marines. While each division had been assigned several thousand Marine replacements, Schmidt wanted the cohesion and combat experience of Colonel Jim Stewart's regimental combat team. Holland Smith argued the replacements would suffice and believed that each replacement Marine in these hybrid units had received sufficient infantry training to fulfill immediate assignment to the frontline outfits.

The next challenge was distributing the replacements in small arbitrary numbers—not teamed units—to plug the gaping holes in the assault battalions. These new men were expected to replace the vital veterans of the Pacific War. These replacement Marines were not only new to combat but also to each other—an assortment of strangers that lacked the life-saving bonds of unit integrity.

One frustrated Marine officer said: "they get killed the day they go into battle." Losses among the replacement Marines within the first forty-eight hours of combat were shocking. Those who survived and learned the ropes established a bond with the veterans and contributed significantly to the battle's victory. Division commanders criticized the wastefulness of this policy and urged for replacements from the veteran battalions of the 3rd Marines.

General Erskine later wrote: "I asked Kelly Turner and Holland Smith to give us the 3rd. They said, 'you got enough Marines on the island now. There are too damn many here already.' I said, 'this is an easy solution. Some of these Marines are tired and too worn out, so take them out and bring in the goddamn 3rd Marines.' They said, 'keep your mouth shut. We made our decision.' And that was that."

Most surviving officers agreed that the decision not to use the veteran 3rd Marines at Iwo was wasteful and ill-advised. But Holland Smith never wavered: "sufficient troops were on Iwo Jima for the capture of the island. Two regiments were sufficient to cover the frontal assault assigned to General Erskine."

On D +14, March 5, General Holland Smith ordered the 3rd Marines to sail back to Guam.

* * *

While Holland Smith may have known the overall statistics of the battle losses sustained by the landing force at that point—he did not fully appreciate the tremendous attrition of experienced junior officers and senior noncoms taking their place every day. For example, the day after the 3rd Marines sailed for Guam, the 2/23 Marines' E Company suffered the loss of their seventh company commander since the start of the battle.

Colonel Cushman's experiences with the 2/9 Marines were typical: "casualties were brutal. By the time Iwo was over, we'd gone through two complete sets of lieutenants and platoon leaders. After that, we had forward artillery observers commanding companies and sergeants leading half strength platoons. It was that bad."

Colonel English wrote: "After twelve days, we'd lost every company commander. I had one company exec left. I'd lost all three of my rifle company commanders killed by the same damn shell."

Many infantry units and platoons ceased to exist. Depleted companies were merged to form half-strength outfits.

NORTHERN ALLIED DRIVE

The Allied drive continued north after the March 5 stand-down. It did not get any easier. The Japanese had changed tactics: fewer big guns and rockets and less observed fire from the highlands. But now, the terrain had deteriorated into narrow gorges, enveloped in sulfur mists—killing zones.

Allied casualties mounted. Gunshot wounds now outnumbered the high explosive shrapnel hits. A myth among Marine units was that the Japanese were nearsighted and poor marksmen. In close quarters fighting in northern Iwo, Japanese riflemen shot down hundreds of advancing Marines in the head or chest with well-aimed fire. Captain Caldwell of the 1/26 Marines said: "Poor marksmen? All the Japs we faced were expert shooters."

Supporting arms coordination became more effective during the battle. Colonel "Buzz" Letcher established the first SACC (Supporting Arms Coordination Center), where senior artillery, naval gunfire, and air support representatives pooled their talents and resources. While Letcher lacked the manpower and communications equipment to run a full-time SACC, his efforts significantly advanced this challenging art.

Colonel McGee's Landing Force Air Support Control Unit worked in harmony with the fledgling SACC. Still, friendly fire incidents happened. Perhaps friendly fire was inevitable on that crowded island, but positive control at the highest level did much to reduce the frequency of these accidents.

The lack of preliminary naval bombardment on Iwo angered Marines. While all hands valued the responsive support received from D-Day onward, the lack of initial fire was blamed for the horrific Marine casualties. The gunfire ships stood in close—less than a mile offshore—and hammered the flanks and front lines. Many ships took hits from the hidden enemy coastal defense batteries. There were no safe zones in or around Iwo Jima.

Two characteristics of naval gunfire on Iwo were notable: The extent ships provided illuminating rounds over the battlefield, especially during the early days before the landing force artillery could assume the bulk of these missions. Second was the degree of assistance provided by the smaller gunships, frequently modified with 4.2-inch mortars, 20mm guns, or rockets. These "small boys" were vital along the northwestern coast as they worked in lockstep with the 5th Marine Division advancing toward The Gorge.

While the Marines comprised most of the landing force on Iwo, they still received support from the army. Two of the four amphibious truck companies on D-Day were army units. The 138th Antiaircraft Artillery Group placed their 90mm batteries around the newly captured airfields. General Jim Chaney (later to become Iwo's island commander) landed on D +8 with elements of the Army's 145th Infantry.

Army units flew into Iwo on March 6 (D +15). The 15th Fighter Group arrived to escort B-29s over Tokyo. This group was a seasoned outfit that included the famous 47th Fighter Squadron and their P-51 Mustangs. While the army pilots had little to no experience in direct air support of ground troops, Colonel McGee was impressed with their "eager beaver attitude" and willingness to learn.

McGee appreciated the fact the Mustangs could deliver thousand-pound bombs. He had the Army pilots trained on how to strike designated targets on nearby islands. In three days, they were ready for duty on Iwo. McGee instructed the Mustang pilots to arm their bombs with twelve-second delay fuses and attack parallel to the front lines approaching from a 45° angle.

These tactics often produced stunning results—especially along the west coast—where the thousand-pound bombs blew sides of entire cliffs off into the ocean. This exposed enemy caves and tunnels to direct naval gunfire from the sea. According to McGee: "those Air Force boys did a lot of good."

The field medical support given to the assaulting Marines

was a major contributor to victory on Iwo. Integrating chaplains, surgeons, and corpsmen within the FMF (Fleet Marine Force) paid valuable dividends. Most times, corpsmen were as tough and combat savvy as the Marines in that company. Wounded Marines knew their corpsman would move heaven and earth to reach them, bind their wounds, and start the long evacuation process.

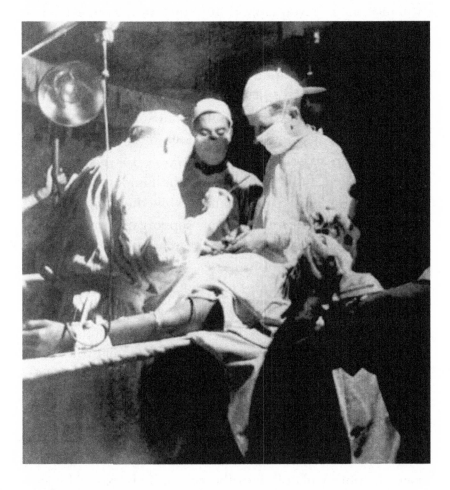

Marines on Iwo Jima echoed the views of Staff Sergeant Al Thomas: "we had outstanding corpsmen. They were our family." The luxury of having first-rate medical help so close to the front took a terrible toll. Eight hundred twenty-seven corpsmen and twenty-three doctors were wounded or killed on Iwo Jima—a casualty rate twice as high as Saipan.

Combat medical support was thoughtfully prepared and provided on Iwo. Past the crude aid stations and toward the rear, the Army and Navy field hospitals arose. Wounded Marines would receive treatment in a field hospital, then recuperate in a bunker before returning to the lines to often receive their second or third wound. The more seriously wounded were evacuated by air to Guam or to one of the several fully-staffed hospital ships operating around the clock. Within the first month of fighting on Iwo, 13,747 Marines and corpsmen casualties were evacuated by hospital ship and another 2,489 by airlift.

When a Marine was wounded, the first few minutes were the most dangerous after going down. Enemy snipers had no hesitations about picking off corpsmen, litter crews, or even the wounded man himself as his buddies tried to slide him out of the fire.

Corporal Ed Canter was a rocket truck crew chief in the 4th Marine Division. Rocket trucks always drew an angry barrage of counter-battery fire from the enemy. A Japanese sniper shot Canter through the stomach. Corporal Canter's comrades knew they had to get him away from that launch site fast. As a nearby motion picture crew recorded the drama, four Marines carried Canter down a mud-covered hillside. They heard the scream of an incoming shell and dumped Canter while they took cover.

The explosion killed the film crew and wounded each of the Marines, including Canter again. The film footage survived and appeared in US newsreels—before becoming a part of the movie *Sands of Iwo Jima*. Corporal Canter survived and was evacuated to a hospital ship and then to different hospitals in Guam and Hawaii before returning to the US. His war was over.

* * *

The shore party personnel and beachmasters performed remarkable feats of logistics to keep the advancing divisions equipped and armed. The logistical management and sheer backbreaking work needed to maintain such a high volume of supplies and equipment moving over these dangerous beaches was hard to imagine. A single beach on the west coast became functional on D +11, but by that time, most of the landing force supplies were already ashore.

The next day after the general unloading was completed, the vulnerable amphibious ships were released from their tether to the beachhead. Shortly after, well-aimed enemy fire detonated the 5th Marine Division's entire ammo dump. Ammunition resupply became vital. Then, the ammunition ship *Columbia Victory* came under direct enemy fire as she approached the western beaches to unload. Waiting Marines held their breath as the *Columbia Victory* was nearly destroyed. She narrowly escaped, but the potential for disaster still loomed.

An entire brigade of the 62nd Naval Construction Battalion (Seabees) extended and repaired the captured runways. Marines returning to the beaches from the northern highlands could scarcely recognize the place they'd first seen on D-Day. There were now over 80,000 Allied troops on the small island, and the Seabees had bulldozed a two-lane road to the top of Mount Suribachi.

Communications had improved dramatically on Iwo compared to previous amphibious campaigns. Handsets and radios were now waterproof and had more frequencies.

Forward observer teams used the backpack SCR-610, while companies and platoons preferred the walkie-talkie style SCR-300 or even lighter portables, the "Spam Can" SCR-536.

Colonel Jim Berkeley, XO of the 27th Marines said: "On Iwo, we had near-perfect communications. It was all any commander could ask for." Marines strung telephone lines between support units and four command posts as the battle raged, elevating the wire along upright posts to avoid damage by tracked vehicles.

Enemy counterintelligence expected to have an easy day splicing into allied phone lines, but Marines baffled them with Navajo code talkers. Each division employed twenty-four trained Navajos. The 5th Marine Division's command post had six established Navajo networks on the island. No one throughout the war could ever crack the Navajo code.

Black American troops played a major role in the capture of Iwo. Black troops drove army amphibious trucks and were active throughout the landing. Black Marines of the 8th Ammunition Company and the 36th Depot Company landed on D-Day and served as longshoremen on those chaotic, bloody beaches. The on-island Black Marines worked with the Shore Party and helped to sustain the momentum of the Allied northern drive. When the Japanese counterattacked penetrated these beach areas, Black Marines dropped their cargo, unslung their carbines, and engaged the enemy with well-disciplined fire.

Colonel Leland Swindler commanded the V Amphibious Corps Shore Party: "the entire body of Black Marines under my command conducted themselves with marked coolness and courage and inflicted more casualties on the enemy than they sustained."

News coverage of the Iwo Jima battle was extensive. Dozens of combat correspondents were embedded with the landing force throughout the battle. Marine Sergeant "Dick" Dashiell was a writer for the Associated Press and assigned to the 3rd Marine Division. Although sometimes terrified and filled with horror, Dashiell endured and wrote eighty-one frontline stories and pounded out news releases on his portable typewriter at the edge of his foxhole. Dashiell's eye for detail always caught the attention of the reader: "All is bitter. Frontal assault always uphill. A ceaseless wind filled the air with a fine volcanic grit." He described how Marines had to stop and clean the grit from their weapons—and how naked that made most Marines feel.

Occasionally, hot food was delivered to the exhausted Marines on the front lines. The deliveries of milk and fruit from nearby ships boosted morale. So did watching the crippled B-29s zoom in for an emergency landing. Sergeant "Doc" Lindsey was a squad leader in Company G, 2/25 Marines. He stated: "It was good to see them land. You knew they'd just come from hitting Tokyo."

DEFIANT TO THE END

General Erskine caught pneumonia but refused to evacuate. His Chief of Staff, Colonel Robert Hogaboom, kept the war moving behind the scenes. The division continued its advance, and when Erskine recovered—Hogaboom adjusted accordingly. The two were an effective team.

Erskine had long wanted to conduct a battalion-size night operation. It bothered him that throughout the war, the Allies had yielded the night to the Japanese. When Hill 362-C continued to thwart his advance, Erskine ordered a predawn assault without the trappings of preparatory fire, which always identified the time and place of attack.

The honor of leading this unusual attack was put to Colonel "Bing" Boehm, CO, 3/9 Marines. But this battalion was new to the sector and received their attack order too late to reconnoiter effectively. Absent of advance orientation, the battalion crossed the line of departure silently at 0500 and advanced toward Hill 362-C. The unit achieved total surprise. Before the sleepy Japanese knew it, the Marines swept across 500 yards of broken ground and roasted enemy outposts and strong points with flamethrowers.

When daylight revealed that Boehm's battalion had captured the wrong hill (Hill 362-C was still 250 yards distant), his battalion was surrounded by a sea of furious and wide-awake and counterattacking enemy infantry. Boehm redeployed his battalion and attacked toward the original hill. This was rough going and took most of the day, but before dark, the 3/9 Marines secured Hill 362-C—a main Japanese defensive anchor.

The Allied positions grew stronger after General Senda's counterattack against the 4th Marine Division. On D +18, a patrol from the 3rd Marine Division reached the northeast coast. The squad leader filled his canteen with saltwater and sent it to General Schmidt marked: "For Inspection, Not Consumption."

Schmidt welcomed the symbolism. The next day, the 4th Marine Division finally secured Turkey Knob and advanced toward The Amphitheater on the east coast. While the end was in sight, the intensity of the Japanese resistance did not fade. In the 5th Division's western zone, the 2/26 reported a casualty rate of seventy percent. General Keller Rockey reported his Marines were: "in a state of extreme fatigue and exhaustion."

Division commanders looked to relieve their shot-up men. General Cates formed a provisional battalion in the 4th Marine Division under Colonel Melvin Krulewitch. He was ordered to attack bypassed enemy positions. While the term "mopping up" was used, it was considered inaccurate by many Allied troops. Countless pockets of Japanese held out—defiant and well-armed to the end. Rooting them out was never easy. Marines used pioneers, motor transport units, and amtracs, as light infantry units to strengthen frontline battalions and conduct combat patrols.

In the extreme rear on Iwo Jima, the men had become overconfident. Movies were shown every night and ice cream could be found on the beach. Men swam in the surf and slept in tents in a deadly and false sense of security.

To the north, Colonel Cushman's 2/9 Marines were engaged in broken terrain east of the airfield. Marines ultimately encircled the enemy's position, but the battle of "Cushman's Pocket," raged on. Cushman's battalion commander reported the action: "The Jap position is a maze of pillboxes, caves, emplaced tanks, stonewalls, and trenches. We beat against them for eight continuous days using every support weapon. Our core objective in the sector still remains. Our battalion is exhausted, and most of our leaders are gone. Our battalion now numbers 387 with 350 replacements."

Cushman's 2/9 was ultimately relieved by elements of the 9th and 21st Marines (equally exhausted) and had just as difficult of a time. General Erskine had no reserves. He ordered Cushman back into the pocket, and by March 16, (D +25) enemy resistance in the thicket of jumbled rocks ended.

* * *

The 4th Marine Division poured over the hills in the east and secured the coastal road by blasting the last Japanese strong points from the rear. Ninety percent of Iwo Jima was in Allied hands. Radio Tokyo announced the fall of Iwo Jima as: "the most unfortunate thing in the whole war situation."

General Holland Smith took the opportunity to declare victory and conduct a flag-raising ceremony. Following that, the old warhorse departed along with Admiral Kelly Turner. Now, General Schmidt and Admiral Hill finally had the campaign to themselves. Survivors of the 4th Marine Division began backloading on board ship—their battle finally over.

The killing continued in the north. The 5th Marine Division entered The Gorge, an 800-yard pocket of broken country the troops called "Death Valley." General Kuribayashi would make his last stand here in a command center in a deep cave. Fighting through this horrid moonscape was a fitting end to the battle—nine days of cave-by-cave assaults with demolitions and flamethrowers. Marine combat engineers used 9,000 tons of explosives to detonate one massive fortification. Progress was bloody and slow. General Rockey's depleted and drained regiments lost one man for every two yards gained. General Schmidt deployed the 3rd Division against Kitano Point in the 5th Division zone to ease the pressure.

Colonel Hartnoll Withers led the final assault with the 21st Marines against the extreme northern tip of the island. General Erskine's pneumonia be damned. He came along to look over Withers' shoulder. The 21st Marines felt the end was near. Their momentum was irresistible. In a few hours of sharp fighting, they cleared out the last of the resistance. Erskine signaled Schmidt: "Kitano Point Taken."

Allied forces tried to persuade Kuribayashi to surrender during these last days. They broadcasted appeals in Japanese and sent him personal messages, praising his bravery, and urging his cooperation. General Kuribayashi was a samurai to the end. In his last message to Tokyo: "We have not eaten or drank for five days, but our fighting spirit is still running high. We will fight to the end for our Emperor."

Imperial Headquarters tried to convey the good news that the emperor had approved his promotion to full general. There was no response from Iwo Jima. It would be a post-humous promotion. Controversial Japanese evidence revealed that he committed *Seppuku* on the night of March 25.

The 5th Marine Division clawed their way forward in The Gorge. The average battalion that landed with thirty-six officers and 885 men on D-Day now only had sixteen officers and 300 men. This included the hundreds of replacements funneled in through the battle. Remnants of the 1/26 and 1/28 Marines squeezed the enemy into a final pocket and destroyed them.

On the evening of March 25 (D +34), the battle for Iwo Jima was over. The island became eerily quiet. Far fewer illumination shells flickered a false light on the shadowy figures moving south toward the airfield. General Schmidt got the good news that the 5th Marine Division had snuffed out the last enemy cave. As the corps commander prepared to declare the end of organized resistance on Iwo Jima—a well-organized enemy force emerged from the northern caves and snuck down the length of the island.

This last spasm of Japanese resistance reflected the enemy's tactical discipline. A 300-man Japanese force took all night to move into position around the island's vulnerable rear area. Newly arrived army pilots from the VII Fighter Command were surprised in their tents. The enemy force attacked the sleeping pilots with grenades, swords, and automatic rifles. The fighting was as savage and bloody as any on Iwo Jima.

Men from the 5th Pioneer Battalion and surviving pilots formed a skirmish line and launched a counterattack. Seabees and redeploying 28th Marines joined the fight. There were few suicides among the Japanese. Most died in battle. Grateful to strike one final blow for their emperor. Sunrise uncovered the carnage—300 dead enemy and over a hundred slaughtered pilots, Seabees, and pioneers along with another 200 wounded. It was a grotesque closing chapter to five savage weeks of killing and carnage.

LEGACY OF IWO JIMA

In thirty-six days of combat, the V Amphibious Corps killed nearly 22,000 Japanese sailors and soldiers. This was achieved at a staggering cost. Marine assault units (along with organic Navy personnel) suffered 24,053 casualties—6,140 killed—the highest single action losses in Marine Corps history. Statistically, for every three Marines who landed on Iwo Jima, one became a casualty.

According to military historian Norman Cooper: "Seven hundred Americans gave their lives for every square mile. For every plot of ground the size of a football field, an average of one American and five Japanese were killed, and five Americans wounded."

Assault units bore the brunt of these casualties. Captain Bill Ketcham's Company I, 3/24 Marines, landed on D-Day with 133 Marines and three rifle platoons. Only nine of these men remained when his company re-embarked on D +35.

Captain Frank Caldwell reported a loss of 220 men from Company F, 1/26 Marines. By the end, a private first class commanded a platoon in Captain Caldwell's merged 1st and 2nd Platoons.

Captain Tom Fields relinquished command of Company D on the eighth day to replace his battalion's executive officer. When he rejoined his company at the end of the battle, Fields was sickened to find only seventeen of the original 250 Marines still alive.

Company B of the 1/28 Marines went through nine company commanders in the fight. Twelve different Marines served as platoon leaders of the 2nd Platoon—including two buck privates. Other divisions reported similar conditions.

The American public reacted with shock and sadness as they had fourteen months earlier on Tarawa. The debate about the high cost of forcibly seizing an enemy island raged in the press while the battle was being fought. The Marine Corps released only one statement on February 22 about detailed battle losses during the fighting. They reported casualties of nearly 5,000.

William Randolph Hearst was an early supporter of the MacArthur for President campaign. Hearst ran a front-page editorial in the *San Francisco Examiner* blaming the horrific Marine losses on poor tactics: "it's the same thing that happened on Saipan and Tarawa." The editorial urged for the elevation of General MacArthur to supreme commander of the Pacific: "HE SAVES THE LIVES OF HIS OWN MEN."

One hundred off-duty Marines disagreed and stormed the offices of the examiner and demanded an apology. But the Hearst editorial had already received wide play. Many families of men fighting in the Pacific were forwarded the clippings. Marines received these in the mail while the fighting still raged on Iwo—an unwelcome blow for morale.

FDR, an expert in manipulating public opinion, kept a lid on the outcry by emphasizing the troops' sacrifice as symbolized by Joe Rosenthal's Suribachi flag-raising. While this photograph was already famous, Roosevelt made it the official logo of the Seventh War Bond Drive. He ordered the six flag raisers be reassigned home to boost morale, but three out of those six men had already been killed in the fighting on Iwo Jima.

The Joint Chiefs studied Iwo's losses. No one questioned the objective: Iwo Jima was an island that had to be secured to launch an effective strategic bombing campaign. The island could not have been bypassed or leapfrogged. There was evidence the Joint Chiefs considered using poison gas during the planning phase. Neither the US nor Japan had signed the international cessation on poison gas, and there were no civilians on the island. The US had stockpiled mustard gas shells in the Pacific Theater. When FDR read the report, he shot down the idea. He publicly stated that the United States would never make *first use* of poison gas. This left the landing force with no other option but a frontal amphibious assault against the most heavily fortified island the United States had ever faced.

The capture of Iwo Jima provided other strategic and symbolic benefits. Marines raised the flag over Suribachi the same day MacArthur entered Manila. The parallel captures of the Philippines and Suribachi were followed immediately by the invasion of Okinawa—accelerating the pace of the war and bringing it at long last to Japan's doorstep. These three campaigns proved to the Japanese command that the Allies had the capability and will to overwhelm even the most resolutely defended islands. Honshu and Kyushu would be next.

The capture of Iwo Jima delivered immediate benefits to the strategic bombing campaign. Marines fighting on the island were reminded of this mission repeatedly as crippled B-29s flew in from Honshu. Securing and rebuilding Iwo's airfields increased the operating range payload and survival rate of the big bombers. The monthly tonnage of high explosives dropped on Japan by the B-29s based in the Marianas increased eleven-fold in March alone. On April 7, eighty P-51 Mustangs took off from Iwo, escorting the B-29s bombing the Nakajima aircraft engine plant in Tokyo.

The great value of Iwo's airfields was that they could be used as emergency landing fields. By war's end, 2,252 B-29s made forced landings on Iwo. These forced landings included 24,765 flight crewmen. Many of these men would have perished at sea without Iwo's safe haven. According to one B-29 pilot: "whenever I landed on that island, I thanked God for the men who fought and died for it."

General Kuribayashi proved to be one of the most competent field commanders the Marines had ever faced. His expert understanding of simplicity and economy of force made maximum use of Iwo's formidable terrain. He deployed his mortars and artillery with great skill and commanded his troops with an iron will—to the end. He was a realist. With no hope of naval or air superiority, he knew he was doomed from the start. Allied forces took five weeks to breach every strong point and exterminate his forces on the island.

Iwo Jima was the pinnacle of Allied amphibious capabilities in the Pacific. The sheer magnitude of planning the assault and sustaining the landing forces made Operation Detachment an enduring model of detailed planning and violent execution. The element of surprise was not available. But the speed of the landing force and the toughness with which assault units withstood the withering barrages amazed the enemy defenders.

Colonel Wornham of the 27th Marines said: "The Iwo landing was the epitome of everything we'd learned over the years about amphibious assaults. Bad as the enemy fire was on D-Day, there were no reports of 'Issue in doubt.'"

Colonel Galer compared his Guadalcanal experience to the battle on Iwo: "then, it was can we hold? On Iwo, the question was simply, when can we get this over?"

While the ship-to-shore assaults were impressive, the actual degree of amphibious effectiveness was seen in the massive, sustained logistical support which flowed over the treacherous beaches. Marines had all the ammunition and flamethrower refills they needed around the clock. They also had many less obvious necessities that marked this battle differently than its predecessors. Marines on Iwo had enough quantities of whole blood, most donated two weeks in advance, flown in, refrigerated, and always available.

Marines had mail call, clean water, radio batteries, fresh-baked bread, and prefabricated burial markers. The Iwo Jima operation was a model of interservice cooperation. Marine and Navy teams functioned efficiently together. The Navy earned the respect of the Marines on D -2 when a flotilla of tiny LCI gunboats fearlessly attacked the coastal defense guns to protect the Navy and Marine frogmen. Marines appreciated the contributions of the Coast Guard, Army, Red Cross, and embedded combat correspondents; all shared in the misery and glory of this battle.

The US Military occupied Iwo Jima until 1968, when jurisdiction was transferred back to Japan. Seventy-seven years later, the island remains a military-only island. It is no longer a baren moonscape, but covered in rich greenery, yet two aspects of this battle are still controversial: inadequate preliminary bombardment and the decision to use piecemeal replacements instead of organized units to strengthen the assault forces. Both decisions were made in the context of several competing factors and were made by experienced commanders in good faith. Iwo Jima's highest cost was the loss of so many combat veterans while taking the island. While this battle created a new generation of veteran heroes among the survivors, many proud regiments suffered devastating losses.

Those veteran regiments had already been designated as crucial landing force components in the Japanese home islands assault—these losses had severe potential implications. It may have been these factors that influenced Holland Smith's unpopular decision to withhold the 3rd Marines from the battle.

To many exhausted Marines and commanders fighting on Iwo Jima, Holland Smith's decision to withhold the 3rd Marines was unforgivable—then and now. But whatever his flaws, General Holland Smith almost certainly knew amphibious warfare better than anyone at the time.

According to Holland Smith: "We had no hope of surprise, either tactical or strategic. There was little possibility for tactical initiative. The entire operation was fought on virtually the enemy's terms. The strength, conduct, and disposition of the enemy's defense required a major penetration of his prepared positions in the center of the Motoyama Plateau and a subsequent reduction of his positions in rugged terrain sloping to the shore on the flanks.

"The terrain and size of the island precluded any Force Beachhead Line. It was a one-phase and one-tactic operation. From the time the engagement was joined until the mission was completed, it was a frontal assault maintained with relentless pressure by a superior force in supporting arms against a position fortified to the maximum practical intent.

"We Americans of a subsequent generation in the profession of arms find it difficult to imagine a sustained amphibious assault under these conditions. In some respects, the fighting on Iwo Jima took the features of the Marines fighting in France in 1918. We sensed the drama repeated every morning on Iwo Jima after the prep fires lifted, when the rifleman, engineers, corpsman, flame tank crews, and armored bulldozers somehow found the fortitude to move out again into The Meatgrinder or Death Valley. Few of us today can study the defenses, analyze the after-action reports, or walk that broken ground without experiencing a sense of reverence for the men who fought and won that epic battle."

While the fighting was raging on Iwo, Admiral Nimitz said: "Among the Americans serving on Iwo Jima, uncommon valor was a common virtue." This line was chiseled into the base of Felix de Weldon's giant bronze sculpture of the Suribachi flag-raising.

On Iwo, Twenty-two Marines, four Navy corpsmen, and one LCI skipper were awarded the Medal of Honor for bravery during the battle—half were awarded posthumously.

General Erskine put the Allied sacrifices into perspective during his remarks at the dedication of the 3rd Marine Division's Cemetery on Iwo Jima: "Our victory was never in doubt. Its cost was. What was in doubt, in all of our minds, was whether there would be any of us left to dedicate this cemetery at the end. Or if the last Marine would die knocking out the last Japanese gunner."

ICONIC FLAG RAISING

There were two flags raised over Mount Suribachi—but not at the same time. On the morning of February 23, 1945, (D +4)

Captain Dave Severance, Company E Commander, 2/28 Marines, ordered Lieutenant Harold Schrier to take a patrol and put up an American flag on the top of Mount Suribachi.

Staff Sergeant Lou Lowery, a *Leatherneck* magazine photographer, joined the patrol. After a short firefight, the 54" x 28" flag was attached to a piece of pipe found at the ridge of the mountain and was raised. This was the flag-raising that Staff Sergeant Lowery photographed. But this flag was too small to be seen from the beach below, and another Marine went on board *LST 779* to get a larger flag. Then, a second patrol took this flag up to the top of Suribachi, accompanied by AP photographer Joe Rosenthal.

In an interview after the war, Rosenthal said: "my stumbling on that picture was in all respects accidental. When I got to the top of the mountain, I stood in a decline just below the crest of the hill with Sergeant Bill Genaust, a motion picture cameraman (later killed on Iwo Jima). We watched a group of five Marines and a Navy corpsman fasten the new flag to another piece of pipe. I turned, and out of the corner of my eye, I saw the second flag being raised. I swung my camera around and held it until I could guess where the peak of the action was and then took the shot."

Some people accused Rosenthal's second flag-raising photograph of being posed. According to Rosenthal's postwar interview: "had I posed that shot, I would, of course, have ruined it. I would've made them turn their heads so they could be identified, and nothing like the existing picture would have resulted. This picture and what it meant to me—and it has a meaning to me—has to be peculiar only to me.

"I can still see blood running down the sand. I can see those awful, impossible positions to take in a frontal attack on such an island, where the batteries opposing you were not only staggered up in front of you but also stood around you as you came ashore. The extraordinary situation they were in before they ever reached that peak. If a photograph can remind us of the sacrifices these boys made—then that was what made the photo important—not the man who took it."

Rosenthal took eighteen photographs that day. Afterward, he went down to the beach to write captions for his undeveloped film packs and, with other photographers on the island, sent his film out to the offshore command vessel. They were flown to Guam, where the photos were processed and censored. Rosenthal's pictures arrived on Guam before Lowery's and were processed and sent to the states for distribution. Rosenthal's flag-raising picture became one of the most famous photographs ever taken in the war—or in any war.

GENERAL HARRY SCHMIDT

Four veteran Marine generals led the assault on Iwo Jima. Each one of these generals received the Distinguished Service Medal for inspired combat leadership in this epic battle.

Major General Harry Schmidt was fifty-eight years old when he was on Iwo Jima. He'd already served thirty-six years in the Marine Corps. Born and raised in Holdrege, Nebraska, he attended the Nebraska Normal College. His expeditionary assignments kept him from serving in World War I, but Schmidt saw considerable small unit action in China, the Philippines, Guam, Mexico, Nicaragua, and Cuba.

Schmidt attended the Army Command and General Staff College and the Marine Corps Field Officer's Course. During World War II, General Schmidt commanded the 4th Marine Division at Roi-Namur and in Saipan before assuming command of the V Amphibious Corps at the Tinian landing.

On Iwo Jima, he commanded the largest force of Marines ever committed to a single battle. According to Schmidt: "it was the greatest honor of my life."

GENERAL GRAVES B. ERSKINE

Major General Graves B. Erskine was forty-seven years old on Iwo Jima, and one of the youngest major generals in the Marine Corps. He'd already served twenty-eight years on active duty by then. A native of Columbia, Louisiana, he received a Marine Corps commission after graduating from Louisiana State University.

Erskine immediately deployed to France for duty in World War I. He served as a platoon commander in the 6th Marines and saw combat at Chateau-Thierry, Soissons, St. Mihiel, and Belleau Wood. He was wounded twice and awarded the Silver Star. He served in China, Cuba, Nicaragua, Santo Domingo, and Haiti in the interwar period.

In World War II, Erskine was Chief of Staff to General Holland Smith during the Marianas, Marshalls, Gilberts, and Aleutians campaigns. He took command of the 3rd Marine Division in October 1944.

GENERAL CLIFTON B. CATES

Major General Clifton B. Cates was fifty-one years old at Iwo Jima. He'd served the last twenty-eight years in the Marine Corps. Cates was one of the rare Marine general officers who had held a combat command at the platoon, company, battalion, regiment, and division levels in his career.

Cates was born in Tiptonville, Tennessee, and graduated from the University of Tennessee. In World War I, he served as a junior officer in the 6th Marines at Blanc Mont, Soissons, Belleau Wood, and St. Mihiel. He was awarded two Silver Stars, the Navy Cross, and a Purple Heart for his service and wounds.

In the interwar years, he served at sea and in China. In World War II, he commanded the 1st Marines at Guadalcanal and the 4th Marine Division at Tinian. Three years after Iwo Jima, General Clifton Cates became the 19th Commandant of the Marine Corps.

GENERAL KELLER E. ROCKEY

Major General Keller E. Rockey was fifty-six years old on Iwo Jima and a thirty-one-year veteran of the Marine Corps. A native of Columbia City, Indiana, he graduated from Gettysburg College and studied at Yale. Like his fellow division commanders, Rockey served in France in World War I and was awarded the Navy Cross as a junior officer in the 5th Marines at Chateau-Thierry.

He earned a second Navy Cross for heroic service in Nicaragua. He also served in Haiti and had two years of sea duty. After spending the first years of World War II at Marine Corps Headquarters in Washington, in February 1944, General Rockey took command of the 5th Marine Division and prepared them for their first and last great battle of the war.

Three other brigadier generals played a considerable role in the amphibious seizure of Iwo Jima:

- Leo Hermle, Assistant Division Commander of the 5th Marine Division.

- Franklin Hart, Assistant Division Commander of the 4th Marine Division.
- William Rogers, Corps Chief of Staff.

GENERAL KURIBAYASHI

According to Colonel Chambers, Battalion Commander of
the 3/25 Marines, whose four days on Iwo Jima resulted in a
Purple Heart and a Medal of Honor: "On Iwo, their smartest
general commanded. This man did not believe in the banzai
business. He ordered each Jap to kill ten Marines—and for a
while, they made their quotas."

Chambers was referring to Lieutenant General Kuribayashi, Commander of the *Ogasawara Army Group* and
Commanding General of the *109th Division*. Tadamichi Kuribayashi was fifty-three years old on Iwo. He was from the
Nagano Prefecture and served the Emperor as a cavalry officer
since graduating from the Military Academy in 1914. Kuribayashi spent several years as a junior officer posted to the
Japanese embassies in Canada and the United States. During
the war in Asia, Kuribayashi commanded a cavalry regiment
in Manchuria and a brigade in northern China. Later he
served as Chief of Staff for the *Twenty-third Army* during the
capture of Hong Kong.

After returning from China, the Emperor chose Kurib-ayashi to command the *Imperial Guards Division* in Tokyo. When Saipan fell in June 1944, he was assigned to command the defense of Iwo Jima.

Kuribayashi was a realist. He believed the crude airstrips on Iwo were a liability for the Empire. They provided nuisance raids against the B-29s but would undoubtedly draw attention from Allied strategic planners. The Iwo Jima airfields in Allied hands would pose a terrible threat to Japan.

Kuribayashi knew he had only two options: blow up the entire island or defend it to the death. Blowing up the entire island would be impractical, so he adopted a radical defensive policy. His troops would not use the suicidal banzai nor linear water's edge tactics used in previous island battles. This caused a massive controversy at the highest levels—Imperial head-quarters even asked the Nazis for advice on how to repel American invasions.

While Kuribayashi made some compromises with his forces on the island, he fired eighteen senior army officers, including his chief of staff. Those who remained would imple-ment Kuribayashi's policy to the letter.

The general knew he was doomed without air and naval support. Still, he proved to be a tenacious and resourceful commander. His only tactical error was in authorizing sector commanders to engage the Allied task force covering the UDT operations on D -2. This gift revealed to the gunners the masked batteries which would have slaughtered more of the landing force assault waves on D-Day.

Controversial Japanese accounts reported Kuribayashi committed *Seppuku* (Japanese ritual suicide) in his cave near Kitano point on March 23, 1945—the thirty-third day of battle. General

Holland Smith said: "of all our adversaries in the Pacific, Kuribayashi was the most redoubtable. Let's hope the Japs don't have any more like him."

JAPANESE SPIGOT MORTAR

One of the deadliest weapons faced on Iwo Jima was the 320mm spigot mortar. These gigantic defensive weapons were placed and operated by the Imperial Japanese Army's *20th Independent Mortar Battalion*.

The mortar tube had a small muzzle cavity. It rested on a steel base plate supported by a wooden platform. Unlike typical mortars, this five-foot-long projectile was placed over the tube instead of dropping down the barrel. The mortar shell's diameter was thirteen inches, while the tube was only a little more than ten inches wide.

This weapon hurled a 675-pound shell over 1,500 yards. The range was adjusted by varying the powder charge, while deflection changes were accomplished by brute force: pushing and shoving the base platform. Although tubes only held out for six rounds, enough shells were lobbed onto Allied positions to make a lasting impression.

A rifleman in the 28th Marines referred to it as "The Screaming Jesus." Most Marines had a healthy respect for the mortar. General Robert Cushman, who commanded the 2/9 Marines on Iwo Jima (later becoming the 25th Commandant of the Marine Corps), recalled the inaccuracy and terror of the tumbling projectiles: "you could see it coming. But you never knew where the hell it was going to come down."

IWO'S AIR SUPPORT

For a few memorable moments before the D-Day landing, the Marines' vision of an integrated air-ground assault team became a reality. As assault troops neared the beach in their tracked amphibian vehicles, dozens of F4U Corsairs swept in and paved the way with rockets and machine-gun fire. According to one Marine: "it was magnificent."

Unfortunately, the Marine fighter squadrons on Iwo Jima that morning came from the fast attack carriers of Task Force 58, not the amphibious task force. Three days later, Task Force 58 left for good in pursuit of more strategic targets. Following that, Navy and Army Air Force pilots provided support for the landing force fighting ashore. Sustained close air support of amphibious forces by Marine air was (once again) postponed for some future combat proving ground.

Other Marine aviation units contributed to the capture of Iwo Jima. One of the first to see action was VMB 612 (Marine Bombing Squadron) out of Saipan. Flight crews on PBJ Mitchell medium bombers ran long-range nightly rocket attacks against enemy ships trying to resupply. These nightly raids, along with the Navy's submarine interdictions, slashed the amount of ammunition and fortifications (mostly barbed wire) delivered to the enemy before the invasion.

Pilots and aerial spotters from Marine observation squadrons flew in from escort carriers or were launched from the infamous *LST 776's* slingshot. These crews played a crucial role in spotting enemy artillery and mortar positions and reporting them.

Marine transport aircraft based in the Marianas delivered critical combat cargo to the island at the height of the battle. Marines relied on aerial delivery before the landing force could establish a fully functional beachhead. On D +1, marine transport squadrons airdropped critically needed machine gun parts, mortar shells, and blood plasma within the lines. On March 3, Colonel Malcolm Mackay landed the first Marine transport aircraft on the island—a Curtiss Commando R5C loaded with ammunition. The three other Marine squadrons followed and brought in much-needed supplies and evacuated the wounded.

On March 8, Marine Torpedo Bomber Squadron 224 flew in from Tinian and took responsibility for day and night anti-submarine patrols. Colonel Vernon Megee had the honor of commanding the first Landing Force Air Support Control Unit (a landmark in the evolution of amphibious combat).

Megee came ashore on D +5 with General Schmidt, but the offloading process was still in such shambles that it took five days to gather communication jeeps. This did not deter Megee. He "borrowed" gear and moved inland to coordinate the Air Liaison Parties. He persuaded Navy pilots to use bigger bombs and listened to the assault commanders' complaints.

McGee's work in training and employing Army P-51 Mustang pilots was masterful. Kuribayashi transmitted to Tokyo "lessons learned" in defending against the Allied amphibious assault during the battle. One of his messages said: "the enemy's air control is strong. At least thirty aircraft flew ceaselessly from early morning to night over this very small island."

SHERMAN ZIPPO TANKS

For many Marines on Iwo Jima, the Sherman M4A3—with the Mark I flamethrower—was the most effective weapon employed in the battle.

On Iwo, Marines had come a long way with the tactical use of fire. Fifteen months earlier on Tarawa, only a handful of backpack flamethrowers were available to fight hundreds of the island's fortifications. While the assault force relied on portable flamethrowers, most Marines saw the value in marrying this technology with armored vehicles for use against the island's toughest targets.

In the Marianas, Marines modified M3A1 light tanks with the Canadian Ronson flame system to a deadly effect. But the small vehicles were vulnerable to enemy fire. On Peleliu, the 1st Marine Division mounted the improvised Mark I system on a thin skin LVT. But again, the vehicle's susceptibility to enemy fire limited the effectiveness of the system. The obvious solution was to mount the flamethrower on a tank.

Early modifications to the Shermans were made by replacing the bow machine gun with the small E4-5 mechanized flamethrower. Replacing the bow machine gun was only a minor improvement. The short-range, limited fuel supply and awkward aiming process did not compensate for losing the machine gun. Each of the three tank battalions used the E4-5-equipped Shermans on Iwo Jima.

The best solution for effective flame projection and mechanized mobility came from the Army's Chemical Warfare technicians on Hawaii before the invasion. Colonel Bill Collins, CO 5th Tank Battalion, inspired this tinkerer group to modify the Mark I flamethrower to operate within the Shermans' turret. By replacing the 75mm main gun with a look-alike launch tube, this modified system could be trained and pointed like any standard turret gun using napalm-thickened fuel. These Zippo tanks streamed 250 yards of flame for eighty seconds—a significant tactical improvement.

But the modification team only had enough time to modify eight M4A3 tanks with the Mark I flame system. The 4th and 5th Tank Battalions were each issued four. The 3rd Tank Battalion on Guam didn't receive any M4A3 Shermans nor field modifications in time for the battle on Iwo Jima. Although several of their A2 tanks kept the E4-5 system mounted in the bow.

The eight Sherman Zippo tanks were ideal against Iwo's rugged caves and concrete fortifications. The enemy was terrified of this weapon. Suicide squads of human bullets would attack flame tanks directly only to be shot down by covering forces or charred by napalm. Enemy fire took a toll on the eight flame tanks—but maintenance crews worked around the clock to keep them in the fight.

Captain Frank Caldwell, Company Commander of the 26th Marines said: "it was a flame tank more than any other supporting arm that won this battle."

The tactical demand for flame tanks never diminished. The 5th Tank Battalion used 10,000 gallons of napalm-thickened fuel a day. When the 5th Marine Division had cornered the last Japanese defenders in "The Gorge," their final after-action report stated the flame tank was one of the weapons that caused the enemy to leave their caves and rock crevices and run for their lives.

BUCK ROGERS MEN

Provisional rocket detachments were attached to the subdivisions of the landing force on Iwo Jima. Marines had a love-hate relationship with the little rocket trucks and their brave crews. These trucks were a one-ton, four wheel drive truck modified to carry three box-shaped rocket launchers containing a dozen 4.5-inch rockets.

Crews fired a ripple of thirty-six rockets within seconds and provided a carpet of high explosives on the target. While effective and deadly, each launch drew heavy return fire from the Japanese—who dreaded the automatic artillery.

The Experimental Rocket Unit was formed in June 1943 and first deployed rail-launched barrage rockets during the fighting in the Solomons. There, heavily canopied jungles limited their efficiency. But once mounted on trucks and deployed in the Central Pacific, these rockets were deadly and effective, especially during the battle on Saipan.

Marines reinforced the trucks' tailgate to serve as a blast shield. They installed hydraulic jacks to raise and lower the launchers. Crude steel rods were welded to the bumper and dashboard to help the driver align the vehicle with the aiming stakes.

A hilly treeless Iwo proved an ideal battleground for the "Buck Rogers Men." The 1st Provisional Rocket Detachment supported the 4th and 5th Marine Divisions throughout the battle on Iwo Jima. The Buck Rogers Men fired over 30,000 rockets to support the landing force.

The Rocket Detachment landed on Red Beach on D-Day and lost one vehicle in the surf and several others to heavy enemy fire or loose sand. When the first vehicle reached its firing position intact, it launched a salvo of rockets against Japanese fortifications on the slopes of Suribachi. It detonated an enemy ammunition dump. The detachment supported the Marines advance to the summit, often launching single rockets to clear suspected enemy positions along the route.

As the fighting advanced north, the rocket launchers' short-range deep angle fire and saturation effect kept them in high demand. They were effective in defilade-to-defilade bombardments. But the distinct flashing telltale blast always caught the attention of the Japanese artillery spotters. The rocket trucks rarely remained in one place long enough to fire more than two salvos. A fast displacement was critical to their survival. Marines knew better than to stand around and wave goodbye—it was time to seek deep shelter from the counter-battery fire sure to follow.

LOGISTICAL SUPPORT

The logistical effort necessary to sustain the assault force on Iwo Jima was complex, enormous, and learned from previous lessons in Pacific amphibious operations. No other element of the emerging art of amphibious warfare had improved so greatly by the winter of 1945.

While Marines had the courage and firepower to tackle a fortress like Iwo Jima, they would have been crippled without the available amphibious logistical support. The procedures, organizations, and concepts took years to develop. But once in place, they enabled the large-scale conquests on Iwo Jima and Okinawa.

On Iwo Jima, the 8th Field Depot was commanded by Colonel Leland Swindler. This depot served as the nucleus of shore party operations. Swindler coordinated the activities of all shore party operations. The logistical support on Iwo was well-conceived and executed. Liaison teams from the 8th Field Depot accompanied the 4th and 5th Divisions ashore. On D +3, field depot units came ashore, took over the unloading, and continued without interruption.

Every imaginable method of delivering combat cargo ashore was used. This involved "hot cargo," carried in by the assault waves. Hot cargo was preloaded in on assault waves or floating dumps. This experimental use of one-shot preloaded amphibious trailers, Wilson drums, and a general loading and unloading would be known to future generations as the "assault follow-on echelon."

Aerial delivery was first by parachute and then via transports landing on the captured runways. The Marine/Navy team experimented with the use of armored bulldozers and sleds loaded with hinged matting delivered by assault waves to clear wheeled vehicles stuck in the soft, volcanic sand. Despite fearsome obstacles: heavy surf, dangerous undertows, foul weather, and formidable enemy fire—the system worked. The combat cargo flowed in and kept casualties and salvaged equipment flowing out.

The occasional shortages were often the result of the

Marines meeting a more robust defensive garrison than initially expected. Urgent calls for more demolitions, grenades, mortar illumination rounds, and blood plasma were common. Transport squadrons delivered many of these critical items directly from the Mariana Islands fleet bases.

The field medical support on Iwo was a model of detailed planning and flexible application. Marines received immediate medical attention from their corpsmen and surgeons. But the system from hospitals to grave registration was mind boggling to some of the older veterans. Moderately wounded Marines received full hospital treatment and rehabilitation—often returning directly to their units—this preserved some of the swiftly decreasing combat experience levels in the frontline outfits. The more seriously wounded were stabilized, evacuated, and treated in offshore hospital ships or taken by air to Guam.

Marines fired an extraordinary half-million artillery rounds to support the assault units. Many rounds were lost when the 5th Marine Division's ammo dump blew up. But the flow never stopped. The shore party used LVTs and amphibious trucks for a fast offloading of ammunition ships dangerously exposed to enemy gunners. Marines helped the shore party hustle munitions onshore and into the neediest hands.

Colonel James Hittle of the 3rd Division (the reserve landing force) shook his head at the "crazy quilt" logistics adopted because of Iwo's geography. Hittle "appropriated" a transport plane and made regular runs to Guam—returning with fresh beef, beer, and mail. Colonel Hittle sent his transport quartermaster out to sea in an LVT full of war souvenirs to trade for bread, eggs, and fresh fruit.

Hittle was amazed at the density of troops funneled onto the small island: "at one point, we had over 60,000 men occupying less than three and a half miles of broken terrain." He directed Marine engineers to dig a well near the beach for a freshwater distilling plant. Instead of a saltwater source, engineers discovered steaming mineral water heated by Suribachi's dormant volcano.

Hittle moved the distilling site, and this spot became a hot shower facility—one of the most popular places on the island.

OPERATION ICEBERG

1945 VICTORY ON OKINAWA

SEIZING SHURI CASTLE

At dawn on May 29, 1945, the 1st Marine Division began their fifth consecutive week of frontal assaults. This was part of the Tenth Army's relentless offensive against Japanese defenses in southern Okinawa.

Operation Iceberg's mission to secure Okinawa was now two months old and badly bogged down. The fast-paced opening had been replaced by weeks of exhausting and bloody attrition warfare against the Shuri Castle.

The 1st Division were hemmed in between two other divisions. They had precious little room to maneuver and had advanced less than a thousand yards in eighteen days. An average of fifty-five murderous yards per day. Their sector was one bristling, honeycombed ridgeline after another—Kakazu, Dakeshi, and Wana.

But just beyond was the long shoulder of Shuri Ridge. Nerve center of the Imperial Japanese *Thirty-second Army.* The outpost of dozens of forward artillery observers, who'd made life miserable for the Allied landing force. On this wet, rainy, and cold morning, things were different. It was quieter. After days of savage and bitter fighting, Allied forces overran Conical Hill to the east and Sugar Loaf to the west. Shuri Castle no longer seemed invincible.

The 1/5 Marines moved out cautiously and expected the usual firestorm of enemy artillery at any moment. But there was none. Marines reached the crest of Shuri Ridge without a fight. Amazed, the company commander looked west along the road toward the ruins of Shuri Castle: a medieval fortress of ancient Ryukyuan kings.

Soldiers in the Tenth Army expected the Japanese to defend Shuri to the death, but the place seemed lightly held. Spiteful small arms fire came from nothing more than a rearguard. Field radios buzzed with this surprising news. Shuri Castle laid in the distance, ready for the taking. Marines asked for permission to seize their long-awaited prize.

General Pedro del Valle, CO of the 1st Marine Division,

didn't hesitate. According to corps division boundaries, Shuri Castle belonged to soldiers of the 77th Infantry Division. General del Valle knew his counterpart, Army General Andrew Bruce, would be furious if the Marines snatched their long-sought trophy before his soldiers could arrive. This was a unique opportunity to grab the Tenth Army's primary objective. General del Valle gave the go-ahead, and with that, the 1/5 Marines raced along the west ridge against light opposition and secured Shuri Castle.

After General del Valle's staff did some fancy footwork to keep peace with their army neighbors, they learned the 77th had scheduled a massive castle bombardment that morning. Frantic radio calls averted the near-catastrophe just in time. General Bruce was infuriated by the Marines' unauthorized initiative. Del Valle later wrote: "I don't think a single Army commander would talk to me after that."

Through the inter-service aggravation, Allied forces had achieved much this morning. For two months, Shuri Castle had provided the Japanese with a superb field of observed fire —covering southern Okinawa's entire five-mile neck. But as the 1/5 Marines deployed into a defensive line within the castle's rubble, they were unaware that a Japanese rearguard still occupied a massive subterranean headquarters underneath them. Marines soon discovered that directly under their muddy boondockers was the underground headquarters of the Japanese *Thirty-second Army*. This mammoth complex was over 1,200 feet long and 160 feet deep: all dug by pick and shovel.

The enemy had stolen a march on the approaching Tenth Army. Japanese forces retreated south during the rains and occupied the third (final) ring of their prepared underground defenses: a series of fortified escarpments on the Kiyamu Peninsula.

Seizing Shuri Castle was an indisputable milestone in the

Okinawa campaign. Still, it was a hollow victory. Like the flag-raising on Iwo Jima's Suribachi signified the end of the beginning of that prolonged battle. The capture of Shuri Castle did not end the fighting. The savage slugfest on Okinawa continued for another twenty-four days—while the plum rains fell and the horrors and dying on both sides continued.

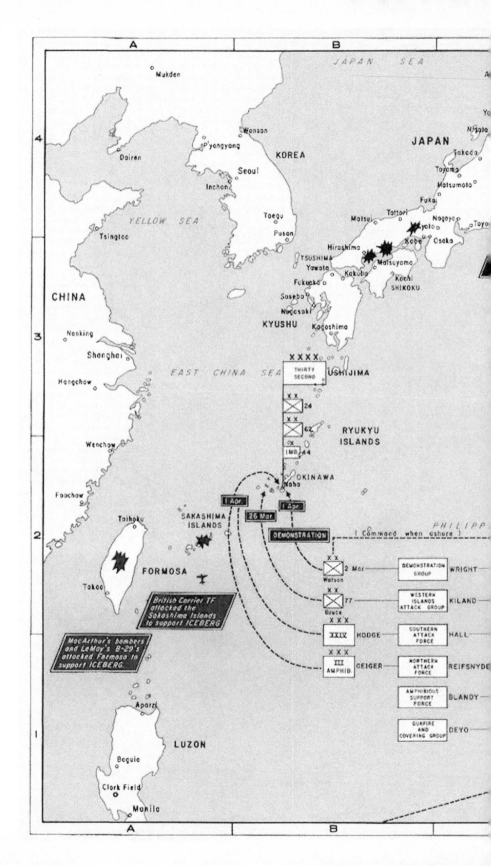

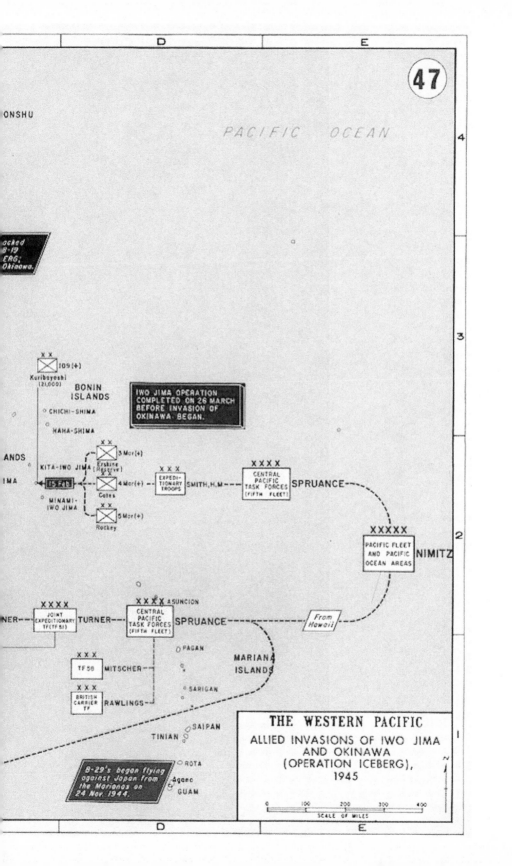

47

PACIFIC OCEAN

ONSHU

acked
B-19
ERG;
Okinawa.

XX
109(+)
Kuribayashi
(21,000)

BONIN
ISLANDS

○ CHICHI-SHIMA

○ HAHA-SHIMA

IWO JIMA OPERATION
COMPLETED ON 26 MARCH
BEFORE INVASION OF
OKINAWA BEGAN.

ANDS

XX
3 Mar(+)
Erskine
(Reserve)

KITA-IWO JIMA

IMA   TF 218   XX
4 Mar(+)
Cates

XXX
EXPEDI-
TIONARY
TROOPS

SMITH, H. M.

XXXX
CENTRAL
PACIFIC
TASK FORCES
(FIFTH FLEET)

SPRUANCE

○ MINAMI-
IWO JIMA

XX
5 Mar(+)
Rockey

XXXXX
PACIFIC FLEET
AND PACIFIC
OCEAN AREAS

NIMITZ

NER

XXXX
JOINT
EXPEDITIONARY
TF(TF 51)

TURNER

XXXX ASUNCION
CENTRAL
PACIFIC
TASK FORCES
(FIFTH FLEET)

SPRUANCE

From
Hawaii

○ PAGAN

XXX
TF 58

MITSCHER

MARIANA
ISLANDS

○ SARIGAN

XXX
BRITISH
CARRIER
TF

RAWLINGS

○ SAIPAN

TINIAN

THE WESTERN PACIFIC

ALLIED INVASIONS OF IWO JIMA
AND OKINAWA
(OPERATION ICEBERG),
1945

○ ROTA

B-29's began flying
against Japan from
the Marianas on
24 Nov. 1944.

Agana
GUAM

0   100   200   300   400
SCALE OF MILES

OPERATION ICEBERG

The battle of Okinawa covered a seven-hundred-mile arc from Kyushu to Formosa. It involved a million combatants— Japanese, Americans, British, and Okinawan natives. This battle rivaled the Normandy invasion because it was the biggest and bloodiest operation of the Pacific War. In eighty-two days of combat, Allied forces and unfortunate noncombatants suffered an average of 3,000 lives lost a day.

By the spring of 1945, the Empire of Japan was a wounded wild animal: desperate, cornered, and furious. Japanese leaders knew Okinawa under Allied control would be transformed into "the England of the Pacific." It would serve as a staging point for the invasion of the sacred homeland. The Japanese would sacrifice everything to avoid the unspeakable disgrace of unconditional surrender and foreign occupation.

The US Navy was presented with its greatest operational challenge to date: how to protect a gigantic and exposed amphibious task force tethered to the beachhead against Japanese *kamikaze* attacks. Okinawa would be the ultimate test of US amphibious power and projection. Could Allied forces in the Pacific Theater plan and execute such a massive assault against a heavily defended landmass? Could the Allies integrate the tactical capabilities of all the services and fend off every imaginable form of counterattack while maintaining operational momentum?

Operation Iceberg was not executed in a vacuum. Preparatory action to the invasion kicked off at the same time campaigns on Iwo Jima and the Philippines were still being wrapped up—another strain on Allied resources. But as dramatic and sprawling as the battle of Okinawa proved to be, both sides saw this contest as an example of the even more desperate fighting soon to come with the invasion of the Japanese home islands. The closeness of Okinawa to Japan was well within medium bomber and fighter escort range. Its valuable military ports, anchorages, airfields, and training areas made this skinny island imperative for Allied forces—eclipsing their earlier plans for the seizure of Formosa.

Okinawa is the largest of the Ryukyuan Islands. The island sits at the apex of a triangle nearly equidistant to strategic areas. Formosa is 330 miles to the southwest, Kyushu is 350 miles to the north, while Shanghai is 450 miles to the west. As on so many Pacific battlefields, Okinawa had a peaceful heritage. Officially an administrative prefecture of Japan (forcibly seized in 1879), Okinawans were proud of their long Chinese legacy and unique sense of community.

Imperial headquarters in Tokyo did little to garrison or fortify Okinawa at the beginning of the Pacific War. After the Allies conquered Saipan, Japanese headquarters sent reinforcements and fortification materials to critical areas within the "Inner Strategic Zone," Peleliu, the Philippines, Iwo Jima, and Okinawa.

Imperial Japanese headquarters on Okinawa formed a

new field army: the *Thirty-second Army*. They funneled different trained components from Japan's armed perimeter in China, Manchuria, and the home islands. American submarines took a deadly toll on these Japanese troop movements. On June 29, 1944, the USS *Sturgeon* torpedoed the transport *Toyama Maru*. She sank with a loss of 5,600 troops of the *44th Independent Mixed Brigade* en route for Okinawa. It would take the Japanese the rest of the year to replace that loss.

In October 1944, US Joint Chiefs decided to act on the strategic value of the Ryukyus. They tasked Admiral Nimitz with seizing Okinawa after the Iwo Jima campaign. The Joint Chiefs ordered Nimitz to seize, occupy, and defend Okinawa before transforming the captured island into an advanced staging base for the invasion of Japan.

Nimitz turned to his most veteran commanders to execute this mission. Admiral Spruance, the victor of Midway and the Battle of the Philippine Sea, would command the US Fifth Fleet (debatably the most powerful armada of warships ever assembled). Admiral Kelly Turner, veteran of the Solomons and Central Pacific landings, would command all amphibious forces under Spruance. But Kelly Turner's military counterpart would no longer be the old warhorse General Holland Smith. Iwo Jima was Smith's last fight. Now the expeditionary forces had grown to the size of a field army with 182,000 assault troops. Army General Simon Buckner (son of the Confederate general who fought against Grant at Fort Donaldson in the American Civil War) would command the newly formed US Tenth Army.

General Buckner made sure the Tenth Army reflected his multi-service composition. Thirty-four Marine officers served on Buckner's staff, including General Oliver P. Smith as his deputy Chief of Staff. Smith later wrote: "the Tenth Army became, in effect, a joint task force."

Six veteran divisions, two Marine and four Army, composed Buckner's landing force. A division from each service was marked for reserve duty—another sign of the growth of Allied amphibious power in the Pacific. Earlier in the war, Americans had landed one infantry division on Guadalcanal, two in the Palaus, and three each on Iwo Jima and Saipan. But by spring 1945, Buckner and Spruance could count on eight experienced divisions besides those still on Luzon and Iwo Jima.

The Tenth Army had three major operational components. Army General John Hodge commanded the XXIV Corps, composed of the 77th and 96th Infantry Divisions (with the 27th Infantry Division in floating reserve and the 81st Infantry Division in area reserve). Marine General Roy Geiger commanded the III Amphibious Corps, composed of the 1st and 6th Marine Divisions (with the 2nd Marine Division held in floating reserve). Marine General Francis Mulcahy commanded the Tenth Army's Tactical Air Force and the 2nd Marine Aircraft Wing.

The Marine components for Operation Iceberg were scattered. The 1st Marines had returned from Peleliu to "Pitiful Pavuvu" in the Russell Islands to prepare for the next fight. The 1st Marine Division had been the first to deploy into the Pacific. They executed brutal amphibious campaigns on Guadalcanal, Cape Gloucester, and Peleliu. Over one-third of the 1st Marines were veterans of two of those battles.

Pavuvu's tiny island limited work-up training, but a large-scale exercise on neighboring Guadalcanal enabled the division to integrate its replacements and returning veterans. General del Valle drilled his Marines in tank-infantry training under the protective umbrella of supporting howitzer fire.

The 6th Marine Division was the only division formed overseas in the war. General Lemuel Shepherd activated the colors and assumed command on September 12, 1944. While this unit was newly formed, it was not green—several former Marine Raiders with combat experience comprised the heart of this Marine division. General Shepherd used his time and the more extensive facilities on Guadalcanal to conduct work-up training from the platoon to the regimental level. He looked ahead to Okinawa and emphasized rapid troop deployments and large-scale operations in built-up combat areas.

General LeRoy Hunt commanded the 2nd Marine Division. Hunt's Marines had returned to Saipan after the conquest of Tinian. The division had absorbed 8,000 replacements and trained for a wide-ranging series of mission assignments as a strategic reserve. The 2nd Division possessed a vital lineage in the Pacific War at Guadalcanal, Tarawa, Saipan, and Tinian. Its presence in the Ryukyus' waters would establish a fearsome "amphibious force-in-being" to distract the Japanese on Okinawa. This division would pay an unequal price for its bridesmaid role in the coming campaign.

The Marine assault force preparing for Okinawa was dealt another organizational change—the fourth of the war. Marine headquarters constantly reviewed "lessons learned" in the war and had just completed a series of revisions to the table of organization for its divisions and components. While it would not become official until a month after the landing, the divisions had already made most changes.

The overall size of each division increased to 19,176 (from 17,465). This was done by adding an assault signal company, a rocket platoon (Buck Rogers Men), a fifty-five man assault platoon in each regimental headquarters, and a war dog platoon. Motor transport, artillery, and service units also received slight increases, as did machine-gun platoons in each rifle company. But the most timely weapons change happened by replacing the 75mm half-tracks with the new M-7s (105mm self-propelled howitzer). Artillery regiment purists did not approve of these weapons being deployed by the infantry. These M-7s would not be used as massed howitzers but as direct fire "siege guns" against the thousands of fortified caves on Okinawa.

Marine Corps Headquarters backed up these last-minute changes by providing the required replacements to land the assault divisions at full strength. Sometimes the skills required did not match. Some artillery regiments absorbed a flood of radar technicians and anti-aircraft artillery gunners from old defense battalions. But the manpower and equipment short-falls that had plagued earlier operations were overcome by the time the assault force embarked on Operation Iceberg.

Even this late in the war, operational intelligence was unsatisfactory before the landing. At Tarawa and Tinian, the pre-assault combat intelligence had been brilliant. But at Okinawa, the landing force did not have accurate figures of the enemy's weapons or abilities.

The cloud cover over the island prevented accurate and complete photo-reconnaissance. Also, the ingenuity of the Japanese commander and the extraordinary digging skills of the enemy garrison helped disguise the island's true defenses.

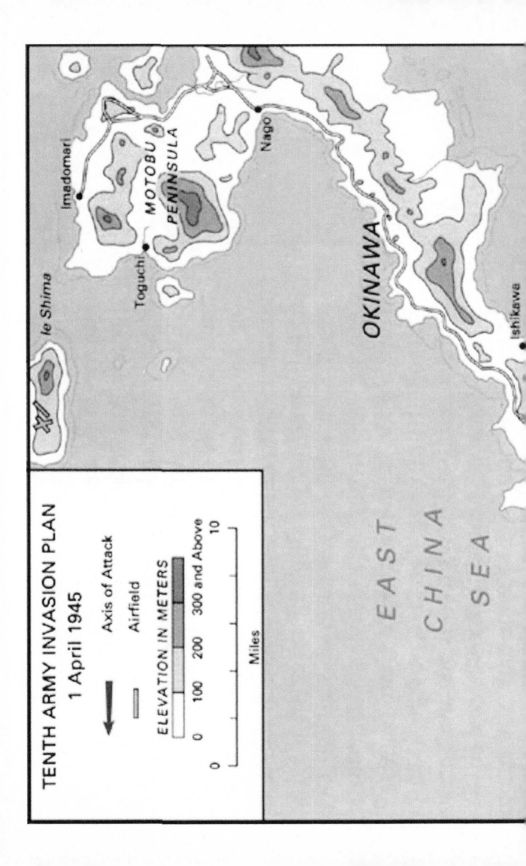

TENTH ARMY INVASION PLAN
1 April 1945

→ Axis of Attack

Airfield

ELEVATION IN METERS

| 0 | 100 | 200 | 300 and Above |

Miles

0 _____ 10

le Shima

Imadomari

Toguchi

MOTOBU PENINSULA

Nago

OKINAWA

Ishikawa

EAST CHINA SEA

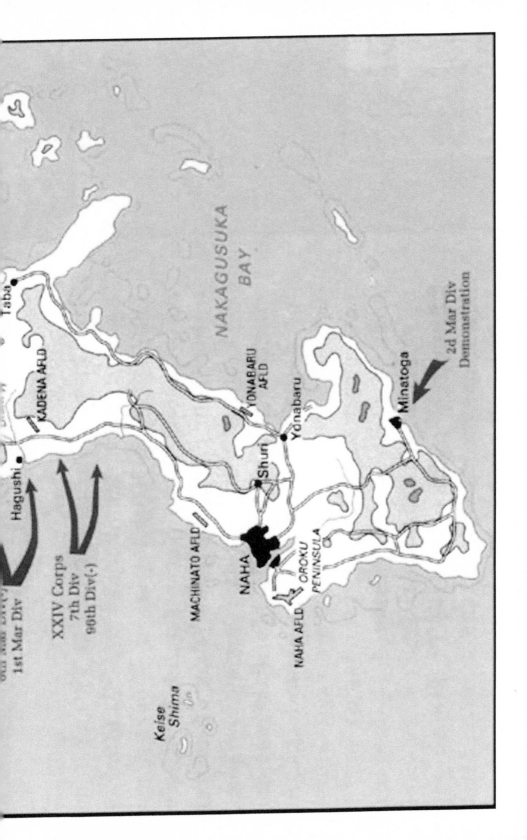

JAPANESE DEFENSES

Okinawa is sixty miles long, but only the lower third of the island had the military objectives of anchorages, ports, and airfields. In August 1944. Japanese General Mitsuru Ushijima took command of the *Thirty-second Army*. He understood the fight would be fought in the south and concentrated his forces there.

He decided to not challenge the probable Allied landings in Hagushi along the broad beaches of the southwest coast. He believed that doing so would lose him the Kadena and Yontan Airfields. This decision allowed him to conserve his forces and fight the only battle that stood a chance: an in-depth defense, underground and protected from the overpowering Allied air and arms superiority.

This clash of cave warfare and attrition would be like the recent battles on Peleliu and Iwo Jima. Each had taken a terrifying cost to Allied invaders. General Ushijima sought to replicate this strategy. He would go underground and sting the Allies with high caliber gunfire from his freshly excavated fireport caves. He believed by bleeding the landing force and bogging down their momentum, he could buy the Imperial Army and Navy's air arms enough time to destroy the fifth fleet with massed *kamikaze* attacks.

General Ushijima had 100,000 Imperial troops on the island, including thousands of Okinawan Home Guard (conscripts known as *Boeitai*). He had a disproportionate number of heavy weapons and artillery in his command. The Allies in the Pacific would not encounter a more formidable concentration of 47mm antitank guns, 320mm spigot mortars, 120mm mortars, and 150mm howitzers. The strategic decision to invade Peleliu, Iwo Jima, and the Philippines before Okinawa gave the enemy seven months to develop their defenses.

Allied forces had already seen what the Japanese could do to fortify a position in a short time. On Okinawa they achieved stunning success. They worked almost exclusively with hand tools: not one bulldozer on the entire island. The Japanese dug miles of underground fighting positions and honeycombed southern Okinawa's ridges and draws. They stocked each position with reserves of food, water, ammunition, and medical supplies. Allied forces anticipated a fierce defense of the southwestern beaches and the airfields, followed by a general counterattack. Then, the battle would be over except for some mop-up and light patrolling.

The Allies could not have been more mistaken.

The assault plan called for the advance seizure of the Kerama Retto Islands after several days of preparatory air and naval bombardment. Followed by a massive four-division assault on the Hagushi Beaches. During the primary assault, the 2nd Marine Division, with a separate naval task force, would duplicate the assault on Okinawa's southeast coast (Minatoga Beaches).

Love-Day (chosen to avoid planning confusion with D-Day being planned for Iwo Jima) would happen on April 1, 1945.

Hardly anyone failed to remark about the irony of April Fool's Day and Easter Sunday.

The US Fifth Fleet was a breathtaking sight as it steamed toward the Ryukyus. Marines who'd returned to the Pacific from the original amphibious offensive on Guadalcanal thirty-one months earlier gaped at the quantity of landing craft in the assault ships. The armada stretched to the horizon—a genuinely incredible, mind-boggling vista.

* * *

On March 26, the 77th Infantry Division skillfully secured Kerama Retto. A move that surprised the Japanese and generated enormous operational dividends. Admiral Turner now had a series of sheltered anchorages to repair ships likely to be damaged by *kamikaze* attacks. Soldiers discovered stockpiled Japanese suicide boats—over 300 powerboats equipped with high explosive rams to sink the thin-skinned troop transports.

Major James Jones commanded the Force Reconnaissance Battalion. His battalion paved the way before each landing with stealthy scouting missions the night before. Jones' recon Marines scouted and found the barren sand spits of Keise Shima undefended. After reporting that welcome news, the Army landed a battery of 155mm "Long Toms" on the small inlets, adding to their significant firepower and the naval bombardment of Okinawa's southwest coast.

Admiral Turner's minesweepers cleared approaches to the southwestern beaches. Navy frogmen and Marines detonated hundreds of man-made obstacles. After seven days of preliminary bombardment, Allied ships fired over 25,000 rounds of 5-inch shells. This shelling produced more of a spectacle than a destructive effect. The Allied forces believed General Ushijima's troops would be arrayed around the beaches and airfields.

While that scale and duration of bombardment would've saved many lives on Iwo Jima: on Okinawa, this precious ordinance was largely wasted and produced few results.

Tensions were high in landing force transports. The 60mm mortar section of Company K, 3/5 Marines learned that the casualty rates on Love-Day were estimated to reach 85%. According to Private First Class Eugene Sledge: "this is not conducive to a good night's sleep."

A Japanese soldier observing the massive armada bearing down on Okinawa wrote in his diary: "it's like a frog meeting a snake and waiting for the snake to eat him."

LAND THE LANDING FORCE

The Allied invasion got off to a roaring start. The few enemy defenders still in the area at dawn on April 1 immediately agreed with the wisdom of conceding the beaches to the landing force.

The massive armada gathered from ports all over the Pacific now bore down on Okinawa's southwest coast: ready to deploy a 182,000-man landing force onto the beach. The ultimate forcible entry—the embodiment of all painfully learned amphibious lessons from the crude beginnings at Guadalcanal and North Africa.

Admiral Turner made his final review of the weather conditions in the objective area. As at Iwo Jima, the amphibious assault was fortunate to have good weather for the critical initial landing. Skies were clear, winds and surf were moderate. The temperature was 75 degrees.

At 0406, Turner ordered: "Land the landing force." That phrase set off a sequential countdown to the first assault waves smashing into the beaches at H-hour. Combat troops crowded the rails of the transports to witness an extraordinary display of Allied naval power. A sustained bombardment by rockets and shells from hundreds of ships. Formations of Allied attack aircraft streaked low over the beaches: strafing and bombing at will. Japanese fire was ineffective and scattered, even against this massive armada assembled offshore.

The diversionary force carrying the 2nd Marine Division set out to bait the Japanese with a feint landing on the opposite coast. This amphibious force steamed into position and launched amphibian tractors and Higgins boats loaded with combat Marines in seven waves toward Minatoga Beach. The fourth wave commander paid careful attention to the clock and crossed the line of departure at exactly 0830—the time of the actual H-hour assault on the western coast. Then, the Higgins boats and LVTs turned away and returned to the transports: mission accomplished.

The diversionary landing achieved its purpose. General Ushijima had placed several front-line infantry and artillery units in the Minatoga Beach area for several weeks as a contingency against an expected secondary landing. His officers reported to Imperial headquarters on Love-Day morning: "enemy landing attempt on east coast blocked with heavy enemy losses."

This deception came at a high cost. *Kamikaze* pilots were convinced this was the main assault. They came in waves and struck the small force that morning, damaging the troopships *LST 844* and *Hinsdale*. The 3/2 Marines and the 2nd Amphibian Tractor Battalion suffered fifty casualties. The troopships lost an equal number of sailors. Ironically, the division that was expected to have the most minor damage or casualties in the battle lost more men than any other division in the Tenth Army that day. According to Operation Officer Colonel Sam Taxis: "we'd requested air cover for the feint but were told the threat was 'incidental.'"

In the southwest, the main assault force faced little resistance. A massive coral reef provided an offshore barrier to the beaches on Hagushi. But by early evening, the reef no longer presented a threat to the landing force. Unlike on Tarawa, where the reef dominated the tactical progress of the battle. General Buckner had over 1,400 LVTs to transport the assault waves from ship to shore without delay.

Eight miles of LVTs churned across the line of departure just behind 360 armored LVT-As that blasted away at the beach with their snub-nosed 75mm howitzers as they advanced the final four thousand yards. Behind the LVTs were 750 amphibious trucks with the first of the direct support artillery battalions. The horizon behind the amphibious trucks was filled with lines of landing boats. They paused at the reef to marry with the outbound LVTs. Marines and soldiers had exhaustively rehearsed transfer line operations—there was no pause in the assault momentum.

The Bisha Gawa river mouth marked the boundary

between IIIAC and XXIV Corps along the Hagushi beaches. The tactical plan called for the two divisions to land abreast— the 6th on the left and the 1st on the right. The endless rehearsal of thousands of hours paid off. The initial assault touched down at 0830: the designated H-hour. Marines stormed out of their LVTs, swarming over the sea walls and berms into the great unknown. The Okinawa invasion had begun. Within the first hour, the Tenth Army had over 16,000 combat troops ashore.

Despite the dire intelligent predictions and their own combat experience, the troops' landing was a cakewalk— almost unopposed. Private First Class Eugene Sledge's mortar section began singing "Little Brown Jug" at the top of their lungs. He later wrote how he couldn't believe his good luck: "I didn't hear a single shot all morning. It was unbelievable."

Many Marine veterans expected enemy fire at any second. Later that day, General del Valle's LVT got stuck in a pothole en route to the beach. "It was the worst twenty minutes I'd ever spent in my life," the general later wrote.

That morning continued to deliver pleasant surprises to the assault force. No mines along the beaches, the main bridge over the Bishi River was still intact, and both airfields were lightly defended. Marines took Yontan Airfield at 1300 while soldiers from the 7th Infantry Division had no problem securing nearby Kadena.

After securing the assault beaches, the landing force left plenty of room for the follow-on forces. Division commanders accelerated the landing of artillery battalions, tanks, and reserves. This massive buildup was hampered by a few glitches. Four artillery pieces went down when their amphibious trucks foundered along the reef. Several other Sherman tanks grounded on the reef. The 3/1 Marines arrived at the transfer line by 1800 but spent an uncomfortable night in their boats because enough LVTs were not available for the last leg at that hour. While only minor inconveniences, by the day's end, the Tenth Army had 60,000 troops ashore and occupied an expanded beach eight miles long and two miles deep.

The landing was not bloodless. Snipers wounded Major John Gustafson, CO of the 3/5 Marines, later that afternoon. Other men went down to enemy mortars and machine-gun fire. But the Tenth Army's entire losses (including the hard-luck 2nd Division) were 159 casualties with twenty-eight killed.

This was less than ten percent of casualties suffered by V Amphibious Corps on the first bloody day of Iwo Jima.

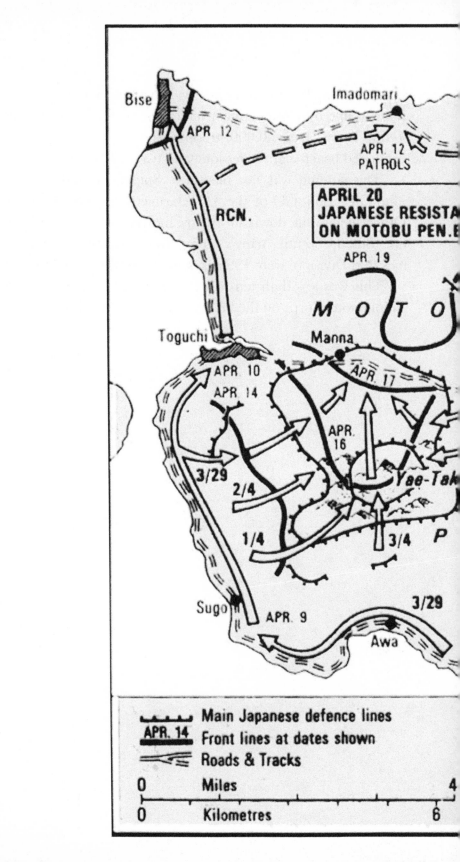

Bise

Imadomari

APR. 12

APR. 12
PATROLS

RCN.

**APRIL 20
JAPANESE RESISTA
ON MOTOBU PEN. E**

APR. 19

M O T O

Toguchi

Manna

APR. 10
APR. 14

APR. 17

APR.
16

3/29

Yae-Tak

2/4

1/4

3/4

P

Sugo

APR. 9

3/29

Awa

Main Japanese defence lines
APR. 14 Front lines at dates shown
Roads & Tracks

0   Miles   4

0   Kilometres   6

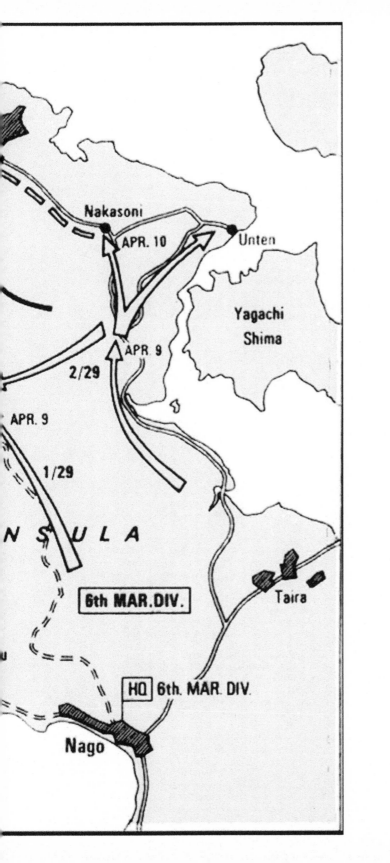

Nakasoni

APR. 10

Unten

Yagachi
Shima

APR. 9

2/29

APR. 9

1/29

N S U L A

6th MAR. DIV.

Taira

HQ 6th. MAR. DIV.

Nago

BATTLE OF YAE TAKE

The assault force's momentum did not slow down after the Tenth Army broke out of the beachhead. The 7th Infantry reached the east coast on the second day. On the third day, the 1st Marine Division secured the Katchin Peninsula and cut the island in two. By now, elements of the III Amphibious Corps had reached their objective initially thought to require eleven days. Colonel Victor Krulak, 6th Marine Division operations officer, recalled General Shepherd's orders: "Plow ahead as fast as you can. The Japs are on the run."

Krulak thought: *Well hell, we didn't have them on the run. They weren't there.*

The 6th Division swung north, while the 1st Marine Division moved to the northwest—their immediate problems stemming not from the enemy but a slow supply system still processing on the beach. The reef-side transfer line worked well for troops but not for cargo.

Navy Seabees worked to build a causeway for the reef. At the same time, the 1st Division demonstrated their amphibious know-how learned on Peleliu. They mounted swinging cranes on powered causeways and secured craft to the seaward side of the reef. When boats pulled alongside, cranes lifted nets filled with combat cargo into open hatches of waiting LVTs and amphibious trucks. This worked so well that the division divided its assets within the Tenth Army.

Beach congestion slowed the logistical process. Both Marine divisions used their replacements as shore party teams. Inexperience combined with a constant call for new replacements caused traffic control problems in establishing functional supply dumps and pilferage. This was not new. Other divisions in earlier operations had had the same problems. The quickly advancing divisions desperately needed bulk fuel and motor transport—but these were slow to land and distribute.

The undeveloped road network on Okinawa made this problem worse. Colonel Ed Snedeker, CO of the 7th Regiment in the 1st Marine Division, wrote: "The movement from the west coast landing beaches on Okinawa across the island was difficult because of the rugged terrain. It was physically exhausting for personnel to be on the transports for such a long time. This also presented an initial impossible supply problem in the Seventh's zone of action because of the lack of roads."

General Mulcahy brought the Tactical Air Force command post ashore on L + 1. Operating out of crude quarters between Kadena and Yontan Airfields, Mulcahy closely watched the Seabees and Army-Marine engineers progress repairing the captured airfields. A Marine observation plane was the first Allied aircraft to land on April 2. Two days later, the airfields were ready to accept fighters. By the eighth day, General Mulcahy could accommodate medium bombers and assumed control of all ashore fleet aircraft.

Mulcahy's fighter arm, the Air Defense Command, was established on shore under the command of Marine General

William Wallace. Graceful F4U Corsairs of Marine Aircraft Group (MAG 31) flew in from escort carriers. Wallace tasked them with flying combat air patrols over the fleet to tackle the vicious mass of *kamikaze* attacks plaguing the fleet. Most Marine fighter pilots' initial missions were combat air patrols, while (ironically) Navy squadrons on board escort carriers handled the close air support jobs.

At dawn, Marine Corsairs took off from the airfields and flew combat air patrols over the far-flung fifth fleet. They passed Navy Hellcats coming in from the fleet to support the Marines fighting on the ground. Other air units poured into the two Army airfields: night fighters, torpedo bombers, and an Army Air Forces fighter wing. The Okinawan airfields were not safe-havens. They received nightly artillery fire from long-range bombing the entire first month ashore. But the two airfields remained in operation around the clock. They were an invaluable asset in support of Operation Iceberg.

* * *

General Roy Geiger unleashed the 6th Marine Division to sweep north while the 1st Division hunted down and destroyed small bands of enemy guerrillas in the center of the island. Riflemen rode topside on tanks and self-propelled guns streaming northward against the fleeing enemy. Not since Tinian did Marines enjoy such invigorating mobility. On April 7, Marines seized Nagano, the largest town in northern Okinawa. The Navy swept for mines and deployed Under-water Demolition Teams to breach obstacles and open the port for direct seaborne delivery of crucial supplies.

Corporal James Day with the 22nd Marines was impressed at the momentum of the operation. He wrote: "Hell, here we are in Nago. It wasn't tough at all. Up until that time, our squad hadn't lost a man." The 22nd Marines continued north through a rugged and broken country. They reached Hedo Misaki at the far end of the island on L +12 after advancing fifty-five miles from the landing beaches at Hagushi.

The honeymoon was coming to a swift end for the rest of the 6th Division. Northwest of Nago, on its bulby nose, the Motobu Peninsula jutted out into the East China Sea. In a six mile area around the 1,200 foot Mount Yae Take, Colonel Takesiko Udo and his *Kunigami Detachment* were in prepared defensive positions. The delaying tactics were over. Udo's force comprised two thousand seasoned troops from the *44th Independent Mixed Brigade*. He had two rifle battalions, a regimental gun company, and an anti-tank company at his disposal.

Mount Yae Take was a defender's dream. Steep vines tangled with dense vegetation. Japanese troops booby-trapped the approaches with mines and mounted 20mm machine cannons and heavier weapons deep inside their caves. According to Colonel Krulak: "They were just there. They weren't going anywhere. They were going to fight to the death. They had a lot of Navy guns that came off disabled ships. They dug them way back in holes where their arc of fire was not more than ten degrees." An artillery battalion of fifteen Marines had the misfortune to lay their guns directly within the narrow arc of a hidden 150mm cannon. "They lost two howitzers before you could spell cat."

The battle of Yae Take was the first real fight for the 6th Marine Division. Five days of difficult and deadly combat against a determined enemy. The 4th and the 29th Marines earned their spurs here. They developed teamwork and tactics, putting them in a good position for the long, bloody campaign ahead.

One aspect of General Shepherd's success in this battle stemmed from his desire to place proven leaders in command of his troops. On the 15th, Shepherd relieved Colonel Victor Bleasdale (a decorated World War I Marine) and installed Guadalcanal veteran Colonel William Whaling as the commanding officer of the 29th Marines. After an enemy sniper killed Major Bernard Greene, commanding the 1/4 Marines, Colonel Alan Shapley assigned his own XO, Colonel Fred Beans (former Marine Raider), as his replacement.

The ferocious fighting continued with three Allied battalions attacking from the west and two from the east. They were protected against friendly fire by the steep pinnacle separating them. Logistics were essential in this fight. Every Marine (from private to general) who climbed that mountain to the front lines carried either a 5-gallon water can or a case of ammo. All hands coming down the mountain helped carry the stretchers of wounded Marines. On April 15, a company of the 2/4 Marines took sixty-five casualties—including three consecutive company commanders.

The next day Marines secured the ridge with the help of the battleship *Tennessee's* 14-inch guns and Marine Corsairs low-level pocket bombing.

Colonel Udo and his troops from the *Kunigami Detachment* died to the last man. On April 20, General Shepherd announced the Motobu Peninsula was secured. His Marines had earned a precious victory, but the cost did not come cheap. The 6th Marine Division suffered 757 wounded and 207 killed in the battle.

In his journal, an impressed General Oliver Smith wrote: "This northern campaign should dispel the belief held by some that Marines are beach-bound and not capable of rapid movement. Our Marines raced over rugged terrain and repaired roads and blown bridges while successfully opening new unloading points. They reached the island's northern tip —over fifty miles away from the landing beaches—in fourteen days. Followed by a seven-day campaign to secure the Motobu Peninsula."

The 77th Infantry Division landed on the island Ie Shima and seized its airfields during the battle for Motobu Peninsula. On April 16, Major Jones' recon Marines paved the way by taking a small islet 6,200 yards offshore called Minna Shima. Here, soldiers positioned a 105mm battery to support onshore operations. The 77th needed plenty of fire support to fight the 5,000 enemy defending the island. The Army soldiers over-whelmed them in six days of hard fighting at the cost of 1,100 casualties.

A popular war correspondent named Ernie Pyle, who'd landed with the Marines on L-Day, was shot in the head by a Japanese sniper. Marines and soldiers alike grieved over Pyle's death just as they'd done six days earlier with the news of FDR's passing.

TYPHOON OF STEEL

The 1st Marine Division fought a different campaign in April than their sister division to the north. They spent their days processing refugees and their nights on ambushes and patrols. Snipers and guerrillas exacted a steady but small toll.

The "Old Breed" Marines welcomed this style of low intensity. After many months in the tropics, they found Okinawa refreshing and rustic. Marines were concerned about the welfare of the thousands of Okinawan refugees streaming in from the heavy fighting.

According to Private First Class Eugene Sledge: "The most pitiful things about the Okinawan civilians were that they were totally bewildered by the shock of our invasion, and they were scared to death of us. Countless times they passed us on the way to the rear with sadness, fear, and confusion on their faces."

Sledge and his companions in the 5th Marines could tell by the sound of the intense artillery fire to the south that the XXIV Corps had smashed into General Ushijima's ring of outer defenses. Inside that first week, soldiers from the 7th and 96th Divisions figured out the riddle: Where the hell are the Japs? By the second week, General Buckner and General Hodge were aware of Ushijima's intentions and the depth and range of his defensive positions.

Along with minefields, caves, and reverse slope emplacements, the Shuri defensive complex contained the most large-caliber weapons the Allies had ever faced in the Pacific. These positions had mutually supporting fires from the adjacent hills and ridgelines—honeycombed with fighting holes and caves. Keeping a strict adherence to these intricate networks of mutually supporting positions required an iron discipline from enemy troops. The enemy's discipline prevailed. Allied forces found themselves entering into savage killing zones.

Japanese tactics along the front were to isolate and contain Allied penetration by grazing fire from supporting positions. Then, they'd overwhelm exposed troops with a storm of

The long battle for the southern highlands of Okinawa was now shifting into gear.

Throughout April and with unparalleled ferociousness, Japanese *kamikazes* punished Fifth Fleet ships supporting the operation. The aerial battles became so intense that the western beaches received a deadly, steady rain of shell fragments from thousands of antiaircraft guns in the fleet. There were no safe havens in this battle.

SITUATION AT SEA

The Japanese strategy to defend Okinawa was to make the most of the nation's shrinking resources and zealous patriotism.

General Ushijima planned to bloody the Allied forces in a lengthy battle of attrition, while the Japanese air forces would savage the Fifth Fleet—tethered to the island to support ground forces. Ushijima's strategy would combine passive ground defense with a violent air offensive. Suicidal *kamikaze* tactics were planned on an unprecedented scale.

By spring of 1945, the Allies understood the enemy's decision to sacrifice planes and pilots in reckless *kamikaze* attacks from their time in the Philippines. Individual suicide attacks by anti-shipping swimmers near Iwo Jima and the "human bullet" anti-tank demolitions on Peleliu were common. Japanese headquarters had escalated these tactics to an overwhelming level at Okinawa. They unleashed their newest weapon: *Operation Kikusui* (floating chrysanthemums) devastating mass suicide airstrikes against the fleet.

While small groups of *kamikazes* struck the fleet nightly and achieved some damage, the worst destruction came from concentrated *Kikusui* raids. The Japanese launched ten separate *Kikusui* attacks during the battle on Okinawa—each with over 350 aircraft. Japanese headquarters coordinated these raids and other tactical surprises, like the sacrificial sortie of the *Yamato* and other formidable counter-attacks. These tactics resulted in a shocking loss of life on both sides.

Kamikaze swarms harassed the Fifth Fleet from the time they entered Ryukyuan waters and throughout the battle. Some senior Navy commanders dismissed the threat—inexperienced pilots and rundown planes launched with insufficient fuel to reach Okinawa. While it was true that many of the 2,377 *kamikaze* pilots did not fulfill their mission, Special Attack

Unit pilots who got through the air and surface screens inflicted a wicked toll on the Fifth Fleet.

At the end of the campaign, the Fifth Fleet had endured thirty-four ships sunk, 360 damaged, and over 9,000 casualties: the worst losses ever sustained in a single battle in the history of the US Navy.

The situation at sea became so devastating that smoke from burning ships and offshore escorts blinded Kadena Airfield and caused four returning combat air patrol planes to crash. As the onslaught continued, Admiral Spruance said: "The suicide plane is an effective weapon which we must not underestimate." Spruance spoke from first-hand experience. *Kamikaze* attacks knocked out his first flagship, the heavy cruiser *Indianapolis*, early in the campaign. Then they damaged his replacement flagship—the battleship *New Mexico* two weeks later.

Enemy pilots attacking the fleet off Okinawa had a new weapon: the *Ohka* (Cherry Blossom) bomb. The Allies called this bomb "Baka" (the Japanese word for foolish). A manned rocket packed with 4,400 pounds of explosives launched at ships from the belly of a twin-engine bomber.

The Ohka bombs were the first antiship guided missiles. They shrieked toward their target at an unheard of speed of 500 knots. This new weapon blew the destroyer *Manert L. Abele* out of the water. But luckily for the Allies, most Ohka's missed their targets—the missiles were too fast for the inexperienced pilots to control in their last seconds of glory.

The ultimate suicide attack was the final sortie of the super battleship *Yamato*. One of the world's last great dreadnoughts. She had 18.1-inch guns that could outrange any US battleship. Imperial headquarters dispatched the *Yamato* on her last mission. A bizarre maneuver with no air cover and only a

DANIEL WRINN

handful of surface escorts—with enough fuel for a one-way trip.

Her mission was to distract American carriers while the Japanese launched a massive *Kikusui* attack against the rest of the fleet. Afterward, the *Yamato* would beach on the west coast of Okinawa and use her massive guns to shoot up the onshore landing force and the thin-skinned amphibious shipping. This daring plan proved to be a complete failure.

This colossal warship would've terrified the fleet protecting an amphibious beachhead in the early years of the war. But not now. US submarines gave Admiral Spruance early warning of the *Yamato's* departure from Japanese waters. Admiral Mark Mitscher asked Spruance: "Shall I take them or will you?" Mitscher commanded the fast carriers of Task Force 58. While Spruance knew his battleship force was eager to avenge their losses at Pearl Harbor—this was no time for nostalgia.

Spruance signaled: "You take them." And with that, Mitscher's Avengers and Hellcats roared into action. They intercepted the *Yamato* a hundred miles from the beach. They sunk her quickly with torpedoes and bombs. It cost the Allied forces eight planes and twelve pilots.

Another bizarre Japanese suicide mission was more effective. On the evening of May 25, seven enemy transport planes loaded with *Giretsu* (Japanese commandos) approached the Yontan Airfield. Vigilant antiaircraft guns flamed five planes, but the surviving plane made a wheels-up belly landing on the airstrip—discharging troops as she slid in sparks and flames along the long surface. Giretsu commandos destroyed eight planes and damaged twice as many more. They ignited 70,000 gallons of aviation fuel, creating chaos and confusion through the night. Jumpy security troops fired into the shadows and injured more of their own men than the Japanese. It took

290

twelve hours to hunt down and destroy the enemy commandos.

Admiral Spruance desperately tried to reduce the effectiveness of the *kamikaze* strikes. His fast-attack carriers hit enemy airfields in Formosa and Kyushu repeatedly, but the Japanese were experts at camouflage. Marine landing parties were sent to seize the outlying islands to establish fire direction and early warning outposts. Fighter aircraft from all three services took to the skies to intercept the massed waves of suicidal enemy planes.

Not all of these enemy airstrikes were *kamikazes*. Equal numbers of fighters and bombers attacked Allied targets while guiding in the suicide planes. The Japanese used several of their later model fighters like the Nakajima in death-defying air-to-air duels over hundreds of miles of blue ocean.

The far-reaching fast carriers usually made the first interceptions. While many pilots were from the Navy, the task force included two Marine fighter squadrons on the carriers *Bennington* and *Bunker Hill*. Marine pilot Lieutenant Ken Huntington flew the only Marine Corsair in the attack on the *Yamato*. Huntington swept through heavy antiaircraft fire to deliver a bomb on the battle ship's forward turret. Described by war correspondent Robert Sherrod: "one Marine, one bomb, and one Navy Cross."

Marine pilots from MAGs 31 and 33 flying out of Yontan Airfield provided most combat air patrol missions over the fleet. Under General Mulcahy's command, the combat air patrol missions surged from an initial twelve planes to as many as thirty-two, with another dozen on alert. These missions involved countless hours of patrolling in rough weather spiked by sudden violent encounters from enemy raiders. Marine planes ran a double risk. Battling with Japanese fighters often brought both planes within range of jittery shipboard antiaircraft gunners—who sometimes shot down both planes.

On April 16, Marine Corsairs raced to help the picket ship *Laffey* under attack from five *kamikaze* planes. Allied aircraft shot down seventeen enemy planes. Only one Corsair was lost in the fight while chasing an enemy *kamikaze* so low that they both clipped the ship's superstructure and crashed.

Major George Axtell and his "Death Rattlers" (VMF-323) intercepted a large flight of enemy raiders approaching the fleet at dusk. Three Marine pilots shot down sixteen enemy planes in twenty minutes. Major Axtell, the squadron commander, shot down five and became an instant ace. He later described these dog fights: "You'd be flying in and out of clouds and heavy rain. Friendly and enemy aircraft would wind up in a big melee. You'd just keep turning into any enemy aircraft that appeared. It was fast and furious, and the engagement would be over within thirty minutes."

Despite the brave efforts of pilots and ground crews, a few *kamikazes* always got through. Kerama Retto's protected anchorage resembled a floating graveyard of severely damaged ships. The small groups of suicide pilots who appeared every night in the fleet were especially vulnerable during the full moon. A naval officer described the nighttime raids as "witches on broomsticks." The main victims of these nocturnal attacks were the "small boys," amphibs and picket ships.

Nick Floros was a 19-year-old signalman who manned a 20mm gun on the tiny *LSM-120*. One moonless night a *kamikaze* appeared out of nowhere. She glided in, cut her engine off, looking like a giant bat. The Japanese plane smashed into the LCM with a horrific explosion before anyone could fire a shot. While the small LSM loaded with landing force supplies somehow survived the fiery blast, she was immediately towed to Kerama Retto's "demolition yard."

* * *

Japanese headquarters believed the exaggerated claims that the *Kikusui* attacks had crippled the US fleet. Wishful thinking. While the Fifth Fleet may have been battered and bruised by the *kamikaze* onslaught, they were too massive of a force to deter. The fleet endured the worst of these endless air attacks. They never wavered from their primary mission of supporting Okinawa's amphibious assault.

Naval gunfire support had never been so effective. Over 4,000 tons of munitions were delivered on L-Day. Frontline regiments received direct support from a "call-fire" ship and one illumination ship throughout the campaign. The quantity and quality of naval gunfire was summed up in this message from General Shepherd: "The effectiveness of our naval gunfire support was measured by the large number of Japanese encountered. Dead ones."

Even through the most intense *Kikusui* attacks in early April, the fleet still unloaded over half a million tons of supplies onto Hagushi's beaches to support the Tenth Army. They opened the port of Nago by clearing mines and obstacles under fire. The only direct consequence from the massed *kamikaze* attacks was the April 6 sinking of ammunition ships *Hobbs Victory* and *Logan Victory*. This caused a shortage of 155mm artillery and delayed General Buckner's first offensive against Shuri by three days. But the Fifth Fleet deserved its nickname "The fleet that came to stay."

But as April dragged into May, the Tenth Army was bogged down because of lackluster frontal assaults along the Shuri line. Admiral Spruance pressured General Buckner to speed up his attack to reduce the fleet's vulnerability. Nimitz was concerned and flew to Okinawa to "counsel" Buckner. Nimitz said: "we're losing a ship and a half each day we're out here. You gotta get this thing moving."

Senior Marine commanders urged Buckner to play the "amphib card" and execute a massive landing on the southeast coast to turn the enemy's right flank. Several Army generals agreed with this recommendation and mentioned that continuing to assault Shuri with frontal assaults was like putting forces through a meatgrinder.

General Vandegrift, Commandant of the Marine Corps, visited the island and seconded the recommendations given to Buckner. Vandegrift pointed out that Buckner still controlled the 2nd Marines. This veteran amphibious outfit had already demonstrated its capability against the Minatoga Beaches on L-Day. Buckner had sent the 2nd Marine Division to Saipan to reduce their vulnerability from *kamikaze* attacks. But the 2nd Division still had combat-loaded ships at hand and could have opened a second front in Okinawa within days.

General Buckner was a capable and popular commander, but his experience with amphibious warfare was limited. His staff warned of a potential logistical nightmare in opening a second front. His intelligence predicted stiff resistance around the Minatoga beachhead. Buckner knew the high cost of the bloody Anzio operation and the consequences of an amphibious landing far from the main effort. Buckner believed the defenses on Shuri would soon crack under a coordinated application of his massive infantry firepower. Buckner rejected the amphibious option. Admirals' Nimitz and Sherman agreed. But not Admirals Turner and Spruance or the Marines.

Spruance wrote in a private letter: "There are times when I was impatient for some of Holland Smith's drive." And

General Shepherd stated: "General Buckner did not cotton to amphibious operations."

Even Colonel Yahara of the *Thirty-second Army*, conceded later under interrogation that he'd been puzzled by the adherence to a wholly frontal assault from north to south: "The absence of a landing in the south puzzled the *Thirty-second Army*. Especially after the beginning of May, when it was impossible to put up anything more than a token resistance in the south."

But by then, the 2nd Marine Division was feeling like a yo-yo preparing for their assigned missions. Colonel Samuel Taxis had sharp words after the war about Buckner's decision. "I will always feel that the Tenth Army should've been prepared the instant they were found bogged down. They should've thrown a left hook down there in the southern beaches. They had one hell of a powerful reinforced division down there—trained to a gnat's whisker."

General Buckner stood by his decision. There was to be no "left hook." Instead, both the 1st and 6th Divisions joined in the Shuri offensive as infantry divisions under the Tenth Army, and the 2nd Division would remain in Saipan.

BLOWTORCH AND CORKSCREW

According to the Tenth Army's after-action report: "Japanese defensive efforts and continued development and improvement of cave warfare was the most outstanding feature of enemy tactics on Okinawa."

General Ushijima selected the best terrain to defend the Shuri highlands across the southern neck of the island. His troops dominated two of Okinawa's strategic features: the sheltered anchorage of Nakagusuku bay (later called Buckner Bay) to the east, and the port of Naha to the west. Because of this, Allied troops would have to force their way into the enemy's preregistered killing zones to secure their objectives.

Everything about the terrain favored the defenders. The elaborate topography of ridges, draws, and escarpments grouped the battlefield into sections of small unit firefights. The lack of dense vegetation gave the Japanese troops full, interlocking fire and observation from immediate strong points.

Like Iwo Jima, the enemy fought primarily from underground positions to counteract the Allied supremacy in supporting arms. The enemy modified thousands of concrete Okinawa tombs to use as combat outposts. While there were blind spots in the defenses, finding and exploiting them was costly in time and blood.

The most savage fighting of the campaign took place on a compressed battlefield. The distance from Yonabaru on the east coast to the Asa River bridge on the other side of the island was only 9,000 yards. General Buckner advanced abreast with two Army divisions. By May 8, he'd doubled his force by adding two Marine divisions from IIIAC and sent them west. His two XXIV Corps Army Divisions were sent east. Each of these divisions fought brutal, bloody battles against disciplined enemy soldiers defending entrenched and fortified terrain.

By rejecting the amphibious flanking plan in late April, Buckner had fresh divisions ready to deploy and join the general offensive against Shuri. The 77th relieved the 96th in the center, and the 1st Marine Division relieved the 27th Infantry in the west. Colonel Ken Chappell's 1st Marines entered the lines on April 30 and took heavy fire the moment they approached. When the 5th Marines arrived to supplement the relief, enemy gunners were pounding anything that moved.

PFC Eugene Sledge later wrote: "It was hell in there. We raced across an open field with Jap shells screaming and roaring around us with increasing frequency. The thunder and crash of explosions was a nightmare. I was terribly afraid."

General del Valle took command of the western zone on May 1 at 1400. He issued orders for a major assault the following morning. That evening, a staff officer brought a captured Japanese map annotated with all the American positions. Del Valle realized that the enemy already knew where the 1st Marine Division had entered the fight.

At dawn, Marines attacked into a jagged country (known as the Awacha Pocket). With all their combat expertise, Marines were no more immune to the relentless storm of shells and bullets than the soldiers they relieved. This frustrating day was a forewarning of future conditions. It rained hard as Marines secured the closest high ground. They came under such intense fire from nearby strongholds and other higher ground that they had to retreat. Dozens of Japanese infiltrators snuck up on the withdrawing Marines and engaged them in savage hand-to-hand combat. According to a Marine survivor: "That, was a bitch."

The 1st Division's veterans from Peleliu weren't strangers to cave warfare. No other division had as much practical experience. While nothing on Okinawa could match the Umurbrogol Pocket's steep cliffs, heavy vegetation, and array of fortified ridges, the "Old Breed" of the 1st Division faced a more numerous and smarter enemy. The 1st Division fought through four straight weeks of hell. The funnel created by the cliffs and draws reduced most of the Allied attacks to savage frontal assaults by fully exposed infantry/tank/engineer teams. General Buckner described this small unit fighting as: "a slugging match with temporary and limited opportunity to maneuver."

General Buckner captured the media's imagination with his "blowtorch and corkscrew" tactics needed for successful cave warfare. But to the Marine and Army veterans of Peleliu, Iwo Jima, and Biak, he was just stating the obvious— flamethrowers were the blowtorch and demolitions the corkscrew. But both weapons had to be delivered from close range by tanks and exposed infantry covering them.

On May 3, the rains finally let up, and the Marines resumed their assault. This time they took and held the first tier of vital terrain in the Awacha Pocket. But even after a methodical reduction of enemy strong points, it would take another full week of fierce fighting. Fire support proved to be an excellent asset. Now it was the Army's time to return the favor of inter-service artillery support. The 27th Division's Field Artillery Regiment stayed on the line with its forward observers and linemen familiar with the terrain.

Here, Japanese defensive discipline began to crack. General Ushijima encouraged discussion and debate from his staff regarding tactical courses of action. These heated discussions were generally between chief of staff, Lieutenant General Cho and conservative operations officer, Colonel Yahara. So far, Yahara's strategy of a "delay and bleed" holding action had prevailed. The *Thirty-second Army* had resisted the massive Allied invasion for over a month. With their Army still intact, they could continue to inflict heavy casualties on their enemies for months while massed *kamikaze* attacks wreaked havoc on the fleet.

But maintaining a sustained defense was not *Bushido* and against General Cho's code of honor and morals. He argued for a massive counterattack. Against Yahara's protests, Ushijima sided with General Cho. The great Japanese counterattack of May 4 was ill-advised and foolhardy. Manning the assault forces would forfeit Japanese coverage of the Minatoga sector and bring Ushijima's troops forward into unfamiliar territory. To deliver the mass of the fire necessary to cover the assault, Ushijima brought most of his mortars and artillery pieces into the open. He planned to use the *26th Shipping Engineer Regiment* and other elite forces in a frontal attack. At the same time, a waterborne double envelopment would alert the Allied forces to a massive counteroffensive. Yahara winced in despair.

General Cho's recklessness was now clear. Navy "Flycatcher" patrols on both coasts interdicted the first flanking attempts by Japanese raiders in slow-moving barges and canoes. On the west coast, near Kusan, the 1/1 Marines and the 3rd Armored Amphibian Battalion greeted the enemy trying to come ashore with deadly fire—killing 727. Farther down the coast, the 2/1 Marines intercepted and killed another 175, while the 1st Reconnaissance Company and the war dog platoon hunted down and destroyed the last sixty-four men hiding in the brush. The XXIV Corps took the brunt of the overland assault. They scattered the Japanese troops into small groups before ruthlessly shooting them down.

Instead of the 1st Marine Division being surrounded and annihilated per the Japanese plan—they launched their own counterattack and advanced several hundred yards. The *Thirty-second Army* took 6,000 front-line troop casualties and lost sixty pieces of artillery in this disastrous counterattack. A tearful Ushijima promised Yahara he would never again disregard his advice. Yahara was the only senior officer to survive the counterattack and described this debacle as: "the decisive action of the campaign."

General Buckner took the initiative and organized a four-division front. He tasked General Geiger to redeploy the 6th Division south from the Motobu Peninsula. General Shepherd asked Geiger to assign his Marines to the seaward flank, to continue receiving the benefit of direct naval gunfire support. Shepherd noted his division's favorable experience with fleet support throughout the northern campaign. There was also another benefit: General Shepherd would have only one nearby unit to coordinate maneuvers and fire with—the veteran 1st Marine Division.

At dawn on May 7, General Geiger reclaimed control of the 1st Marine Division and his Corps Artillery and set up his forward command post. The next day, the 22nd Marines came in to relieve the 7th Marines on the lines north of the Asa River. The 1st Division had suffered over 1,400 casualties in the last six days while trying to cover a vast front. The two Marine divisions advanced shoulder to shoulder in the west. They were greeted by heavy rains and ferocious fire as they entered the Shuri lines. The situation was dire along the front. On May 9, the 1/1 Marines assaulted Hill 60 in a spirited attack but lost their commander, Colonel James Murray, to a sniper. Later that night, the 1/5 Marines joined in savage hand-to-hand fighting against a force of sixty Japanese troops —appearing like phantoms out of the rocks.

The heavy rains delayed the 22nd Regiment's attempt to cross the Asa River. Engineers built a narrow footbridge under intermittent fire one night. Hundreds of infantry troops raced across before two enemy soldiers wearing satchel charges strapped to their chests darted into the stream and blew themselves and the bridge to pieces. Engineers spent the next night building a more stable "Baily Bridge." Allied troop reinforcements and vehicles poured across it, but the tanks had a hell of a time traversing the soft mud along the banks. Each attempt was a new adventure. But the Marines were now south of the river in force: encouraging progress on an otherwise stalemated front.

On May 10, the 5th Marines finally fought clear of the hellish Awacha Pocket, ending a week of frustration and point-blank casualties. Now it was the 7th Marines' turn to engage their own nightmarish terrain. South of their position was Dakeshi Ridge. Buckner urged his commanders to keep up the momentum and declared a general offensive along the entire front. This announcement was probably in response to the growing criticism Buckner had been receiving from the Navy and in the media for his attrition strategy.

But the rifleman's war had progressed past high-level persuasion. The assault troops knew full well what to expect—and had a good idea of what the price in blood would be.

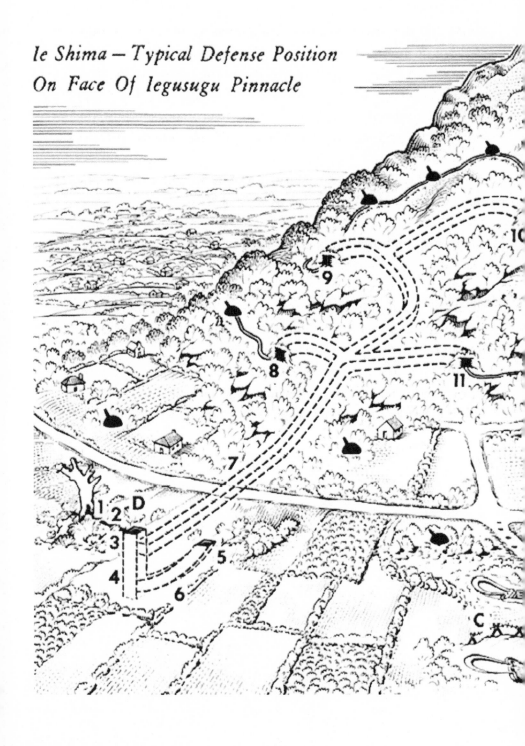

Ie Shima — Typical Defense Position On Face Of Iegusugu Pinnacle

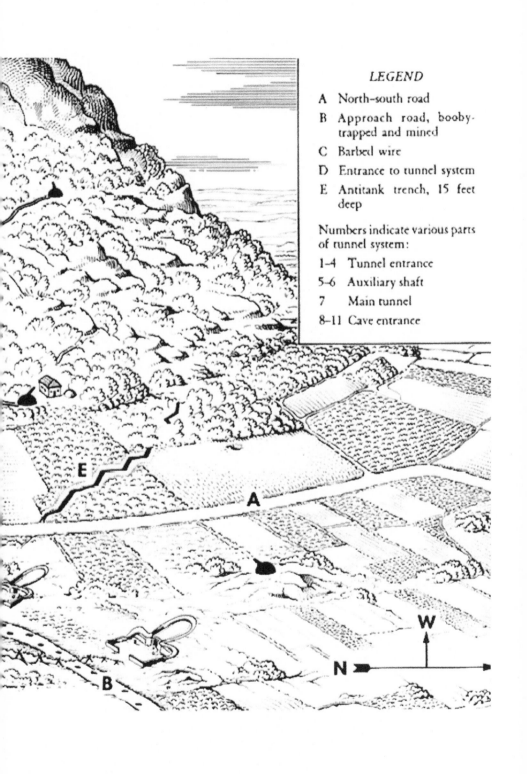

LEGEND

A North–south road
B Approach road, booby-trapped and mined
C Barbed wire
D Entrance to tunnel system
E Antitank trench, 15 feet deep

Numbers indicate various parts of tunnel system:

1–4 Tunnel entrance
5–6 Auxiliary shaft
7 Main tunnel
8–11 Cave entrance

SUGAR LOAF HILL

Colonel Edward Snedeker was a veteran commander with experience fighting on Bougainville and Guadalcanal. "I was fortunate on Okinawa," Snedeker said, "in that each of my battalion commanders had fought at Peleliu. Still, our regiment had its hands full on Dakeshi Ridge. It was our most difficult mission."

After a full day of ferocious fighting, Colonel John Gormley's 1/7 Marines fought their way to Dakeshi's crest but withdrew after enemy counterattacks swarmed them like a hive of angry hornets. The next day, the 2/7 Marines retook the crest and cut down the Japanese counterattacks pouring out from the reverse slope bunkers. Now the 7th Marines were on Dakeshi to stay—another major Allied breakthrough.

The Old Breed Marines briefly celebrated this achievement before the difficulties to come dawned on them. Advancing the next 1,200 yards would take eighteen days of brutal fighting. Their most formidable obstacle would be the steep and twisted Wana Draw rambling off to the south—a lethal killing ground surrounded by towering cliffs, pockmarked with caves and mines, and covered by interlocking fire at every approach. According to General Oliver Smith: "Wana Draw was the toughest assignment the 1st Division ever encountered on Okinawa." The remains of the Japanese *62nd Infantry Division* was prepared to defend Wana to the death.

Historians have paid little attention to the 1st Division's fight against the Wana Draw defenses. Mainly because the celebrated 6th Division's assault on Sugar Loaf Hill happened at the same time. But the Wana Draw battle was just as deadly of a man-killer as the Sugar Loaf Hill battle. Colonel Arthur Mason (now leading the 1st Marine Regiment) began the assault on the Wana complex on May 12. All three infantry regiments took turns assaulting this narrow gorge to the south. The division made full use of their medium Sherman tanks and attached Army flame tanks. Both were instrumental in their assault and fire support roles. On May 16, the 1st Tank Battalion fired over 5,000 rounds of 75mm and 175,000 rounds of 30-caliber along with 650 gallons of napalm.

Crossing the gorge was a heart-stopping race through a gauntlet of enemy fire—and progress came slowly. Typical of the fighting was the division's summary for its progress on the 18th: "Gains were measured by yards won, lost, and then won again." On May 20, Colonel Stephen Sabol's 3/1 Marines improvised a new method to dislodge enemy defenders from their reverse slope positions.

In five hours of grueling, muddy work, troops manhandled several drums of napalm up to the north side of the ridge. There, Marines split the barrels open and tumbled them into the gorge, setting them on fire by dropping white phosphorus grenades in their wake. These small successes were undercut by the Japanese ability to reinforce and resupply their positions during darkness—usually screened by small-unit counterattacks.

The close-quarters fighting was a vicious affair. General del Valle watched his casualties mount daily at an alarming rate. The 7th Marines lost 700 men taking Dakeshi and another 500 in the first five days of fighting for the Wana Draw. On May 16, Colonel E. Hunter Hurst's 3/7 Marines lost twelve officers among his rifle companies. The other regiments suffered just as terribly. From May 11-30, the division lost 200 Marines for every one hundred yards gained.

Heavy rains started again on May 22 and continued in a torrential downpour for ten days. The 1st Marine Division's sector had no roads. General del Valle committed his LVTs to deliver ammo and extract the wounded. Valle resorted to using replacements to hand-carry food and water to the front. This was not acceptable for General del Valle. He brought in torpedo bombers from Yontan Airfield and airdropped supplies by parachute. The low ceilings, heavy rain, and intense enemy fire made for hazardous duty. General del Valle did everything in his power to keep his troops supported, reinforced, supplied, and motivated—even through these grim and treacherous conditions.

To the west, the 6th Marine Division advanced south below the Asa River and collided into a trio of low hills in the open country leading to Shuri Ridge. The first of these hills was steep and unassuming (soon to be known as Sugar Loaf Hill). In the southeast was Half Moon Hill, and in the southwest was the village of Takamotoji and Horseshoe Hill. These three hills represented a singular defensive complex: the western anchor of the Shuri line.

An attack on any one of the mutually supporting defenses of these three hills would prove ineffective unless the others were simultaneously assaulted. Colonel Mita and his *15th Independent Mixed Regiment* would defend this sector to the last man. Its anti-tank guns and mortars were expertly placed to cause maximum damage to the enemy. The western slopes of Half Moon Hill had some of the most sophisticated machine-gun nests the Marines had encountered in the Pacific War. Sugar Loaf Hill had intricate, concrete-reinforced, reverse-slope positions. All approaches to this complex lay within a no-man's-land of heavy artillery from Shuri Ridge, dominating the battlefield.

Sugar Loaf Hill had an elevation of 245 feet, Half Moon at 220, and Horseshoe at 190. In comparative terms, Sugar Loaf though steep, only rose fifty feet above the northern approaches—it was no Mount Suribachi. The significance of Sugar Loaf was in the genius of the defensive fortifications and the unbridled ferocity with which the Japanese would counter-attack every US assault.

The Sugar Loaf complex was like a smaller version of Iwo Jima's Turkey Knob. As a tactical objective, Sugar Loaf lacked the physical dimensions to accommodate anything larger than a rifle company. But after eight days of fighting, that small ridge managed to chew up a handful of companies from two regiments.

Corporal James Day was a squad leader from Weapons Company 2/22. He "debatably" had the best seat in the house to watch the battle. Corporal Day's squad spent four days and three nights isolated in a shell hole in Sugar Loaf's western shoulder. On May 12, Day got orders to cross the Asa River and support Company G's attack against the small ridge. Corporal Day's squad arrived too late to do anything more than cover the fighting withdrawal of G Company. His company lost half their number in the all-day assault, including their gutsy commander, Captain Owen Stebbins (shot in both legs by a Japanese machine gunner). Corporal Day later wrote that Stebbins was: "a brave man whose tactical plan for assaulting Sugar Loaf became the pattern for all successive units to follow."

Concerned about unrestricted fire from the Half Moon Hill area, Major Henry Courtney, battalion XO, took Corporal Day and his squad with him. They moved out on the morning of May 13 on a dangerous trek to reach the 29th Marines and coordinate the upcoming assault. The 29th Marines were then committed to protecting the 2/22 Marines' left flank. Courtney tasked Corporal Day and his squad to support Company F in the following day's assault.

Day's rifle company comprised seven Marines. On the 14th, they joined Company F's assault on Sugar Loaf Hill and scampered up the left shoulder. Day got orders to backtrack his squad around the hill and take up defensive positions on the right western shoulder—this was not easy. By late afternoon Company F had been driven off their exposed left shoulder, leaving Corporal Day with just two of his squad mates in a large shell hole on the opposite shoulder.

That evening, Major Courtney led forty-five volunteers from George and Fox Companies up the left shoulder of Sugar Loaf. In a frantic battle of close-quarters fighting, the Japanese killed Major Courtney and half of his force. According to Corporal Day: "We didn't know who they were. Even though they were only fifty yards away, they were on the opposite side of the crest, we were out of visual contact. But we knew they were Marines, and we knew they were in trouble. We did our part by shooting and grenading every Jap we saw moving in their direction."

Then, Corporal Day heard the sounds of Courtney's force getting evacuated from the hill and knew they were alone on Sugar Loaf. Nineteen-year-old Corporal Day's biggest concern was letting the other Marines know where they were and replenishing their ammo and grenades. "Before dawn, I went back down the hill and there were a couple of LVTs trying to deliver critical supplies to the folks who made it through the earlier penetration. But both had been knocked out just north of the hill. I was able to raid those disabled vehicles several times for ammo, rations, and grenades. We were fine."

On May 15, Corporal Day and his men watched another Marine attack come from the northeast. This time Marines on the eastern crest of the hill were fully exposed to raking fire from the mortars on Half Moon and Horseshoe Hills. Corporal Day's Marines directed their rifle fire into a column of enemy troops running toward Sugar Loaf from Horseshoe: "we really needed a machine gun."

But good fortune provided them with a 30-caliber air-cooled M1919A4 left behind in the wake of the withdrawing Marines. Day's gunner put the weapon into action on the forward parapet of their hole. But an enemy 47mm crew opened up from Horseshoe Hill, killing the Marine gunner and destroying the gun. Now there were only two riflemen left on the ridgetop.

DAY AND BERTOLI

On May 15, tragedy struck the 1/22 Marines. A crushing Japanese bombardment caught the command group assembled at their observation post while they planned their next attack. Shellfire killed the CO, Major Tom Myers. Every other company commander was wounded, including the CO and XO of the supporting tank company. General Shepherd wrote: "it was the greatest single loss the division had sustained. Major Myers was an outstanding leader."

Major Earl Cook, the battalion XO, took command and continued to make assault preparations. Division staff released a warning: "The enemy is able to accurately locate our OPs and CPs because of the commanding ground he occupies. The dangerous practice of permitting unnecessary crowding exposure in these areas will have serious consequences."

That warning was worthless. Commanders had to observe the action to command. Exposure to interdictive fire was a risk you had to take as an infantry battalion commander. The following day, Colonel Jean Moreau, CO of the 1/29 Marines, suffered a serious wound when an enemy shell hit his observation post. His XO, Major Robert Neuffer, took over, and the battle raged on.

According to Corporal Day's last surviving squad mate, Private First Class Dale Bertoli: "The Japs were the only ones up there, and they gave us their full attention. While we had plenty of grenades and ammo, it was still pretty hairy."

Sugar Loaf Hill's south slope was the steepest. Japanese troops swarmed from their caves on the reverse slopes but had a tough climb to get at the Marines on the ridge. Day and Bertoli greeted enemy troops scrambling up the rocks with grenades. The Japanese troops who survived this mini-barrage were backlit by flares as they struggled over and back down the ridge. Day and Bertoli were back to back in the dark side of the crater—an excellent position to shoot down fleeing Japanese troops.

According to Corporal Day: "I believed that Sugar Loaf would fall on the 16th. We looked back and down and saw the battle shaping up. A great panorama." The two squad mates hunkered down while artillery, mortars, and tanks hammered the ridge. Day saw the fire coming from the enemy had not slackened: "Sugar Loaf's real danger wasn't the hill where we were, it was a 300-yard kill zone the Marines had to cross to approach the hill from the north. It was a grim sight. Men falling, tanks getting knocked out . . . division must've suffered over 600 casualties in that one day." Looking back, the 6th Marine Division considered May 16 to be the bloodiest day of the entire campaign.

The battered 22nd Marines were down to forty percent effectiveness. General Shepherd relieved them with the 29th and installed fresh regimental leadership, replacing the CO and XO with Colonels Harold Roberts and August Larson. When the weather cleared during the late afternoon on the 16th, Day and Bertoli could see well past Horseshoe Hill and all the way to the Asato River. Steady columns of Japanese reinforcements surged northward through Takamotoji village and toward the battlefield. Day and Bertoli kept firing at them from 600 yards away, keeping a small but persistent thorn in the enemy's defenses. Their rifle fire drew substantial attention from crawling squads of nighttime enemy raiders.

Corporal Day recalled: "They came at us from 2045 and on all night. All we could do was to keep tossing grenades and firing at them with our M-1s. Marines north of Sugar Loaf tried to help us with mortar fire, but it came a little too close, and both me and Bertoli were wounded by shrapnel and burned by white phosphorus."

At dawn on the 17th, a runner from the 29th Marines

scrambled up to their shell-pocked crater with orders to "get the hell out of there." A massive naval, air, and artillery bombardment was underway. Day and Bertoli did not hesitate. They were exhausted and partially deaf, but still had the energy to stumble back down the hill to safety. Day and Bertoli endured a series of debriefings from staff officers, while a roaring bombardment crashed down on the three hills.

May 17 was the fifth day of battle for Sugar Loaf Hill. It was 2/29 Easy Company's turn to attack the complex's defenses. While brave and persistent, Easy Company's several assaults fared little better than their predecessors. During one of these ferocious attacks, the 29th Marines reported to division: "E Company moved to the top of the ridge and had thirty men south of Sugar Loaf. [E Co.] sustained two close-in charges and killed a hell of a lot of Nips. Moving back to base to reform and at dusk, we are going again, We will take it."

But Sugar Loaf did not fall. At dusk, after overcoming another savage onslaught of bayonets, flashing knives, and hand-to-hand combat against a brutal counterattack, Easy Company withdrew—taking 160 casualties.

May 18 marked the beginning of incessant rain. In this soupy mess, Dog Company, 2/29 Marines, attacked Sugar Loaf Hill. They were supported by tanks that braved the minefields on both shoulders of Sugar Loaf to penetrate the no-man's-land just to the south. When the enemy swarmed out of their reverse-slope caves for another counterattack—tanks destroyed them. Dog Company earned the honor of becoming the first rifle company to hold Sugar Loaf overnight. Marines would not give up that bloody and costly ground.

The shot-up and exhausted 29th Marines still needed to take Half Moon and Horseshoe Hills. General Geiger adjusted the tactical boundaries westward and brought the 1st

Marine Division into the fight for Horseshoe Hill. Geiger also released the 4th Marines from Corps reserve.

General Shepherd deployed the fresh Marines into the battle on the 19th. The battle raged, and the 4th Marines took seventy casualties just relieving the 29th Marines. But with Sugar Loaf now in Allied hands, the battle's momentum shifted. On May 20, Colonel Reynolds Hayden's 1/4 Marines (with help from the 2/4 and 3/4) made notable gains on both flanks. By the end of the day, Marines had secured Half Moon Hill and a good portion of Horseshoe.

Enemy reinforcements funneled into the fight from the southwest. The Marines prepared for nighttime visitors at Horseshoe Hill. Japanese troops came in massive numbers: 700 sailors and soldiers smashing into Marine defenders throughout much of the night. Colonel Bruno Hochmuth's 3/4 Marines had six artillery battalions in direct support of the attack and fifteen battalions at the height of the fighting. Throughout the crisis on Horseshoe, Hochmuth kept in radio contact with Colonel Bruce Hemphill, who commanded the support artillery battalions.

This exchange between commanders reduced the number of short rounds and allowed Marines to provide accurate fire on the Japanese. This hellish rain of shells blew massive holes into the ranks of every Japanese advance: Marine riflemen met those who survived with their bayonets. The enemy counter attackers died to the man.

The victory at Sugar Loaf lacked a climactic finish. There was no celebration ceremony here. The sniper-infested ruins of Naha loomed ahead, with Shuri Ridge in the distance. The 1st Marine Division sidestepped the last of the Wana defenses to the east. The 6th Marine Division crept west while the 4th Marines crossed the chest-high Asa River on May 23. The III

Amphibious Corps stood primed on the outskirts of Okinawa's capital city.

* * *

The Army's XXIV Corps matched the Marines' break-throughs and success. On the east coast, the 96th Division secured Conical Hill (opposite Sugar Loaf on the Shuri anchor line) after weeks of fierce fighting. On May 22, the 7th secured Yonabaru.

Now, the Japanese Thirty-*second Army* faced a real risk of being cut off from both flanks. General Ushijima (this time) took Colonel Yahara's advice. Instead of fighting to the death at Shuri Castle, the remaining Japanese troops took advantage of the awful weather. They streamed southward to their last line of prepared defenses in the Kiyamu Peninsula. General Ushijima masterfully executed this maneuver. While Allied pilots spotted and interdicted the southbound columns, they reported other columns moving north. General Buckner believed the Japanese were rotating units in defense of Shuri. But these northbound troops were ragtag units tasked with a suicide rearguard action. At this, they succeeded.

On May 29, a South Carolina company commander raised the "Stars and Bars" Confederate flag over the abandoned Shuri Castle. According to General del Valle: "every damn OP that could see that flag started telephoning me and raising Cain. I had one hell of a hullabaloo on the telephone. I agreed to replace that rebel flag with the Stars and Stripes, but it took two days to get it through the Japs rear guards."

On May 31, Colonel Richard Ross, CO of the 3/1 Marines, raised the Stars and Stripes over Shuri Castle and then took cover. Unlike Sugar Loaf Hill, Shuri Castle could be seen from all over southern Okinawa. Every Japanese gunner within range opened up on the hated American colors. Even though the Stars & Stripes fluttered over Shuri Castle, and the formidable enemy defenses had been breached, the Japanese *Thirty-second Army* still remained as deadly a fighting force as ever. The enemy would sell their lives dearly for the final eight shell-pocked, rain-soaked miles of southern Okinawa.

SCREAMING MIMI

Withdrawing Japanese troops did not easily escape from their Shuri defenses. US Navy spotter planes found the southbound column and called in a devastating fire from every available attack craft and half a dozen ships.

Soon after, many miles of that muddy road were littered with wrecked field guns, trucks, and corpses. General del Valle congratulated the Tactical Air Force: "Thanks for the prompt response this afternoon when the Nips were caught on the road with their kimonos down."

Still, most of General Ushijima's *Thirty-second Army* survived and made it to their "Alamo" on the Kiyamu Peninsula. The Tenth Army missed an opportunity to end the battle a month early—stalled by heavy rains and deep mud—simply too encumbered to swiftly respond.

Allied infantry trudged south, cursing the weather but glad to be past the Shuri line. Every advance exacted a price in blood. A Japanese sniper killed Colonel Horatio Woodhouse, CO of the 2/22 Marines (and General Shepherd's cousin) as he led his battalion toward the Kokuba Estuary. Shepherd grieved privately at the loss of his young cousin and put the battalion XO, Colonel John G. Johnson, in command.

As troops of the III Amphibious Corps continued south, Marines came upon a series of east-west ridges that dominated open farmlands. Colonel Snedeker wrote: "The southern part of Okinawa consisted primarily of cross ridges that stuck out like the bones of a fish." In the meantime, divisions from the Army's XXIV Corps carefully approached the towering escarpments in their zone. The remaining Japanese troops had gone to ground again along the ridges and peaks—lying in wait to ambush the Allied advance.

Rain and mud plagued the advancing Allied forces. In Eugene Sledge's book, he described this battlefield as a "five-mile sea of mud." PFC Sledge wrote: "The mud in camp on

Pavuvu was a nuisance. But the mud on that Okinawan battle-field was misery beyond description."

The 96th Division reported the results of a full day's efforts under these conditions: "those on the reverse slope slid back and those on the forward slope down—otherwise no change."

Marines chafed at the heavy-handed controls of the Tenth Army, which seemed to stall at each encounter with a Japanese outpost. General Buckner preferred a massive application of firepower and destroying every obstacle before committing troops into the open. Colonel Shapley, CO of the 4th Marines, disagreed: "I'm not too sure that sometimes when they whittle you away, ten to twelve men a day, that maybe it would be better to take a hundred losses a day to get out sooner."

Colonel Wilburt "Bigfoot," Brown, CO of the 11th Marines (legendary veteran artilleryman) believed the Tenth Army relied too heavily on firepower. "We dumped a tremendous amount of metal into those Jap positions. Nothing could have lived through that churning mass of roaring and falling shells—but when we advanced, the Nips were still there—and mad as hell." Colonel Brown also had strong feelings about the overuse of star shells for night illumination: "It was like we were the children of Israel in the wilderness: living under a pillar of fire by night and a cloud of smoke by day."

This heavy reliance on artillery support stressed the amphibious supply system. The Tenth Army's demand for heavy ordinance grew to over 3,000 tons of ammunition per day. Each round had to be delivered to the beach and distributed along the front. This reduced the availability of other supplies, including rations. Frontline troops began to go hungry. Partial support came from the friendly skies when Marine torpedo-bombers air-dropped rations during the first three days of June.

Offshore, the fleet endured waves of *kamikaze* attacks. On

May 17, Admiral Turner announced an end to the amphibious assault phase and departed. General Buckner now reported to Admiral Spruance. Admiral Harry Hill assumed command of the enormous amphibious force still supporting the Tenth Army. On May 27, Admiral "Bull" Halsey relieved Spruance. And the Fifth Fleet officially became the Third Fleet: same crew, same ships, different designation. Turner and Spruance began plotting their next amphibious assault—Operation Downfall—the invasion of the Japanese home islands.

General Shepherd appreciated the vast amphibious resources available and decided to inject some tactical mobility into this sluggish campaign. For the 6th Division to secure the Naha Airfield, Shepherd had to first overcome the Oroku Peninsula. The hard way of achieving this would be to attack from the peninsula's base and scratch seaward. Or Shepherd could launch a shore-to-shore amphibious assault and surprise the enemy on their flank. "The Japanese expected us to cross the Kokuba," Shepherd said. "I wanted to surprise them."

Shepherd convinced General Geiger of the wisdom of this approach, but getting General Buckner's approval took much longer. Eventually, Buckner agreed but only gave the 6th Marine Division thirty-six hours to plan and execute this division-level amphibious assault.

Colonel Krulak relished this challenge. Scouts from Major "Cold Steel" Walker's 6th Recon Company crept across the statuary at night to gather intelligence on the enemy defenders and Nishikoku Beaches. Scouts confirmed a cobbled force of Japanese Navy units under an old adversary. The final opposed amphibious landing of the Pacific War would be launched against one of the last surviving SNLF (Special Naval Landing Force) commanders—Admiral Minoru Ota.

Admiral Ota was fifty-four years old and a graduate of the

Japanese Naval Academy. A veteran of the elite SNLF service from as early as 1932 in Shanghai. Ten years later, he commanded the *2nd Combined Special Landing Force* meant to assault Midway but was prevented by the catastrophic naval defeat suffered by the Japanese.

In November 1942, he commanded the *8th Combined Special Landing Force* in the Solomons, defending Bairoko against the 1st Marine Raiders. By 1945, the SNLF had mostly disappeared. Ota was in command of a motley outfit of several thousand coastal defense and antiaircraft gunners, aviation mechanics, and construction specialists. Ota still breathed fire into his forces. He equipped his ragtag troops with hundreds of machine cannons from wrecked aircraft and made them sow thousands of mines.

Shepherd knew he was in for a fight and that he faced a skilled opponent; he also realized that he had the advantage of surprise if his forces could act quickly. The final planning details centered on problems with the division's previously dependable LVTs. The hard-fighting onshore had taken a hefty toll on the tracks and suspension systems of these amphibious assault vehicles—and there were no repair parts available. Worse, the first typhoon of the season was approaching, and the Navy was getting jumpy. General Shepherd remained resolute in executing the assault on June 4, and Admiral Halsey backed him up.

Shepherd chose Colonel Shapley to lead the 4th Marines in the assault. Shapley divided the 650-yard Nishikoku Beach between the 1/4 Marines on the right and the 2/4 on the left. Despite the heavy rains, the assault jumped off on schedule. The Oroku Peninsula exploded in smoke and flame under the hammering of hundreds of naval guns, aerial bombs, and artillery batteries. Scouts secured Ono Yama island while the 4th Marines swept across the statuary. LCIs and LCMs loaded with tanks appeared from Loomis Harbor in the north.

The amphibious force achieved total surprise. Many of the busted-up LVTs broke down en route, causing delays, but enemy fire was negligible. Empty LVTs from the first waves quickly returned to rescue the stranded troops. The 4th Marines rapidly advanced with Colonel Whaling's 29th Marines close behind. By dusk, Marines occupied 1,200 yards on Oroku Peninsula. A furious Admiral Ota redeployed his sailors to the threat from the rear.

This amphibious assault had been near-perfect and a model for future study in amphib ops. The typhoon blew through while the Marines occupied the peninsula and captured the airfield in two days. On June 7, when the 1st Division reached the southwest coast north of Itoman, Admiral Ota's force had no chance of escape. General Shepherd ordered a threefold enveloping movement with his regiments—leading to the inevitable outcome.

The battle for the Oroku Peninsula was savage. Admiral Ota was no ordinary enemy commander. His 5,000 troops fought with a warrior's spirit and were heavily armed. No similar size Okinawan force had so many automatic weapons or so effectively placed mines. Marines encountered devastating enemy weapons at short range—rail-mounted 8-inch rockets, "the Screaming Mimi," and massive 320mm spigot mortars firing "Flying Ashcans."

On June 9, the 4th Marines reported: "Stubborn defense of high ground by MG and 20mm fire. Character of opposition unchanged. L Hill under attack from two sides. Another tank shot on right flank, thinking 8-inch gun."

Admiral Ota saw the end coming. On June 6, he reported to Tokyo: "The troops have fought valiantly in the finest tradition of the Japanese Navy. While fierce bombardments may have deformed the mountains of Okinawa, they cannot alter the loyal spirit of our men." Three days later, Ota sent his final message to General Ushijima: "Enemy tank groups now attack our cave headquarters. The naval force will have a glorious death." Ota committed ritual suicide—his duty now done.

General Shepherd had defeated a competent and worthy foe. In his Oroku operation after-action report he said: "In ten days of fighting we killed 5,000 Japanese and took 200 prisoners. Mines disabled thirty of our tanks. One tank was destroyed by two direct hits from an 8-inch naval gun at point-blank range. 1,608 Marines were wounded or killed."

WRAPPING UP THE FIGHT

When the 1st Marine Division reached the coast near Itoman, it was the first time the division had access to the sea in over a month. This relieved the veteran division's extended supply lines. Colonel Snedeker, CO of the 7th Marines, wrote: "As we reached the shore we were helped a great deal by amphibian tractors that had come down the coast with supplies. Otherwise, there was no way in hell we could get supplies overland."

The wide-open southern country allowed General del Valle to further refine the deployment of his infantry-tank teams. No unit in the Tenth Army surpassed the 1st Marine Division's synchronization of these two supporting arms. Using those painfully learned tactical lessons from Peleliu, the 1st Division never allowed their tanks to range beyond the support of accompanying artillery and infantry. This resulted in the 1st Tank Battalion being the only armored unit in the battle not to lose a tank to Japanese suicide squads—even during the swirling close-quarter combat at Wana Draw.

General del Valle appreciated his attached Army 4.2

mortar battery: "My tanks had such good luck because the 4.2s were vital in Okinawa. We developed the tank infantry training to a fare-thee-well in those swales—backed up by the 4.2-inch mortars."

According to Colonel "Bigfoot" Brown of the 11th Marines: "Working with Lieutenant Colonel 'Jeb' Stuart and the 1st Tank Battalion, we developed a new method of protecting tanks and reducing infantry vulnerability during the assault. We'd put an artillery observer in one of those tanks with a radio to one of the 155mm howitzer battalions. We used both packs of the 75mm, and LVT-As with the airburst capabilities. If any Jap [suicider] showed his face anywhere, we opened fire with an airburst and kept a pattern of pattering shell fragments around the tanks."

On June 10, Colonel Jim Magee's 2/1 Marines used similar tactics in a bloody all-day assault on Hill 69—west of Ozato. Magee's Marines lost three tanks to enemy artillery in the approach. But they still took the hill and held it through a savage enemy counterattack that night.

Kunishi Ridge loomed beyond Hill 69. A steep coral escarpment dominated the surrounding grasslands and rice patties. Kunishi was longer and higher than Sugar Loaf, but equally honeycombed with enemy caves and tunnels. While it lacked cover with Half-Moon and Horseshoe on its rear flanks, it was still protected from behind by Masato Ridge—500 yards south. Fragments of the veteran *32nd Infantry Regiment* defended the many hidden bunkers. This was the last of General Ushijima's organized frontline troops. Kunishi Ridge would be as deadly a killing ground as the Marines would ever face in the Pacific War.

On June 11, enemy gunners repelled the first tank-infantry assaults by the 7th Marines. Colonel Snedeker had a different plan: "I realized, due to the losses of experienced leadership, we'd never be able to take Kunishi Ridge in the daytime. I thought a night attack could be successful."

Snedeker flew over his objective and devised his plan. Tenth Army night assaults were rare in this campaign—especially Snedeker's ambitious plan of deploying two battalions. But General del Valle approved his plan, and at 0330 the next morning, the 1/7 and 2/7 departed the combat outpost for the dark ridge. By 0500, lead companies of both battalions swarmed over the crest and surprised several enemy groups calmly cooking breakfast. Then, a brutal battle to expand the toehold on the ridge exploded into action.

As dawn broke, enemy gunners targeted relief infantry columns as Marines clung to the crest and endured showers of shrapnel from grenades and mortar rounds. According to General del Valle: "This situation was one of the tactical oddities in this type of peculiar warfare. We were *on* the ridge, and the Japs were *in* the ridge, on both the forward and reverse slopes."

Marines on Kunishi desperately needed supplies and reinforcements. The growing number of wounded needed evacuation. Only the medium Shermans had the bulk and the ability to provide relief. Over the next several days, the 1st Tank Battalion (even losing twenty-two Shermans to enemy fire) made remarkable achievements. They removed two crewmen to make room for six replacement riflemen inside each tank. Once on top of the hill they exchanged replacements for wounded, but no one could stand without getting shot. So, all the exchanges had to take place through the escape hatch in the bottom of the tanks.

This became a familiar sight on Kunishi Ridge: a buttoned-up tank lurching up to besieged Marine positions while replacements slithered out via the escape hatch carrying ammo, rations, water, and plasma. Then, other Marines crawled under the Shermans, dragging their wounded on ponchos—manhandling them through the small escape hatch. For those severely wounded, they had the unsavory privilege of riding down to safety lashed topside behind the turret. Tank drivers provided maximum protection to their exposed stretcher cases by backing down the entire 850-yard gauntlet. In this meticulous way, tankers delivered fifty fresh troops and evacuated thirty-five wounded men the day after the 7th Marines' night assault.

General del Valle was pleased with these results and ordered Colonel Mason to execute a similar night assault in the 1st Marine sector of Kunishi Ridge. This mission went to the 2/1 Marines, who accomplished it on the night of June 13 despite careless lapses of illumination fire by forgetful supporting arms.

Furious Japanese swarmed out of their bunkers in a massive counterattack. Losses mounted quickly in Colonel Magee's ranks. One company lost six of seven officers that morning, before the 1st Tank Battalion came to the rescue delivering reinforcements and evacuating 110 wounded Marines by nightfall.

General del Valle wrote: "The Japs were so damn surprised. They used to counterattack us at night all the time. I bet they never felt we'd have the audacity to go out and do it to them."

During Colonel Yahara's interrogation, he admitted the Marine night attacks effectively caught his troops off-guard—psychologically and physically.

By June 15, the 1st Marines had been fighting for twelve straight days: sustaining 500 casualties. The 5th Marines replaced them with an elaborate nighttime relief on June 15.

The 1st Marines, back in the safety of division reserve, received their newest orders: *If not otherwise occupied, you will bury Japs in your area.*

The battle for Kunishi Ridge raged. PFC Sledge approached the embattled escarpment with dread. He later wrote: "That crest looked so much like Bloody Nose that my knees nearly buckled. I felt like I was back on Peleliu and had to go through that hell all over again." The fighting along that crest and its slopes took place at point-blank range—even for Sledge's 60mm mortars. His crew then became stretcher-bearers in this highly hazardous duty. Half of his company was wounded within the next twenty-two hours.

Getting wounded Marines off Kunishi Ridge was no easy task. The seriously wounded needed to endure another half day of evacuation by field ambulance over bad roads and enemy fire. Then, pilots stepped in with a great idea. Engineers cleared a rough landing strip suitable for "Grasshopper" observation aircraft. Corpsmen hustled to deliver casualties from Kunishi and Hill 69 to the crude airfield. They were gently loaded into waiting "Piper Cubs" and flown back to the field hospitals in the rear—an eight-minute flight. This was the dawn of tactical medevacs, which saved so many lives in the subsequent Asian wars. Marine pilots flew out 640 casualties in eleven days: saving countless lives.

The 6th Marine Division joined the southern battlefield after securing the Oroku Peninsula. The *32nd Infantry Regiment* died a hard death after the combined forces of III Amphibious Corps swept north and overlapped Mezado Ridge and could smell the sea along the south coast. In Ira Saki, Marines from Company G (2/22) raised the 6th Division's colors on the island's southernmost point.

The long-neglected 2nd Marine Division finally got into the fight in the closing week of the campaign. Colonel Clarence Wallace and his 8th Marines arrived from Saipan to capture the two outlying islands—Aguni Shima and Iheya Shima—this would give the fleet more early warning radar sites against *kamikaze* raids. Colonel Wallace commanded a considerable force (essentially a brigade), including the 2/10 Marines and the 2nd Amphibian Tractor Battalion. General Geiger assigned the 8th Marines to the 1st Division, and on June 18, they relieved the 7th Marines and swept southeast with ferocity.

PFC Sledge recalled the arrival of the 8th Marines: "We scrutinized these Marines with the hard professional stare of old salts sizing up another outfit. Everything we saw brought forth remarks of approval."

General Buckner was interested in observing the 8th Marines' first combat deployment. Earlier, he'd been impressed with Colonel Wallace's outfit during an inspection visit to Saipan. Buckner went to a forward observation post on June 18 to watch the 8th Marines advance along the valley floor. Enemy gunners on the opposite ridge saw the official party and opened up. A shell struck a close coral outcrop and drove a lethal splinter into the general's chest. Buckner died in ten minutes. One of the few senior American officers killed in action in World War II.

General Geiger assumed command. His third star became effective immediately. The Tenth Army was in capable hands. Geiger became the only Marine—and the only pilot of any service—to command a field army. The Okinawan soldiers had no qualms about this. Senior Army echelons elsewhere did. Army General Joseph Stillwell received urgent orders to Okinawa. Five days later, he relieved Geiger. But by then, the battle was over.

When news of General Buckner's death reached the *Thirty-second Army* headquarters in its cliff-side cave near Mabuni—the enemy officers cheered—but General Ushijima remained silent. He respected Buckner's military ancestry and appreciated that they'd both once commanded their respective service academies: Buckner at West Point and Ushijima at Zama.

Ushijima knew his end was approaching fast. The 7th and 96th Divisions were nearly on top of Japanese command. On June 21, General Ushijima ordered his men to "save themselves so they could tell the story to Army headquarters." Then he committed *Seppuku*. Ushijima plunged his *Tantō* (short knife) into his belly, drawing the blade from left to right before Colonel Yahara shot him in the back of the head—Ushijima collapsed into a pool of his own blood.

General Geiger declared the end of organized resistance on Okinawa the same day. True to form, a final *kamikaze* attack struck the fleet that night, and sharp fighting broke out on the 22nd. Undeterred, General Geiger ordered the 2nd Marine Aircraft Wing in action and ran up the American flag at Tenth Army headquarters.

The long battle was finally over.

GENERAL ROY GEIGER

Marine commanders on Okinawa were well-versed and seasoned combat veterans of joint service operations. These qualities contributed to the ultimate victory of the US Tenth Army.

General Roy Geiger was a 60-year-old native of Middleburg, Florida. He graduated from Florida State and Stetson University law schools before commanding III Amphibious Corps. He enlisted in the Marines in 1907 and became a naval aviator (the fifth Marine ever) in 1917.

Geiger flew combat missions in World War I France and commanded a squadron of the Northern Bombing Group. In 1942 on Guadalcanal, he commanded the 1st Marine Aircraft Wing. The following year, he took command of the 1st Marine Amphibious Corps on Bougainville for the invasion of Guam and the Palaus.

Geiger knew combat. Even on Okinawa, he made frequent visits to the front lines of combat outposts. On two separate occasions, he "appropriated" an observation plane to fly over the battlefield for his own personal reconnaissance.

After the death of General Buckner, Geiger took command of the Tenth Army and was immediately promoted to lieutenant general. Geiger also relieved General Holland Smith as commanding general of the Fleet Marine Force Pacific. Geiger was one of the few Marines invited to attend the Tokyo Bay Japanese surrender ceremony on the USS *Missouri*, September 2, 1945.

Geiger was an observer at the 1946 atomic bomb tests at Bikini Lagoon. His solemn evaluation of the vulnerability of future surface ship-to-shore assaults of atomic munitions spurred the Marine Corps to develop the transport helicopter. General Geiger died from lung cancer in 1947.

GENERAL PEDRO DEL VALLE

General Pedro del Valle commanded the 1st Marine Division. He was a 51-year-old native of San Juan, Puerto Rico. In 1915 he graduated from the Naval Academy. He commanded a Marine detachment on board the battleship *Texas* in the North Atlantic during World War I.

Years of expeditionary campaigns and sea duty in the Caribbean and Central America gave del Valle a vision of how Marines could better serve the Navy and their country at war. In 1931, General Randolph Berkeley appointed del Valle (then a major) to the "Landing Operations Board" in Quantico. This was the first organizational step taken by the Marine Corps to develop a working doctrine for amphibious assaults.

In February 1932, he published a provocative essay about ship to shore amphibious operations in the *Marine Corps Gazette*. He challenged his fellow officers to think seriously of executing an opposed landing.

A decade later, del Valle (now a veteran artilleryman) commanded the 11th Marines with distinction during the

Guadalcanal campaign. Many surviving Japanese admired the superb artillery of the Marines. Following that, del Valle commanded corps artillery for III Amphibious Corps long before assuming command of the "Old Breed" on Okinawa. General del Valle died in 1978 at the age of 84.

GENERAL LEMUEL SHEPHERD JR.

General Lemuel Shepherd Jr. was a 49-year-old native of Norfolk, Virginia. He graduated from the Virginia Military Institute in 1917 and served with distinction with the 5th Marines in France. He was wounded three times and received the Navy Cross. Shepherd became one of those rare infantry officers who'd commanded every possible echelon from division all the way down to rifle platoon. Early in the Pacific, he commanded the 9th Marines and served as assistant commander of the 1st Marine Division at Cape Gloucester before taking command of the 1st Provisional Marine Brigade on Guam.

In September 1944, Shepherd became the first commanding general of the newly formed 6th Marine Division and served with honor on Okinawa. After the war, he commanded the Fleet Marine Force Pacific for the first two years of the Korean War. In 1952, he became the 20th Commandant of the Marine Corps. General Shepherd died at age 94 from bone cancer in La Jolla, California.

GENERAL FRANCIS MULCAHY

General Francis Mulcahy commanded the Tenth Army Tactical Air Force. He was a 51-year-old native of Rochester, New York, and graduated from Notre Dame before his commission in 1917. He attended naval flight school the same year, and like Roy Geiger, Mulcahy flew bombing missions in World War I France. He pioneered the Marine Corps' close air support and ground operations in the interwar years of expeditionary campaigns in Central America and the Caribbean.

After the attack on Pearl Harbor, Mulcahy served as an observer with the British Western Desert Air Force in North Africa. When he deployed to the Pacific, he took command of the 2nd Marine Aircraft Wing. In the final months of the Guadalcanal campaign, Mulcahy served with distinction in command of all Allied Air Forces in the Solomons. Mulcahy worked meticulously at the airfields on Yontan and Kadena to coordinate combat deployments against the *kamikaze* threats to the fleet.

General Mulcahy received three Distinguished Service

Medals for his heroic accomplishments in France, the Solomons, and Okinawa before his death in 1973.

BLOOD AND IRON

Army infantry and Marines faced fierce opposition from over 100,000 enemy troops under the command of General Ushijima. Allied intelligence originally estimated Ushijima's *Thirty-second Army* strength at 65,000. But many other reinforcing organizations traveled to Okinawa from previous posts on Manchuria, China, and Japan.

The *9th Infantry Division* was the first to arrive. They were an elite veteran unit—the backbone of Ushijima's defense forces. Following them was the *44th Independent Mixed Brigade* (which lost part of their strength when one of their ships was torpedoed). The *15th Independent Mixed Regiment* was flown to Okinawa and added to the remains of the *44th*. The next large unit was the *24th Infantry Division*, coming from Manchuria. They were well-trained and equipped, but had not yet been bloodied in battle. The final major infantry unit to arrive was General Fujioka's *62nd Infantry Division* comprising two brigades of four independent infantry battalions.

Imperial Japanese headquarters saw the battle of Okinawa as a fixed defensive fight. Other than the *27th Tank Regiment,* Ushijima was not given any strong armored force. Japanese headquarters diverted large weapon shipments and troops to Okinawa because of the hopeless situation in the Philippines and their inability to deliver reinforcements and supplies. The *Thirty-second Army* possessed a heavier concentration of artillery under a single command than had been available to other Japanese commanders anywhere else in the Pacific War.

Total Japanese artillery strength was grouped into the *5th Artillery Command*. General Wada's command comprised two independent artillery regiments and artillery elements of the *44th Brigade* and the *27th Tank Regiment*. He also had thirty-six howitzers and eight 150mm guns with the *1st* and *2nd Medium Artillery Regiment*.

Wada also had the *1st Independent Heavy Mortar Regiment* firing the 320mm spigot mortars first encountered by Marines on Iwo Jima. Their ninety-six 81mm mortars were assigned for close infantry support and controlled by sector defense commanders.

Potential infantry replacements varied from excellent with the *26th Shipping Engineer Regiment* to meager at best with the various rear area service units. The *10th Air Sector Command* provided 7,000 replacements composed of airfield mainte- nance and construction units at the Kadena and Yontan Airfields. Seven sea-raiding squadrons based at Kerama Retto had one-hundred handpicked men whose only assignment was to smash explosive-loaded suicide craft into the sides of cargo vessels and assault transports.

A native Okinawan home guard (called *Boeitai)* rounded out the *Thirty-second Army*. These men were trained and inte- grated into Army units. The *Boeitai* gave Ushijima another 20,000 extra men to use as he pleased. Add to this 1,700 Okinawan children (thirteen years old and up) organized into volunteer youth groups called "Blood and Iron" for the Emperor's duty units.

US ARMY TROOPS

The US Army played a significant role in the victory on Okinawa. The Army deployed as many combat troops, suffered comparable casualties, and fought with an equal heroism and bravery as the Marines.

Army battles for Conical Hill, Kakazu Ridge, and the escarpment at Yuza Dake were just as bloody and memorable as Nishi Ridge and Sugar Loaf for the Marines. The Okinawa campaign still serves today as a model of joint service cooperation despite its isolated cases of sibling rivalry.

In mid-1943, the Joint Chiefs identified three divisions in the Pacific with amphibious "proficiency." The 1st and 2nd Marine Divisions were veterans of Tulagi and Guadalcanal, while the 7th Infantry was fresh from fighting in the Aleutians. These three units joined with four other divisions and constituted the Tenth Army bound for Okinawa. The number of divisions with experience in amphibious operations in the Pacific had now expanded sevenfold.

Three assault units in General John Hodge's XXIV Corps had recent experience with amphibious landings in the Battle for Leyte Gulf. It was the 96th Division's first campaign and the third amphibious operation for the 7th Division after Kwajalein and Attu. The veteran 77th Division executed a daring landing at Ormoc, which surprised and slaughtered the enemy defenders.

The 27th was a National Guard unit still bitterly regarded by Marines after their flail on Saipan, but still a proud unit with amphibious experience in the Marianas and Gilbert Islands. No other army divisions had the luxury of extended preparations for Okinawa. General MacArthur didn't release the underfed and under-strength XXIV Corps (after 112 days of combat on Leyte) to the Tenth Army until seven weeks before L-Day on Okinawa. The 27th Division had more time but endured inadequate training in the jungles of Espiritu Santo.

There were many examples of Marines and Army units

cooperating in the Okinawan campaign. Army Air Force P-47 Thunderbolts flew long-range bombing and fighter missions for General Mulcahy's Tactical Air Force. Army and Marine Corps units supported opposite services regularly during the long drive to the Shuri line. Marines gained a healthy respect for the Army's 8-inch howitzers. These heavy weapons were often the only way to breach a well-fortified enemy strong point.

General Buckner attached deadly "Zippo tanks" from the 713th Armored Flame Thrower Battalion along with 4.2-inch mortar batteries to both Marine divisions. The 6th Marine Division also had the 708th Amphibian Tank Battalion attached for the entire battle. Each of these units received a Presidential Unit Citation for service with their parent Marine units.

The Army often gave logistical support to the Marines as the campaign slogged south during the endless rains. The Marines' fourth revision of their table of organization still did not provide enough transfer assets to support such a lengthy campaign conducted far from the forces' beachhead. A shortage of amphibious cargo ships assigned to the Marines also reduced the number of LVTs and wheeled logistics vehicles available. Often, the generosity of the supporting Army units determined if the Marines would eat that day.

An example of this cooperative spirit happened on June 4, when soldiers from the 96th Division gave rations to Colonel Richard Ross's starving and exhausted Marines. This brightened the battalion on a day otherwise known as "the most miserable day spent on Okinawa."

In short, Okinawa was too difficult and too large for one service to undertake. In this eighty-two-day campaign against a well-armed, resolute enemy, victory required teamwork and cooperation from several services.

MARINES AVIATION UNITS

According to Colonel Vernon McGee, landing force air support commander during the battle: "Okinawa was the culmination of the development of air support doctrine in the Pacific. The procedures we used there were results of all lessons learned in preceding campaigns—including the Philippines."

Marine aviation units on Okinawa operated across a range of missions: from bombing enemy battleships to supply drops.

Over 700 Marine planes took part in the Okinawa campaign. An estimated 450 of these were engaged in combat for half the battle. Most Marine air units served under the Tenth Army's TAF (Tactical Air Force) commanded by General Mulcahy. Outside of the TAF, Marine fighter squadrons were assigned to fleet carriers or escort carriers and long-range transports.

Admiral Spruance commanded all Allied forces for Operation Iceberg. He believed the enemy's air arm was the biggest threat to the mission's success. Spruance made the Tenth Army's first objective to secure the Kadena and Yontan Airfields and support land-based fighter squadrons.

Assault forces achieve this on L-Day. The next day, General Mulcahy moved his command post ashore and began TAF operations. His top priority was to maintain air superiority over Okinawa and the Fifth Fleet. Because of the massed *kamikaze* attacks unleashed by the Japanese, this mission kept Mulcahy preoccupied for many weeks.

Army and Marine aviation units composed Mulcahy's Tactical Air Force. His force had fifteen Marine fighter squadrons, ten Army fighter squadrons, two Marine torpedo bomber squadrons, and sixteen Army bomber squadrons. Marine fighter pilots flew F4U Corsairs and radar-equipped, night-fighting F6F Hellcats. Army pilots flew P-47 Thunderbolts, and their night fighters were P-61 Black Widows.

Allied pilots fought air-to-air duels against *kamikazes* and plenty of other late-model "Franks" and "Jacks." Altogether, the Tactical Air Force pilots shot down 627 planes. Colonel Ward Dickey's Marine Aircraft Group (MAG-33) set the record with 215 kills—more than half claimed by the "Death Rattlers"—Major George Axtell's squadron VMF-323.

The need to protect the Fleet caused some ground

commanders to worry that their own close-in air support would be "short-sheeted." But escort carrier Naval squadrons picked up the slack. They flew over sixty percent of the close-in support missions between April 1 and the end of June. The combined TAF and carrier pilots flew over 14,000 air support sorties. Over 5,000 of these supported Marines on the ground. Pilots dropped over 150,000 gallons of napalm on enemy positions.

Air Liaison Parties accompanied the frontline divisions and directed aircraft to the target. Coordinating these lower echelon requests became the responsibility of three Marine Landing Force Air Support Control Units. One represented the Tenth Army to the fleet while the others were responsive to IIIAC and the XXIV Corps. This technique refined experiments McGee had started on Iwo Jima. In most cases, close air support for the infantry was extremely effective. Several units reported safe and prompt delivery of ordnance on target within 150 yards. But there were also accidents and delays (less than a dozen) and situations where lines were simply too intermingled for any air support.

Other Marine aviation units helped in the victory on Okinawa. Marine torpedo bomber pilots flew their Avenger "torpeckers" in zero-zero weather. They dropped over 40,000 pounds of medical supplies, rations, and ammunition to forward-deployed ground units. The fragile and small Grasshoppers of the Marine Observation Squadrons flew 3,487 missions of artillery spotting, medical evacuations, and photo-reconnaissance. One artillery officer described the Grasshopper pilots as: "the unsung heroes of Marine aviation. They'd often fly past cave openings and look in to see if the Japs were hiding a gun in there."

Marine pilots served on Okinawa with panache. During a

desperate dogfight, one pilot radioed: "Come on up here and help me. I got two Franks, and a Zeke cornered." Those were his last words, but his fighting spirit persisted. According to a destroyer skipper who'd just been rescued from swarms of *kamikazes* by Marine Corsairs: "I'd take my ship to the shores of Japan if I could have those Marines with me."

ARTILLERY ON OKINAWA

Because of the tactics selected and the nature of enemy defenses, Okinawa was the most significant battle in the war for artillery units. General Geiger landed with fourteen firing battalions with the IIIAC. And when the 2/10 Marines came ashore to support the 8th Marines—the total rose to fifteen firing battalions.

General David Nimmer commanded the III Corps

Artillery with three batteries of 155mm howitzers and three 155mm "Long Tom" guns. The Marines had considerably enhanced their firepower since the initial Pacific campaigns.

While one 75mm howitzer battalion still remained, the 105mm howitzer had become the norm for division artillery. Infantry units on the front line were supported by the 75mm fire of medium tanks and LVT-As. New self-propelled "siege guns" with 4.5-inch multiple rocket launchers fired by the "Buck Rogers" men and attached Army 4.2 mortar platoons caused chaos on Japanese positions.

Colonel Fred Henderson described this devastating array of fire support: "Not many people realize that the Tenth Army's artillery, plus the LVT-As and naval gunfire gave us a guns/mile of front ratio on Okinawa that was higher than any US effort in all of World War II."

General Buckner tasked his commanders to integrate field artillery support early in the campaign. General Geiger sent his corps artillery and 11th Marines (not fully committed in the opening weeks) to help the XXIV Army Corps in their early assaults against the outer Shuri defenses. From April 7 to May 6, these artillery units fired over 55,000 rounds in support of the XXIV Corps. But this was only the beginning. Once both IIIAC Marine divisions entered the lines, they benefited from Army artillery support and organic fire support—two Marine and two Army.

By the end, the Tenth Army artillery rockets had fired over two million rounds downrange. In addition, 707,000 mortars, rockets, and five-inch or larger shells were fired from naval gunfire ships offshore. Half of the artillery rounds were from 105mm howitzer shells and the M-7 self-propelled guns. Compared to these bigger guns, the older 75mm pack howitzers were the battlefield's "Tiny Tims." Their versatility and mobility proved valuable through the long haul.

According to Colonel Brown, who commanded the LVT-As firing similar ammunition: "The 75mm was plentiful and contrasted with the heavy calibers, so we used it for fire interdiction and harassing missions across the front."

Generals del Valle and Geiger expressed interest in the army's larger weapons. Geiger respected the Army's 8-inch howitzer 200-pound shell. It had much more penetrating and destroying power than the 155mm gun's ninety-five-pound shell—largest in the Marine's inventory. Geiger urged Marine Corps Headquarters to form 8-inch howitzer battalions for the next attack on Japan. Geiger also praised the accuracy, range, and power of the Army's 4.2-inch mortars, and recommended their inclusion in the Marine division.

On several occasions, artillery commanders were tempted to orchestrate all this killing power into one mighty concentrated attack. Time on target (TOT) missions frequently occurred in the early weeks, but their high consumption rates were a drawback. Late in the campaign, Colonel Brown coordinated a massive TOT with twenty-two battalions against enemy positions in southern Okinawa. This sudden concentration worked brilliantly, but Brown failed to inform the generals and woke everyone from a sound sleep. Brown "caught hell" from all sides.

Geiger insisted the LVT-As were also trained as field artillery. While this was done, the opportunity for direct fire support in the assault waves fizzled on L-Day when the enemy chose to not defend the Hagushi breaches. Colonel Lewis Metzger's 1st Armored Amphibian Battalion LVT-As fired over 20,000 rounds of 75mm shells in an artillery support role after L-Day.

Marines made great advances in refining supporting arms coordination during the battle for Okinawa. Commanders established Target Information Centers (TIC) at every level from battalion up to Tenth Army. The TICs provided centralized target information and a weapons assignment system responsive to both assigned targets and targets of opportunity. All three component liaison officers: air, artillery, and naval gunfire, were staffed with target intelligence information officers.

This commitment to innovation led to significant support improvements for the foot-slogging infantry. As one rifle battalion commander later wrote: "It wasn't uncommon for a battleship, artillery, tanks, and aircraft to be supporting the efforts of a single platoon during the assault on Shuri."

SHERMAN M-4 TANKS

Seven Marine and Army tank battalions were deployed on Okinawa. They were a deadly weapon—but only when coordinated with accompanying infantry. The Japanese tried to separate the two components by boldness and fire.

Before the invasion, General Ushijima said: "The strength of the enemy's forces is with his tanks." Ushijima's anti-tank training received the highest priority within his *Thirty-second Army*. These preparations proved successful on April 19, when the Japanese knocked out twenty-two out of the thirty Sherman tanks of the 27th Division—mostly by suicidal demolitionists.

The Marines fared better. They learned in earlier campaigns how to integrate artillery and infantry in a close protective over-watch of their tanks and to keep the "human bullet" suicide squads at bay. While enemy mines and guns took their toll on the Shermans, only one Marine tank sustained damage from a Japanese suicide attack.

Colonel Arthur Stewart commanded the 1st Tank Battalion on Okinawa. His unit had fought with distinction at Peleliu six months earlier, despite shipping shortfalls that kept a third of his tanks out of the fight. Stewart insisted on keeping the battalion's older M-4A2 Shermans because their twin (General Motors) diesel engines were safer in combat: "The tanks were not so easily set on fire and blown up under enemy fire," Stewart wrote after the war.

Colonel Rob Denig preferred the newer Sherman model M-4A3 for his 6th Tank Battalion. Denig's tank crews liked the greater horsepower provided by the water-cooled Ford V-8 engines. They considered the reversion to gasoline from diesel an acceptable risk. The 6th Tank Battalion faced its greatest challenge against Admiral Ota's naval guns and mines on the Oroku Peninsula.

Sherman tanks were harshly criticized in the European

theater for coming up short against the heavier German Tiger Tanks. But they were ideal for island fighting in the Pacific. On Okinawa, the Sherman's limitations were obvious. Their 75mm gun was too light against most of Ushijima's fortifications. But the new M-7 self-propelled 155mm gun worked well. Shermans were never known for their armor protection. At thirty-three tons, their strength was more in mobility and reliability. Japanese anti-tank weapons and mines reached the height of their deadliness on Okinawa. The Sherman's thin-skinned weak points (1.5-inch armor on the rear and sides) caused considerable concern.

Marine tank crews sheathed the sides of their tanks with lumber to thwart hand-lobbed Japanese magnetic mines as early as the Marshalls. By Okinawa, the Shermans were draped with spot-welded track blocks, sandbags, wire mesh, and clusters of large nails—designed to enhance armor protection.

Both tank battalions had their Shermans configured with dozer blades (valuable for cave fighting), but neither deployed with flame tanks. Despite the rave reports of the USN Mark I turret-mounted flame system installed on the Shermans in the Iwo Jima battle, there was no retrofit program for the Okinawa-bound Marine tank units. All flame tanks on Okinawa were provided courtesy of the US Army's 713th Armored Flamethrower Battalion. Company B of that unit supported the Marines with three brand-new H1 flame tanks. Each carried 290 gallons of napalm thickened fuel— good for two-and-a-half minutes of flame at a range of 200 yards.

Marines used the new T-6 "tank flotation devices" to get the initial waves of Shermans ashore on L-Day. The T-6 was a series of floating tanks welded around the hull. They had a provisional steering device that made use of the tracks and electric bilge pumps. Once ashore, the crew jettisoned the bulky rig with built-in explosive charges.

The April 1 landing for the 1st Tank Battalion was truly "April Fool's Day." An LST (Landing Ship Tank) captain carrying six Shermans equipped with a T-6 launched the vehicles an hour late and eleven miles out to sea. It took them five hours to reach the beach (losing two tanks on the reef at ebb tide). Most of Colonel Stewart's other Shermans made it ashore before noon, but some of his reserves could not make it across the reef for another forty-eight hours.

The Sixth Tank Battalion had better luck. Their LST skippers launched their T-6 tanks on time and close in. Two tanks were lost: one sank after its main engine failed, and the other broke a track and swerved into a hole. The other Shermans surged ashore and were ready to roll.

Enemy gunners and mine warfare experts knocked out three Marine Shermans in the battle. Many more tanks took damage from the fighting but were repaired by the hard-working maintenance crews. Because of their ingenuity, the assault infantry battalions never lacked armored firepower, shock action, and mobility.

AMPHIBIOUS RECONNAISSANCE

A series of smaller amphibious operations around the periphery of Okinawa helped contribute to victory. These landing forces varied in size from the company level to an entire division. Each reflected the apex of amphibious expertise learned in the Pacific theater by 1945. These landings produced fleet anchorages, auxiliary airfields, fire support bases, and expeditionary radar sites, giving an early warning to the fleet against the dreaded *kamikazes*.

The Amphibious Reconnaissance Battalion commanded by Major James Jones provided outstanding service to landing force commanders in a series of audacious exploits in the Marianas, Marshalls, Gilberts, and on Iwo Jima. Before L-Day on Okinawa, these Marines supported the Army's 77th Division with stealthy landings on Awara Saki, Keise Shima, and other islands in the East China Sea. Later in the battle, this recon unit executed night landings on the islands guarding the eastern approaches to Nakagusuku Wan (later known as Buckner Bay).

On one of those islands—Tsugen Jima, the main Japanese outpost—Jones and his recon Marines had a ferocious firefight before he could extract his men through the darkness. The Army's 105th Infantry stormed ashore on Tsugen Jima three days later and eliminated the stronghold and all resistance. On April 13, Jones' Marines then sailed northwest and executed a night landing on Minna Shima to seize a firebase supporting the 77th's main landing on Ie Shima.

The post-L-Day amphibious operations with the 27th and 77th Divisions were helpful—but not decisive. By mid-April, the Tenth Army had waged a campaign of massive firepower against the primary Japanese defenses. General Buckner chose not to employ amphibious resources to break the gridlock. Buckner's long deliberation of whether to use the "amphib card" was not helped by a lack of flexibility by the Joint Chiefs, who kept strings attached to the use of the Marine divisions. The Japanese *Thirty-second Army* in southern Okinawa was the enemy's center of gravity in the Ryukyu Islands. But still, the

Joint Chiefs let weeks pass before scrubbing earlier commitments to send the 2nd Marine Division into attack Kikai Shima—an obscure island north of Okinawa.

General Buckner used the 8th Marines in a pair of amphibious landings on June 3 to seize outlying islands for early warning radar facilities against the *kamikaze* raids. Then, the commanding general attached the reinforced regiment to the 1st Marine Division for the final overland assaults on the south.

Buckner consented to the 6th Marine Division's request to conduct its own amphibious assault below Naha to surprise the Naval Guard Force on the Oroku Peninsula. This was a jewel of an operation in which the Marines used every component of amphibious warfare to their great advantage.

If the 77th Division's amphibious landings on Ie Shima or the 6th Marine Division's landing on Oroku had been executed separately from the Okinawan campaign, they would both have received major historical study for the size of forces, brilliant orchestration, and intensity of the fighting.

While both operations provided valuable objectives: unrestricted access to Naha's ports and Ie Shima airfields. They were only secondary to the more extensive campaign and barely received a passing mention. The Oroku operation would be the final unopposed amphibious landing of the war.

LEGACY OF OKINAWA

The exhausted Marines on Okinawa showed little joy at the official proclamation of victory. The death throes of the *Thirty-second Army* kept the battlefield deadly. The last of General

Ushijima's infantry may have died defending Yuza Dake and Kunishi Ridge, but the remaining mishmash of support troops sold their lives dearly to the last man.

On June 18, diehard enemy survivors wounded Major Earl Cook, CO of the 1/22 Marines, and Colonel Hunter Hurst, CO of the 3/7. Even Day and Bertoli, who'd survived so long in that crater on Sugar Loaf, watched their luck run out in the final days. Private First Class Bertoli died in action. Corporal Day was seriously wounded by a satchel charge and required urgent evacuation to the hospital ship *Solace*.

The butcher's bill on Okinawa was costly to both sides. Over 120,000 Japanese died defending the island, while 7,000 surrendered at the end. The native Okinawans suffered the worst. Recent studies show that over 150,000 civilians died in the fighting—one-third of the island's population. The Tenth Army suffered over 45,000 combat casualties, including 7,264 dead Americans. An additional 26,000 nonviolent casualties were incurred: primarily cases of combat fatigue.

The Marine Corps' overall casualties: air, ship detachments, and ground were 19,821. In addition, 562 members of the Navy Medical Corps were wounded or killed. General Shepherd described the corpsmen on Okinawa as: "the finest and most courageous men that I'd ever known. They did a magnificent job."

Losses within the infantry (as usual) were disproportionate with other Allied outfits. Colonel Shapley reported his losses as 110 percent in the 4th Marines. This number represents the replacements and their high attrition in the battle. Corporal Day of the 2/22 Marines experienced the death of his battalion and regimental commanders, plus the killing and wounding of his two company commanders, seven platoon commanders, and every other member of his rifle squad.

The legacy of this epic battle can be defined through the following points:

Foreshadow to the Invasion of Japan

Admiral Spruance described the Okinawan battle as: "the bloody and hellish prelude to the invasion of Japan." As wicked a nightmare as Okinawa was, every survivor knew the subsequent battles on Honshu and Kyushu would be worse. The operational plans for invading Japan specified the use of surviving veterans from Iwo Jima and Luzon. The reward for the Okinawan survivors would be to land on the main island of Honshu. Most of the men were fatalistic—no man's luck could last through those hellish infernos.

Mastery of amphibious tactics

The massive and nearly flawless amphibious assault on Okinawa happened thirty years (to the month) after the disaster at Gallipoli in World War I. By 1945, the Allied forces had refined this difficult naval mission into an art form. Admiral Nimitz had every advantage in place for Okinawa: specialized ships and landing craft, a proven doctrine, mission-oriented weapons systems, flexible logistics, trained shock troops, and unity of command. Everything clicked and everything worked. The projection (and execution) of 60,000 combat troops landed ashore on L-Day validated an amphibious doctrine earlier considered suicidal.

Attrition style warfare

Ignoring the great opportunities for maneuver and surprise available in the amphibious task force, the Tenth Army executed most assaults on Okinawa using an unimaginative attrition style of warfare, which played to the Japanese defenders' strength. This unrealistic reliance on firepower and siege tactics only prolonged the fighting. The Oroku Peninsula and Ie Shima Landings (despite being successful) comprise the only division-level amphibious assaults after L-Day. Also, the few night attacks made in unison by the Army and Marine forces (which were successful) were not encouraged. The Tenth Army squandered several opportunities for tactical innovations that could have hastened a breakthrough into enemy defenses.

Unity of service

Excluding squabbles between the 77th Infantry Division and 1st Marine Division after the Marines' seizure of Shuri Castle (in the Army's zone), the battle for Okinawa represented joint service cooperation at its finest. This was General Buckner's finest achievement, and General Geiger continued with this level of teamwork after Buckner was impaled through the chest and killed in action. The battle of Okinawa today is still a model of study in inter-service cooperation for succeeding generations of military professionals.

The best training

Marines deployed in Okinawa received the most practical and thoroughly advanced training of the war. Well-seasoned and battle-hardened division and regimental commanders anticipated Okinawa's requirements for cave warfare. They built-up areas to conduct realistic rehearsals and training. This battle produced few surprises.

Many Marines who survived Okinawa went on to top positions of leadership that influenced the Marine Corps for the next two decades. Two Marine Corps commandants emerged from this hellish ordeal: General Lemuel Shepherd of the 6th Marine Division and Colonel Leonard Chapman, CO of the 4/11 Marines. Oliver Smith and Vernon McGee were promoted to the rank of four-star general. At least seventeen others achieved the rank of lieutenant general—including George Axtell, Alan Shapley, Ed Snedeker, and Victor Krulak.

Corporal James Day recovered from his wounds and returned to Okinawa forty years later as a Major General in command of all Marine Corps bases on the island.

During the taping of the battle's fiftieth anniversary, General Victor Krulak gave a fitting epitaph to the brave men who gave their lives on Okinawa. Speaking on camera, he said: "The cheerfulness with which they went to their death has stayed with me forever. What is it that makes them all the same? I watched them in Korea, I watched them in Vietnam, and it's the same. American youth is one hell of a lot better than he is usually credited."

* * *

Building a relationship with my readers is one of the best things about writing. I occasionally send out emails with details on new releases and special offers. If you'd like to join my free readers group and never miss a new release, go to danielwrinn.com to sign up for the list.

REFERENCES

Allen, Robert E. *The First Battalion of the 28th Marines on Iwo Jima: a Day-by-Day History from Personal Accounts and Official Reports, with Complete Muster Rolls.* McFarland, 1999.

Alexander, Colonel Joseph. "'In for One Hell of a Time': Bloody Sacrifice at the Battle of Iwo Jima." HistoryNet.com and World War II magazine. HistoryNet.com and World War II magazine, February 2000.

Alexander, Joseph H. *The Final Campaign: Marines in the Victory on Okinawa.* Washington, D.C.: Marine Corps Historical Center, 1996.

"Amphibious Operations: Capture of Iwo Jima." Naval History and Heritage Command, October 23, 2019.

Anderson, Charles R. *Western Pacific.* The U.S. Army Campaigns of World War II. U.S. Army Center of Military History, 1994. CMH Pub 72-29.

Antill, Peter D. "The Battle for Iwo Jima." History of War, April 6, 2001.

Appleman, Roy Edgar, James Burns, Russel Gugeler, and Stevens John. *Okinawa: The Last Battle.* Washington: United States Army Center of Military History, 1948.

Bradley, James, and Ron Powers. *Flags of Our Fathers.* New York: Bantam Books, 2006.

Bradley, James. *Flyboys: a True Story of American Courage.* Boston: Little, Brown, 2003.

"Breaking the Cycle of Iwo Jima Mythology: A Strategic Study of Operation Detachment." *The Journal of Military History* 68, no. 4 (October 2004)

Buell, Hal. *Uncommon Valor, Common Virtue: Iwo Jima and the Photograph That Captured America.* New York, NY: Berkley, 406AD.

Burbeck, James. "Invasion of Peleliu". *Animated Combat Map.* The War Times Journal, 2008

Burrell, Robert S. *The Ghosts of Iwo Jima.* College Station: Texas A&M University Press, 2006.

Chen, C. Peter "Palau Islands and Ulithi Islands Campaign". *World War II Database.* Archived from the original on October 6, 2007.

Gayle, Gordon D., BGen USMC. *Bloody Beaches: the Marines at Peleliu*. Washington, D.C.: Marine Corp Historical Center, 1996.

Fisch, Arnold G. *Ryukyus*. Washington, D.C.: U.S. Army Center of Military History, 2004.

Gypton, Jeremy. "Bloody Peleliu". MilitaryHistoryOnline, 2008.

Hallas, James H. *The Devil's Anvil: The Assault on Peleliu*. Praeger Publishers, 1994

Hammel, Eric M. *Iwo Jima: Portrait of a Battle: United States Marines at War in the Pacific*. St. Paul, MN: Zenith Press, 2006.

Hastings, Max. *Retribution: the Battle for Japan, 1944-45*. New York: Alfred A. Knopf, 2009.

Hearn, Chester G. *Sorties into Hell: The Hidden War on Chichi Jima*. Guilford, CT: Lyons Press, 2005.

HistoricalResources. "Ivo Jima Maps - February 19, 1945–March 26, 1945." Historical Resources About The Second World War RSS, September 15, 2008.

Hobbs, David. *The British Pacific Fleet: the Royal Navy's Most Powerful Strike Force*. Barnsley, South Yorkshire: Seaforth Publishing, 2012.

Horie, Yoshitaka, Robert D. Eldridge, and Charles W. Tatum. *Fighting Spirit: The Memoirs of Major Yoshitaka Horie and the Battle of Iwo Jima*. Annapolis, MD: Naval Institute Press, 2011.

Hough, Frank O. *The Assault on Peleliu*. Washington, D.C.: Historical Division, Headquarters, U.S. Marine Corps, 1950.

Kier, Mike. "PELELIU". Archived from the original on December 19, 2006.

Kindersley, Dorling. *World War II: The Definitive Visual History*. New York: DK Publishing, 2009.

Lacey, Laura Homan. *Stay Off the Skyline: The Sixth Marine Division on Okinawa: an Oral History*. Potomac Books, 2005.

Manchester, William. *Goodbye Darkness*. Boston, Mass: Little, Brown and Co., 1980.

Moran, Jim, and Gordon L. Rottman. *Peleliu 1944: the Forgotten Corner of Hell*. Oxford: Osprey, 2002.

Morison, Samuel Eliot. *Victory in the Pacific, 1945 Vol. 14 of History of United States Naval Operations in World War II*. Urbana: University of Illinois Press, 2002.

Morison, Samuel Eliot. *Leyte: June 1944-January 1945, vol. 12*. Boston: Little, Brown and Company, 1958.

Nash, Douglas. *Battle of Okinawa III MEF Staff Ride Battle Book*. U.S. Marine Corps History Division, 2015.

Nichols, Chas S., and Henry I. Shaw. *Okinawa: Victory in the Pacific (PDF)*. Washington, D.C.: Government Printing Office, 1955.

"'Rare Photos of the Battle of Iwo Jima from the U.S. National Archives and the Department of Defense, USMC.'" Awesome Stories. Accessed June 2021.

Ross, Bill D. *Peleliu: Tragic Triumph: the Untold Story of the Pacific War's Forgotten Battle*. New York: Random House, 1991.

Rottman, Gordon L. *Okinawa, 1945: the Last Battle*. Oxford: Osprey Pub., 2002.

Salomon, Henry. *Victory at Sea Volume 23: Target Suribachi*. United States of America: The National Broadcasting Company, 1954.

Shively, John C. *The Last Lieutenant: A Foxhole View of the Epic Battle for Iwo Jima*. Bloomington: Indiana University Press, 2006.

Shread, Paul. "The Battle of Peleliu and the scars of war". *The Concord Monitor*. Archived from the original on September 19, 2014.

Sledge, E. B. *With the Old Breed: At Peleliu and Okinawa*. New York: Oxford University Press, 1991.

Sledge, E. B., and Paul Fussell. *With the Old Breed At Peleliu and Okinawa*. New York: Oxford University Press, 1991.

Sloan, Bill. *Brotherhood of Heroes: the Marines at Peleliu, 1944: the Bloodiest Battle of the Pacific War*. New York: Simon & Schuster, 2005.

Sperling, Milton. *To the Shores of Iwo Jima.* United States of America: United States Navy and United States Marine Corps, 1945.

The Battle for Iwo Jima 1945. Stroud: Sutton, 2006.

Toll, Ian W. *TWILIGHT OF THE GODS: War in the Western Pacific, 1944-1945.* S.l.: W W NORTON, 2020.

Veronee, Marvin D. *A Portfolio of Photographs: Selected to Illustrate the Setting for My Experience in the Battle of Iwo Jima, World War II, Pacific Theater, as a Naval Gunfire Liaison Officer with the First Battalion, 28th Marines, 19 February-26 March 1945.* Quantico: Visionary Pub., 2001.

Wells, Keith. *Give Me Fifty Marines Not Afraid to Die: Iwo Jima.* Abilene, TX: Produced by Quality Publications, 1995.

Wheeler, Richard. *Iwo.* Annapolis, MD: Naval Institute Press, 1994.

World War 2 Pictures. "Iwo Jima Pictures." WW2-Pictures.com, April 16, 2010.

World War 2 Pictures. "Okinawa Pictures." WW2-Pictures.com, April 16, 2010.

Wright, Derrick. *Iwo Jima 1945: The Marines Raise the Flag On Mount Suribachi.* Oxford: Osprey Publishing Ltd, 2004.

Wright, Derrick. *To the Far Side of Hell: the Battle for Peleliu, 1944.* Tuscaloosa: University of Alabama Press, 2005.

ALSO BY DANIEL WRINN

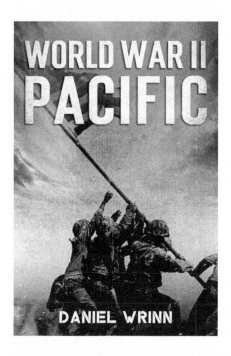

WORLD WAR II PACIFIC: BATTLES AND CAMPAIGNS FROM
GUADALCANAL TO OKINAWA 1942-1945

*"A brisk and compelling game changer for the historiography of the Pacific
Theater in World War II."* – Reader

**An enlightening glimpse into nine battles and
campaigns during the Pacific War Allied offensive.**

Each of these momentous operations were fascinating feats of
strategy, planning, and bravery, handing the Allies what would
eventually become a victory over the Pacific Theater and an
end to Imperialist Japanese expansion.

Operation Watchtower, a riveting exploration of the spark that set off the Allied offensive in the Pacific islands, detailing the grueling struggle for the island of Guadalcanal and its vital strategic position.

Operation Galvanic, an incredible account of the battle for the Tarawa Atoll and base that would give them a steppingstone into the heart of Japanese-controlled waters.

Operation Backhander, a gripping retelling of the war for Cape Gloucester, New Guinea, and the Bismarck Sea.

Battle for Saipan, Marines stormed the beaches with a goal of gaining a crucial air base from which the US could launch its new long-range B-29 bombers directly at Japan's home islands.

Invasion of Tinian, is the incredible account of the assault on Tinian. Located just under six miles southwest of Saipan. This was the first use of napalm and the "shore to shore" concept.

Recapture of Guam, a gripping narrative about the liberation of the Japanese-held island of Guam, captured by the Japanese in 1941 during one of the first Pacific campaigns of the War.

Operation Stalemate, Marines landed on the island of Peleliu, one of the Palau Islands in the Pacific, as part of a larger operation to provide support for General MacArthur, who was preparing to invade the Philippines.

Operation Detachment, the battle of Iwo Jima was a major offensive in World War II. The Marine invasion was tasked with the mission of capturing airfields on the island for use by P-51 fighters.

Operation Iceberg, the invasion and ultimate victory on Okinawa was the largest amphibious assault in the Pacific Theater. It was also one of the bloodiest battles in the Pacific, lasting ninety-eight days.

This gripping narrative sheds light on these often-overlooked facets of WWII, providing students, history fans, and World War II buffs alike with a captivating breakdown of the history and combat that defined the ultimate victory of US forces in the Pacific.

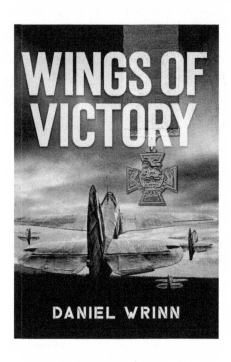

WINGS OF VICTORY: WORLD WAR II ADVENTURES IN A WAR-
TORN EUROPE

"Historical fiction with a realistic twist." – Reviewer

Thrilling World War II adventures like you've never seen them before.

As the Nazis invade Europe on a campaign for total domination, a brutal war begins to unfold which will change the course of the world forever—and John Archer finds himself caught in the middle of it. When this amateur pilot joins the Allied war effort and is tasked with a series of death-defying missions which place him deep into German-occupied territory, his hair-raising adventures will help decide the fate of Europe.

In **War Heroes**, John is caught up in the devastating Nazi invasion of France while on vacation. Teaming up with ambulance driver Barney, John will need his amateur pilot skills and more than a stroke of luck to pull off the escape of the century.

In **Bombs Over Britain**, the Nazis have a plan which could change the course of the entire war . . . unless Archer can stop them. Air-dropped into Belgium on a top-secret mission, Archer must retrieve vital intelligence and make it out alive. But that's easier said than done when the Gestapo are closing in.

And in **Desert Scout**, Archer finds himself stranded beneath the scorching Libyan sun and in a race against time to turn the tide of the war in North Africa. But with the Luftwaffe and the desert vying to finish him off, can he make it out alive?

Packed with action and filled to the brim with suspense, these thrilling stories combine classic adventures with a riveting and historical World War II setting, making it ideal for history buffs and casual readers. If you're a fan of riveting war fiction novels, WW2 aircraft, and the war for the skies, Archer's next adventure will keep you on the edge of your seat.

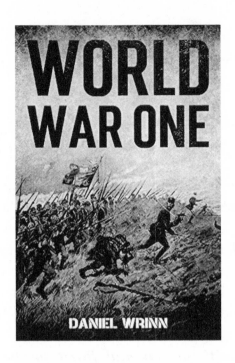

WORLD WAR ONE: WWI HISTORY TOLD FROM THE
TRENCHES, SEAS, SKIES, AND DESERT OF A WAR TORN
WORLD

"Compelling . . . the kind of book that brings history alive." –
Reviewer

**Dive into the incredible history of WWI with these
gripping stories.**

With a unique and fascinating glimpse into the lesser-known
stories of the War to End All Wars, this riveting book unveils
four thrilling stories from the trenches, seas, skies, and desert
of a war-torn world. From one captain's death-defying mission
to smuggle weapons for an Irish rebellion to heroic pilots and
soldiers from all corners of the globe, these stories shed light

on real people and events from one of the greatest conflicts in human history.

• **WWI: Tales from the Trenches**, a sweeping and eerily realistic narrative which explores the struggles and endless dangers faced by soldiers in the trenches during the heart of WWI

• **Broken Wings**, a powerful and heroic story about one pilot after he was shot down and spent 72 harrowing days on the run deep behind enemy lines

• **Mission to Ireland**, which explores the devious and cunning plan to smuggle a ship loaded with weapons to incite an Irish rebellion against the British

• And **Journey into Eden**, a fascinating glimpse into the lesser-known battles on the harsh and unforgiving Mesopotamian Front

World War I reduced Europe's mightiest empires to rubble, killed twenty million people, and cracked the foundations of our modern world. In its wake, empires toppled, monarchies fell, and whole populations lost their national identities.

Each of these stories brings together unbelievable real-life WWI history, making them perfect for casual readers and history buffs alike. If you want to peer into the past and unearth the incredible stories of the brave soldiers who risked everything, then this book is for you.

ABOUT THE AUTHOR

Daniel Wrinn writes Military History & War Stories. A US Navy veteran and avid history buff, Daniel lives in the Utah Wasatch Mountains. He writes every day with a view of the snow capped peaks of Park City to keep him company. You can join his readers group and get notified of new releases, special offers, and free books here:

www.danielwrinn.com

Made in the USA
Monee, IL
29 June 2021